MY FIRST EIGHTY YEARS

THE AUTHOR, AGED 86

[*Frontis.*]

MY FIRST
EIGHTY YEARS

by

ALBERT VICTOR BAILLIE, K.C.V.O., D.D.

Formerly Dean of Windsor

LONDON

JOHN MURRAY, ALBEMARLE STREET, W.

First Edition . . *1951*

Printed in Great Britain by Butler & Tanner Ltd., Frome and London
and published by John Murray (Publishers) Ltd.

FOR MY SON
EAN

CONTENTS

ILLUSTRATIONS

"If you find anyone uninteresting you may be sure that it is because you are too stupid to find out what is interesting in them."

MY MOTHER.

INTRODUCTION

DEAR ROBERT PALMER,

Our work together on the final revision of my memoirs has at last come to an end. Really I am a little sorry to lose the pleasure of this labour which has brought me so many new friends, among them Mary Berry, who patiently and perfectly took down the first draft of the manuscript from dictation ; Wyndham Haslitt, who carried out the unenviable task of a first revision ; and lastly yourself, with whose help I prepared the book for publication. Our year's work together has taught me much, but above all two things seem to me the most important : firstly, that I am still in sympathy with the young—or that the young are still in sympathy with me—and secondly, that every man of eighty-five is justified in writing the story of his life.

In combing out the matted skeins of my personal history I have gained a quite new perspective and understanding of those full years through which I have passed. It is curious, for instance, how insistent a pattern of life can be in asserting itself. In my life, this pattern has taken the form of contrast. While Queen Victoria was my godmother, I acted as a kind of unofficial godfather to a group of slum boys in Tyne Dock. It was from the cramped industrial areas of East London, where I was a curate, that I travelled west to be married in Westminster Abbey, in whose Cloisters I lived as a youth with my Uncle Dean Stanley. Though it gives me great pleasure to know that my grandfather danced with Marie Antoinette, I gain even greater pleasure from the memory of my personal association with the Marx Brothers in Hollywood. My friendships with actors of Irving's day may have caused you at times to think of me as a fossil washed up by the Flood, but that I am not quite so decayed as this may be seen in my recent connection with the incomparable Lunts, who played for me at Windsor. And so the contrasts go on, my seemingly continuous movement between extremes.

Of course, the greatest contrast of all for an old man is that between the society of great individuals which he knew in his youth, and the world of social averages which he has seen grow up about him within the last thirty years. The Prince who welcomed me in state during a tour through Hungary has become a creature of musical plays : the old reality turned into a contemporary romance. Now you will complain that I am talking like a man of the past, but it is not so. I believe in your generation and in its ability to endure. The past is simply my teacher : the present is my tonic, and the future just one more exciting mystery for me to wonder at. I fully intend to walk with you as far as I can into our unborn history, but when I falter and stay behind in Time, this book will be my shadow on your library shelves.

Yours,

A. V. B.

BALDOCK, *July*, 1951.

PART I
BEGINNINGS

CHAPTER I

CARLSRUHE

I AM seven years older than the German Reich. My father, in the diplomatic service, was appointed Chargé d'Affaires at Carlsruhe, the capital of the independent state of Baden, in the year 1864, when I was born.

Few details of my early life in Carlsruhe remain with me. The long span of years between then and now cloud my memory, like steam on a window-pane. A few characters step clearly out against the screen of my past childhood, walk, talk and then are gone again. The atmosphere only remains with me, and some traditions, still fresh and exciting as they were when I was a boy. How curiously vivid to me, even now, is the story of the building of Carlsruhe, which stood in a semicircle at the edge of a great forest, on the main road from Durlach to Baden.

I was told that some two hundred years previously the Grand Duke Carl of Baden, after hunting in the forest, lay down to sleep and dreamed of building a new capital, in the shape of a fan, on that very spot. On awakening, he translated his dream into reality and gave to his new capital the name of Carlsruhe, which means Carl's Rest.

The royal palace formed the handle of the fan and paths or roads radiated from it like the sticks, through gardens, until they reached a semicircle of little two-storied Baroque houses, continuing beyond the semicircle in the form of streets lined by similar houses as far as the main high road, which cut right across the top of the fan. After it entered the town this high road became the Langestrasse.

It was in the Langestrasse that I found my first home. Our landlord, Herr Muntz, was an upholsterer and saddler who kept the ground floor of the house as a shop. I remember

3

a vast window facing on to the street like a transparent stable wall, behind it an immense wooden horse on the back of which was displayed one of Herr Muntz's saddles. We lived above the shop and below the Muntz's living quarters, in a first-floor flat. Our drawing-room, with my mother's bedroom on one side and my father's dressing-room on the other, had three windows overlooking the street. It was not a beautiful room. One side was all windows and in the centre of each of the remaining three sides there were large folding doors. In one corner was the stove, in another stood my father's piano ; in the middle was a round table surrounded by very Victorian rosewood chairs upholstered with red velvet. There were no pictures or ornaments. All the rest of the rooms in the flat looked into the courtyard where many things happened, interesting and exciting to my young eyes. I was particularly thrilled by an old woman who held a goose tightly under her arm and stuffed food down its throat with her thumb, to swell its liver in preparation for its being turned into *pâté de foie gras*. Another event of great fascination (not shared by the rest of the family as the smell was past belief !) was the periodical arrival of an engine to pump out the cesspool under the house.

One of our first German playfellows came from this house in the Langestrasse. We called him " Muntzlie ", or " little Muntz ", as he was our landlord's son. In later years the world knew him as Carl Muntz, a distinguished opera singer. Besides Carl we counted the Grand Duke's children among our playmates. The eldest son was already away doing his military training, but his sister, afterwards Queen of Sweden, was my sister's contemporary and friend. One reason why the Grand Duchess encouraged a close association between her daughter and my sister was her belief that it was a natural thing for girls to be fond of dolls and she hoped my sister, who loved dolls, would correct her daughter's disinclination in that respect. The youngest son, Prince Ludwig, was my friend. But above all other playmates of this period in my life I must raise Hannah Hechler, my first sweetheart. Hannah

4

was the daughter of our Anglican clergyman. A little older than myself, she became the object of my passionate affection. Afflicted with a violent squint, she was not beautiful ; but I positively adored her and my love affair was one of our family jokes.

My family are an integral part of that German background to my first nine years. I remember my father as a most dignified presence, with a charming smile, who seemed to be always sketching or playing the piano. I cannot recall his smallest personal intervention in the lives of my sister, my two brothers or myself, apart from occasionally, on Sundays, drawing delightful imaginary animals for us and telling us thrilling stores about them. His general aloofness, however, was not repellent ; we both liked and admired him. After his death I heard him spoken of constantly and, ten years later when I returned to Germany, learned much from many of our old friends whom I visited. People always laid great stress on his beauty, his dignity and his charm. There is one interesting illustration of the influence which his distinctive presence and personality gave him. In the days when he was a young Attaché at the Court of Wurtemberg it had been the immemorial custom of the King to give a reception on Sundays, at which the different diplomats were expected to attend. My father intimated that it was against his principles to go to a Sunday entertainment ; whereupon the King and Queen, instead of thinking it an impertinence and being annoyed, transferred the reception to a week-day. This was a remarkable homage to accord a young Attaché of no especial importance.

With his intense love of art and his own considerable artistic talents, my father made of our home in the Langestrasse a rendezvous for the artists and musicians who thronged Carlsruhe. Some of my earliest memories are of seeing him play duets with various distinguished musicians. Once, on running into the drawing-room, I found sitting next to him at the piano an old gentleman with long white hair. It was the Abbé Lizst, with whom he had formed an enduring friendship whilst Attaché in Vienna.

Actors, I think, did not come to our home. My father
was a strict Evangelical and as such regarded the theatre
with horror. I have a series of letters with represent his
side in a controversy he had with my mother on the subject, during their engagement. I only wish I had also my
mother's defence in reply to his indictment of her theatre-
going. The matter was finally closed by their agreeing to
differ ; certainly my mother's nature was much too honest to
pretend to agree with a restriction which conflicted with her
own beliefs. Incidentally, I fancy that my parents' final way
of settling this controversy had a good deal to do with his
complete non-intervention in his children's religious teaching.

My father's strong Evangelical opinions found militant
expression in the distribution of tracts, a habit which, at
Baden, the then Monte Carlo of Europe, mortified my
sixteen-year-old sister whenever she went out with him. I
recollect years later lunching with my father's first cousin,
Alec Baillie, of whom I was very fond. He was a little, dry
retired soldier : a student of Eastern languages, an agnostic
and my father's exact opposite. " Dear Evan ! " my cousin
remarked to me. " He had astonishing charm. He used to
present tracts right and left and people positively liked it ! "
Yet, all in all, my memory of my father remains vague ; my
general impression being of a rather indolent man, with a
deep love of art on the one hand and a quite stern piety on
the other.

My mother provided an almost complete contrast and was
the determining influence in the growth of my character from
the beginning. Perhaps the most striking quality about her
was her vitality. Everything she felt, she felt intensely. Life
for her was at bottom an almost severely serious affair, balanced
always by a bubbling sense of fun and a gorgeous joy in living.
Whatever she thought, did or said was instinct with energy ;
a little too much so, I thought, during our walks together,
when she moved a great deal further and faster than I cared for.

My mother's religion, while quite as deep and sincere as
that of my father, had none of the taboos inherent in his strict

Evangelicalism. She never seemed to inhibit one's inclinations or to find fault, yet one always felt she was expecting the very best from one and trusting one not to fail her.

Hannah's father, Herr Hechler, the Anglican clergyman who ministered to us at Carlsruhe, was formerly a Jew and a missionary. He was an extreme Calvinist and held services in a barrack-like hall, with wooden benches and a desk upon the platform from which he preached. If I remember aright, there was no music at all. While the services must have been extraordinarily dreary, my mother quite clearly did not find them so. The Prayer Book by itself gave her all the joy she needed. She fixed it firmly in my mind by her example that I must try and mean the words I used in speaking to my God. She herself obviously spoke the words with intense earnestness and enjoyment. She gave me no actual lessons on the Prayer Book, but left the meaning to explain itself.

I do not remember hearing my mother ever criticising Herr Hechler's sermons. In later years, however, my sister told me that she had agreed with her in finding them very trying, since they dealt exclusively with Hell. In those days nobody would have dreamed of taking children out before the sermon and, as Hell was not considered a fit topic for our young ears, my mother solved the problem by telling us that that portion of the service was not meant for us. To prevent our fidgeting in idleness we were given picture books to look at. The books chosen for us were not exclusively religious in character ; I distinctly recall Landseer's picture of a Newfoundland dog in one of mine.

But my contemplation of Landseer's dog did not interfere with my religious education. Besides my mother's example in matters of faith I had always the stern guidance of *Me-me*, my nurse. Whitley, for that was her correct name, came to us when my sister was born. She took each of us boys in turn and finally became maid to my mother when I went to school, remaining with the family for a quarter of a century, when she died.

Whitley believed in the innate dignity of her own class.

Her family had lived for two hundred years in the village of Hoddesdon, on the borders of Essex and Hertfordshire. The Whitleys were tailors. In a town a tailor belonged to the tradesman class, but in a village he ranked as an artisan. As *Me-me* thought and I learned to feel, an artisan who conscientiously fulfilled his duty was a very noble person. I can still see her old father and mother sitting in Windsor chairs on either side of the fireplace, with groups of silhouettes of past members of the family looking down on them from over the mantelpiece. My nurse's stories about various members of this gallery laid the foundation of my knowledge of the finer possibilities of human character and the dignity of individual life. There was a great-uncle, for instance, a carpenter, whom she taught me to admire as a man of outstanding quality; when later I read *Adam Bede* I felt it was just such a man that George Eliot had in mind. A cupboard made by this great-uncle for his wife as a wedding present was left me by my nurse. She had always used it to illustrate her belief in the splendour of any work into which a man put his best efforts; but even more splendid where that best was given unselfishly and with devotion. All *Me-me*'s relations were not great-uncles, however, nor all as admirable: she offered the example of some of her family to me as warnings. I still chuckle when I recall her telling me with indignant insistence about an aunt who created wholesale mischief with her unbridled tongue.

The one thing I shall be ever grateful for was my nurse's insistence upon reverence. She taught it through details of personal conduct. It mattered how we knelt at our prayers; it was important that we should never be careless in handling the Prayer Book or the Bible. Little matters, but wonderfully effective in education. And after all it was the method Moses used in training the Jews to a similar end. He insisted that every step in the building and use of the Tabernacle should be carried out reverently. Nothing might be done carelessly or casually, even to the driving in of a tent peg, because it had to do with the House of God; and he gave dignity to the work by declaring that craftsmen were inspired in their skill by the spirit of God.

Our secular education during these years in Carlsruhe came from two very different sources. My mother did not believe in governesses and we were, consequently, put under a tutor : a tall raw-boned Scotsman named Barclay. We came to love him : he had that rare capacity in a teacher of injecting a spirit of fun and discovery into our lessons. Under him I learnt my letters and gradually had laid down the foundation on which was to be raised the superstructure of my future education.

Heinrich Schmidt was the second source of our education : he taught us discipline. Heinrich came to the family some years before I was born. He began as my father's servant and continued as butler, first to my mother and on her death to my eldest brother, until I was over fifty. None of our friends for the next half-century could think of us without him. Heinrich was a short, egg-shaped German with a broad fresh-complexioned face and prominent blue eyes, extremely efficient but hot-tempered and self-willed. In small things he ruled my father completely, giving him every morning the amount of pocket money he considered necessary for the day. If he did not agree with an order that had been given him, he merely remarked " I shall not " and that was the end of the matter. None the less, behind his little eccentricities there was ever the most astonishing affection for us all. When he was old and very rheumaticky a friend of our family said to him : " Surely, Heinrich, it would be better for you to retire and go and live quietly with your children ? " To which came the reply : " I shall not ! Mr. James, Mr. Augustus and Mr. Albert are much more like my children than my children are."

Heinrich was an admirable trainer of young servants, though his methods were somewhat rough. One of his footmen years afterwards told me he owed everything to the old man. He added laughingly, however, that his schooling at Heinrich's hands had been no easy affair ; if he did anything of which the old man disapproved, Heinrich simply knocked him down.

To the end of his life my eldest brother, when he was his master and himself past middle age, never used to give Heinrich an order but only made suggestions; always, if the suggestions did not meet with his favour, Heinrich would produce his time-honoured " I shall not ! "

2

Just at the end of my first seven years came the upheaval of the Franco-Prussian War. We heard that the Emperor Napoleon III had ordered the complete destruction of Carlsruhe, so a big Union Jack was kept ready on a pole in my mother's room for display in an emergency. Inevitably all our sympathies lay with Germany, whose patriotic songs we children chanted with our German playfellows. I remember the excitement of the ladies making lint for bandages and the ragged streams of French prisoners pouring into the town. But the war was soon over : in 1871 France collapsed and we were at peace again.

During the celebrations that followed the German victory we drove round the illuminated streets with Baroness Bunsen,[1] who described to us the illuminations she had seen in London after Napoleon's defeat at Waterloo. The Baroness was a close friend of my mother. I remember her as a gracious old lady with all the social gifts of a great hostess. She lived in a tiny house with her two daughters and a single maid. As soon as I could walk I used to carry her a bouquet on her birthday, one of which I thought so beautiful that it was only with the greatest difficulty that I was induced to give it up. I can still see that bouquet—a mass of violets, with here and there a sprig of lily of the valley.

Baroness Bunsen's two daughters were known to us as Tante Frances and Tante Mim. Tante Frances was a little on the grim side. She was an extreme Calvinist who con-

[1] The Baroness Bunsen was the subject of an exhaustive biography by Augustus Hare. She was English by birth, niece of the Mrs. Delaney mentioned so frequently in Fanny Burney's Journal, and widow of the famous scholar, Baron Bunsen.

CARLSRUHE, 1869

The author's parents, with Victoria

Victoria, the author, Augustus and James

James, the author and Augustus, with their
tutor, Mr. Barclay

Heinrich, with one of his own children

[10]

sidered churches and clergymen wrong. Shortly after we left Germany she died but Tante Mim I found still there in later years. For me she was the symbol of a vanished world ; her dignity and her charm exuded the spirit of the great society of her youth. The people of Carlsruhe treated her with great deference. Towards the end of her life she moved about very little, but once every year she paid a small round of visits to her three greatest friends, all of whom happened to be queens.

A characteristic feature of German society of this period was its insistence on purity of descent as a condition of social acceptance. In Austria, for example, nobody without the requisite number of quarterings was allowed to go to court. Similarly, in Bavaria no member of a family descended from union with an Englishwoman, irrespective of rank, was eligible to hold the highest order of chivalry. This rule did not arise from any contempt for the English aristocracy ; on the contrary, they were always welcomed with the utmost respect ; but they were considered careless in the matter of marriages : an English ancestress might have some blot in her pedigree, and so vitiate the blood of the house into which she had married.

In Carlsruhe this rigidity was not so intense : society was not based exclusively on claims of birth. There was rather the natural friendliness of a small English country town, without its provincialism. In the first place the capital was the seat of a real court and parliament. The state government was an independent one : it had a full diplomatic corps in residence, in which my father represented England along with the accredited representatives of all the other states of Germany, and the larger states of Europe.

Another enlivening and vitalising influence in that little social world consisted in all the small German rulers vying with each other in fostering universities, operas, theatres and schools of painting. Some of these institutions attained international celebrity : Weimar, whose intellectual influence was an impulse throughout Europe ; Dresden or Bayreuth or later

Darmstadt, whose operas attracted talent and interest from countries all over the globe.

With all its variety of interest and breadth of outlook, Carlsruhe's social atmosphere was very simple. Everyone knew everybody else ; but while many of the inhabitants were great aristocrats, they had singularly little money. Indeed, in those days, luxury or ostentation was synonymous with vulgarity. Only one person in the town could afford to keep a carriage, namely the Grand Duke's Lord Chamberlain, and on the nights of the receptions at the Palace the Chamberlain's carriage used to run to and fro fetching his friends. Everyone lived in little houses or flats, generally with a single servant. There were no luncheon or dinner parties, although coffee parties were constant. All the ladies knitted, and many years afterwards when I returned to Germany, nothing struck me more than the complete disappearance of what I had known as a universal habit. In those earlier days, even when the ladies walked to the opera or the theatre, they went in their bonnets carrying their knitting.

We remained in this Carlsruhe society for almost a year after the birth of the German Reich, at the end of the Franco-Prussian War. During that period my mother took me with her on a visit to Paris. She had been brought up in the French capital and spoke French like a native. We travelled along the line of the recent battlefields and the peasants, believing my mother to be a Frenchwoman, spoke of the kindness of the conquering German soldiery that contrasted sharply with their treatment at the hands of their own army. Paris itself provided a startling spectacle. It was just like London after the blitz ; public buildings were in many instances no more than blackened shells and entire streets had been burnt to the ground. The whole thing was the deliberate work of the Communists during their brief bid for power following the retirement of the Germans. Immense numbers of the trees and avenues had been cut down during the siege of the capital at the end of the war, adding to the sense of general desolation. We met various people who had been through both the siege and the Commune and who had grim stories to relate of life during that time. I thought it very exciting that all the dogs and cats, rats and mice, and the animals in the Zoo had been eaten up! Even though I was a very small boy, what I saw and heard remained etched deeply in my mind.

This visit to Paris coincided with my father's transfer to Darmstadt. Princess Alice,[1] wife of the Grand Duke of Hesse-Darmstadt, who was a lifelong friend of my mother, had requested this transfer. Although we had come to love Carlsruhe the move to our new home was one that caused me the greatest excitement. In a short time the Royal children became our friends and we were constant companions. One day when the two boys were playing in their mother's bedroom, leaning out of the windows to shout to one another, the youngest overbalanced and fell two storeys to the pavement below. This was the beginning of a series of disasters that claimed almost every member of the family. The second sister as the widow of the Grand Duke Sergius was murdered by the Bolsheviks; the third sister married Prince Henry of Prussia, brother of the deposed Kaiser; the fourth sister as the Tzarina of Russia shared her Consort's brutal end after the Russian Revolution. The eldest brother grew up only to die, with his wife, his eldest son and his daughter-in-law, in an aeroplane accident on the way to England for his second son's wedding. Only the eldest girl, Lady Milford Haven, escaped her family's unhappy destiny. She has lived to see her second son gain distinction as Lord (Louis) Mountbatten and her grandson married to the heiress presumptive to the English throne.

When I was nine years old this opening chapter in my life came to a close. We had been in Darmstadt for only a few months when my father's health forced him to relinquish his duties and return with his family permanently to England.

[1] Queen Victoria's second daughter.

CHAPTER 2

BOYHOOD

IT was summer when we arrived in England. We settled immediately at Culduthel, one of the houses on my grandfather's property of Dochfour in the Highlands. My father straightway entered into the life of the country, though his sketching and music went on. My brothers went away to school and I had the summer mainly to myself. There were many occupations for a boy at Culduthel ; for me, riding was the most important. Some three years previously, during a holiday from Germany, we stayed at Megginch Castle, the home of my Drummond relations, where I was very nearly frightened off riding for life. I used to be taken out on Donald, a Shetland pony on which all of us learned to ride, in charge of somebody with a leading-rein. One day, as we were passing a point where the road ran close to the railway lines, a train went by. In those days horses were very nervous of trains and Donald, twitching himself free, bolted for home. I was half-crazed with fright and ended by being decanted on to the ground in the stable-yard. I ran upstairs to the nursery where *Me-me*, because of my state of mind, put me to bed. Everyone was out at the time, with the exception of old Mr. Drummond, who, hearing of my mishap, at once came to the nursery. Standing by my bed, he said, solemnly : "This won't do. Gentlemen must never give way to fear." My awe of him quieted me and, after making *Me-me* dress me, he took me down and mounted me on Donald again, holding the leading-rein himself. During the long ride that followed he talked to me quietly and naturally until he had restored me to a perfectly normal frame of mind. No reference to what had occurred was made on our return home and the following day I went out riding as usual. But deep down in my soul there was a sense of shame ; shame at having given way to my nerves. The lesson I learned then has remained with me throughout my life, and I owe the dear old man one of the greatest debts any human being can owe another—the conquest of fear.

At Culduthel the riding lessons for which Mr. Drummond had fitted me continued. I was sent out daily on the faithful Donald all by myself. He was a cheerful pony, with a great sense of fun and absolutely no vice. Every day in the course of our outing he would suddenly run away and equally suddenly stop dead, shooting me over his head and then waiting for me to get on again. My mother never took these tumbles of mine seriously, or even inquired if I was hurt. On the contrary, she made a joke of them, declaring that no one could learn to ride until they had had twenty-five falls.

Notwithstanding my continuous riding and the bumps and tumbles that came from it, I never quite defeated my nervousness and indolence. My eldest brother and my sister regarded these signs of what they called " effeminacy " with great contempt, or at least wished me to think so. As I was said to be an exceptionally pretty little boy, they thought that outsiders would spoil me. By their drastic efforts at redressing the alleged deficiencies and hardening me up, they gave me an inferiority complex which lasted right up to my university days.

My sister was seven years my senior, and such was the terror with which she inspired us that we were never entirely free from it to the day of her death, when she was over eighty. I, perhaps, eventually got over it more than my brothers did, but it was truly comic the way in which the other two, when they were quite elderly men, showed very palpable nervousness in her presence. She had an absolutely unrivalled power of snubbing one and she kept all of us, my mother included, as far as possible on the outside of her life. If, for example, we asked her at lunch where she had been for her morning walk, she would answer tersely, " Out." In big things as well as small we were allowed to know as little as possible about her affairs. After my father's death she persuaded herself that nobody understood her, that my mother was only interested in us boys, and her isolation became even more pronounced. Poor Victoria was another instance of that most fatal of evils, self-pity. She would have been an altogether different woman if only she could have let herself go. She was clever, and during the years when she was first Maid of Honour, and then one of the personal secretaries of Queen Victoria, she did extremely well. Her very reticence was of great value at Court, while her complete straightforwardness and integrity of nature were qualities that no one could fail to respect.

In that summer when I was with my sister at Culduthel she acted for a time as my governess and made my lessons frightening to a degree I never experienced with another teacher. In her old age she told a niece that there was no more irritating child to teach than myself, since while I apparently paid not the least attention I always got my answers right.

My two brothers were a very different matter. It is true James also considered I stood radically in need of education, and being six years my senior he was able to give me little or no chance of entering into his life and amusements, so that it was later that we became friends. But Augustus, who came between us, was the most delightful of all companions. There was never anybody with a more glorious sense of humour. Even so, both James and Augustus were so much older than myself as to make my position virtually that of an only child.

At the end of those first summer holidays after settling down at Culduthel I turned ten years old and had my first experience of school, at Wixenford in the parish of Eversley. Not many weeks later there came a morning when I was summoned by the headmaster and told, very gently and kindly, that my father was dead. I went to London and joined Augustus, who had come up from Marlborough. James had gone straight to Edinburgh from Eton. It was dark when Augustus and I reached the hotel where my father had died. I shall always remember, as it might be a scene

The Author at Marlborough

from a play, being greeted by our sister carrying a single bedroom candle before her through the gloomy hotel hall. I can still see her dim outline moving up the stairs ahead of us, the light from the thin flame of the candle throwing each step into shadowy relief.

The circumstances of my father's illness and death were doubly tragic. He had just retired from diplomacy, and the Queen had asked my mother to become Lady-in-Waiting to the Duchess of Edinburgh, who was lately married. My father remained in Scotland while my mother went to London, and during her absence went to Edinburgh to undergo a trifling operation. Antiseptics were not understood at that time and he developed blood poisoning. In London my mother was on the point of leaving for the Opera in attendance on the Duchess when my uncle, Sir William Colville, Comptroller of the Duke of Edinburgh's Household, rushed in with a telegram to say that my father was dying. She left just as she was, in full evening dress with bare neck and arms ; there was barely time to drive to the station to catch the night train north. It was in November and in those days trains were without heating ; my mother had only a light opera cloak and a greatcoat lent her by Sir William to keep her warm. The shock of losing my father combined with the terrible cold she caught on her journey resulted in an illness from which she nearly died and from which she never entirely recovered.

After our arrival that night Augustus and I were allowed no more than the merest glimpse of her. Of the funeral and the depressing days that followed I remember hardly anything. I suppose I returned to school ; but we spent the holidays that Christmas in lodgings in Edinburgh, where my mother was still lying in a very serious condition.

When at length she was sufficiently recovered to review her position, my mother was exercised in mind to know what she should do for the best. She felt quite definitely that we could not return to Culduthel. This was made impossible by her relation to my father's mother, or rather my grandmother's relation to her. Lady Georgiana was very possessive and hated her daughters-in-law for standing between her and her sons. She also hated my grandfather and created a most difficult atmosphere in the family by teaching her children to regard him with contempt. I may have known something of this unfortunate background in a vague way, but as she was kind to me I could never bring myself quite to believe in my grandmother's reputedly hard, cruel nature. She was the most beautiful old woman I have ever seen, with an astonishing charm of manner and very witty. To her favourites, of whom I happened to be one, nobody could be more delightful. But beneath this façade she was abnormally hard and cold. One finds references in memoirs to similar qualities in her father, the Duke of Manchester, who was himself conscious of it in his sister, the Duchess of Montrose, described by him as " colder than a dog's nose ". At a later date I was to reconsider all I had heard told against my grandmother. I inherited a bundle of letters which, over many years, she had written to her eldest daughter : in these, behind a mask of Evangelical piety she revealed a heartlessness so horrible that I burned the letters out of hand. Her daughters were trained by her to a spirit of intrigue. She would say to them : " It doesn't matter if your father doesn't approve. He need never know."

My father, while he had a great affection and admiration for his mother, was aware of the poison in the family atmosphere, and warned my mother before she had ever seen her relatives that she would never be able to live among them. I have sometimes felt the story of Isaac, Rebecca and Jacob to be very like that of my poor grandfather's home-life. It would have been next to impossible, therefore, for my mother to have attempted to live without my father close to Dochfour and she decided instead to get a house in London.

2

With my father's death it was inevitable that my mother should be the most powerful single influence in my life. It was through the example of members of her family that she taught us our duty to one another and to society. Her education was a rich and, for those days, unconventional one. She was only four years old when her father, Thomas, Earl of Elgin and Kincardine, best known in connection with the Elgin Marbles, died in Paris. My grandmother [1] remained in Paris after his death, and it was against the glowing tapestry of contemporary French society that my mother and her sisters, Augusta and Charlotte, grew to womanhood.

The *salon* was still a feature of French life but without the artificiality which had marked it before the Revolution. The only refreshments provided were weak tea and *eau sucré*, that curious drink composed of a glass of water with a lump of sugar in it affected by Frenchmen at that period, and which even I can remember. My grandmother had her own *salon*, to which serious intellects were attracted by her outstanding mental ability. Some of the old aristocrats my grandfather had known in pre-Revolution days, having seen the society to which they belonged shattered and their relatives and friends dragged away to the guillotine, emerged from their ancient family houses to attend my grandmother's *salon*, where they exchanged stories of their vanished youth. If she were interested my grandmother would talk, and talk well; if she were bored she frankly yawned, to the amused distress of her daughters. As the girls grew up they busied themselves with the management of the parties and cultivated a social talent that was to last them throughout their lives. As a result of the Paris life my mother and her sisters were free of the rigid conventionalities of thought and behaviour that restricted the lives of so many of their class at home.

My Aunt Charlotte died when I was very young. She and her husband, Fred Locker, were to form an interesting circle of their own. To their house Thackeray brought *The Rose and the Ring* to read to my aunt before it was published, while Browning, who had been a friend of my grandmother and used to read to her, would come and wander round the rooms. Indeed, most of the contemporary men of letters were frequent visitors and enjoyed the only hospitality that the Lockers,

[1] The second Lady Elgin, formerly Miss Elizabeth Oswald of Dunnikeir.

owing to their small means, were able to provide—a teapot, a loaf of bread, and a pot of jam. Fred Locker had a considerable reputation in his day as a writer of light verse. In his wife's lifetime, however, he was overshadowed by her more brilliant wit. I recall the surprise with which people came to realise after her death how amusing he was and what good company he could be.

My Aunt Augusta's appointment as Lady-in-Waiting to the Duchess of Kent introduced yet another interest to my mother's life. The Duchess wrote her dozens of little letters to Paris, asking for details of her clothes and the parties she attended and requiring any amusing caricatures to be sent to England, especially of Napoleon III who was regarded then as a slightly ridiculous adventurer.

Aunt Augusta remained with the Duchess for twenty years. Hers was not, however, merely a formal relationship limited to part of the year; she resided the whole year round at Frogmore and Clarence House, and became practically like a daughter to the Duchess. She was responsible for the management of the social side of life, receiving and entertaining guests, and generally doing all she could to brighten the old lady's days. The Duchess, on her side, adopted my aunt's brothers and sisters, throwing her home open to the former when they returned from different embassies and governorships and welcoming my mother on her visits to England after she was eighteen.

As a result my aunt, and in a lesser degree my mother, came to be very intimate with the Queen and her children, who came down to see their grandmamma every day. On the Duchess's death the Queen invited my aunt to go to her in a similar capacity, living with her throughout the year. Lady Augusta's extraordinarily sympathetic nature made her the repository of all the little difficulties arising with the Royal Family, and kept her so busy during the day that she acquired the practice of dealing with her vast correspondence through the night, which contributed materially to her early death. Fortunately the court life did not last for many more years, but while it lasted it was an intense strain. At the Prince Consort's death, and for some months afterwards, she was the only person the Queen saw, apart from her children. Although she was constantly overworked, nothing could damp the joyousness of her nature or narrow her wealth of sympathy, which embraced everyone with whom she came into contact. Her position, however, made her very reticent and discreet, with the result that her manner was sometimes thought artificial.

Throughout those years spent in attendance on the Duchess of Kent and the Queen there developed in my aunt a spirit of unselfishness that found full expression in her devoted care of her husband, Arthur Penrhyn Stanley, Dean of Westminster, whom she married shortly before I was born.

3

Before my mother got a house in London my Aunt Augusta died. Her long years of unremitting service with the Royal Family and later her tireless public activities in Westminster had hastened her death and left my uncle, Dean Stanley, by himself at the Deanery. Automatically, we made the Deanery our home, my mother sharing the task of running my uncle's household with his sister, Miss Stanley, and her cousin, Mrs. Drummond.

By their personal qualities my uncle and aunt during their years together made the Deanery a centre towards which interesting people from home and abroad seemed naturally to gravitate. But even without my aunt, my uncle's magnetic personality drew a great collection of people regularly to the Deanery. His vast popularity depended not on what he did but simply on the natural vivacity of his spirit. Matthew Arnold, in the poem he wrote about him after his death, spoke of his

> Bright wits, and instincts sure,
> And goodness warm, and truth without alloy,
> And temper sweet, and love of all things pure,
> And joy in light, and power to spread that joy.

That description could not be bettered. Everything connected with humanity, whether of the past or of the present, was vividly interesting to him. Any striking public event in any part of Europe would send him scurrying off to see the people engaged in it. The Abbey was a stirring place to him and every monument in it held an exciting story of human life ; he used to thrill the parties of working men he took round on Saturdays just as much as the cultivated visitors that flocked there from all over the world. For my own part, walking with him in London was always an adventure, every street providing some entrancing story and every outing coloured by the people we encountered. I can still see Disraeli shivering one cold day as he stood talking to my uncle, or old Carlyle, another of his great friends, whom we once came upon seated solitary on a Chelsea Embankment bench.

Dean Stanley's extraordinary interest in everybody and everything was, I believe, his compensation for a certain lack of physical senses. The ordinary senses meant nothing to him. He had no sense of taste or smell ; musical sounds were a mere noise to him, the only tune he recognised being the " Dead March in Saul " and that because of the drums (which being omitted at one performance puzzled and infuriated him) ; scenery and pictures only affected him when they told some definite story, such as a portrait of a man in whom he was interested or a striking event which deeply moved him, otherwise the beauty of nature or the meaning of colours were lost on him entirely. It was noticed when he was a schoolboy at Rugby that he remained totally unconscious of the coarse sensual vice prevalent in the school during that time. And, indeed right through life he was never able to recognise the evil effects of the senses in anyone. He had always to be carefully fed to make him eat at all ; his dressing had to be watched or it would have been left hopelessly unfinished. There were only two things that appeared to awake his senses : tea and a hot fire. Of the first he drank great quantities and was, I suppose, conscious of some exhilarating effect from it ; while before the latter his whole being seemed visibly to expand.

In the presence of company or topics congenial to him his refined little face would light up to an astonishing brightness ; on the other hand he seemed literally to shrivel into nothingness if anyone persisted in talking about something beyond his experience, or when something happened that he did not understand.

Intellectually he had one marked limitation : arithmetic meant absolutely nothing to him, and his brother-in-law Fred Locker insisted that he was unable to see the difference between eighteen pence and one and eightpence. In illustration of this Locker told a delightful story. The cook of a friend of his won £10,000 in a lottery, the winning number being 23. On being asked if she had any special reason for choosing that number, the good woman explained that she had dreamed three times of the number 7. When Locker told the story, Arthur Stanley remained earnestly puzzling for several moments before remarking, with childlike simplicity : " Oh, then I suppose three times seven is not twenty-three ? "

It was a wonderful experience for a boy with my tastes to be constantly in Dean Stanley's company ; and it was an education to watch crowding round him at the Deanery, as he poured out his enchanting talk, many of the greatest thinkers of the day. I remember Tennyson, Browning, Matthew Arnold, Dobson and many other poets ; scientists like Tyndall and Owen, historians like Lecky and Froude ; Scottish, English and foreign ecclesiastics, among whom were to be found those who disapproved of my uncle's views just as much as those who were his close personal friends and understood him. In actual fact, he did not have any intellectually definable views. The intellectual definitions of theology were as meaningless to him as arithmetic ; but he did have a deep spiritual grasp of religious truths, and a vital faith that expressed itself in simply piety. He was often misunderstood because of the chivalry with which he defended heretics of all sorts, simply from an innate love of freedom and justice.

The possession of such a background for the first eighteen years of one's life was a rare privilege.

4

My formal education continued at Wixenford, whose Principal, Mr. Powles, was a genuine educator and a remarkable man. He wore his hair neatly brushed up into two horns above his ears—a fashion you can see in Cruikshank's illustrations of Dickens—and from time to time he would stroke those horns with his fingers. A life-long friend of Charles Kingsley, he had moved his school from Blackheath to Wixenford so as to be in Kingsley's parish. When I arrived at the school Kingsley was nearing his end ; I only once heard him preach in the little parish church, but I had known him well at the Deanery at Westminster where he was one of the Canons, and I attended his funeral, which Dean Stanley came down to take. It was an impressive sight : a great crowd filled Eversley churchyard, among which were hunt servants in their pink, gypsies from all the country round-about, country neighbours, farmers and many people from London.

Mr. Powles was personally responsible for giving me the inestimable advantage of writing a good hand. His own handwriting was exquisite, and I can still feel the infinite trouble that he took with us, individually, to ensure that we held our pens the right way and made every stroke correctly. Two of the assistant masters were also first-rate teachers. Mr. Wilkins was our History Master, and while I believe that nowadays *memoria technica* are very much out of favour, I owe an immense amount to that method. Mr. Wilkins gave us *memoria technica* of the kings and queens of England which he composed as we went along. Ever since, those schoolboy jingles have served as a useful framework into which all my serious historical reading fitted ; they are as fresh today as they were then :

William the First by conquest and tricks
    Obtained the crown in 1066 ;
William the Second by Will was given
    The English crown in 1087
Henry the First for England fought
With Robert his brother 1100.

Another instance of the Wilkins method occurred in
Divinity lessons. I venture to think there can be few people
who can give an accurate list of the judges in the Pentateuch,
but this I am still able to do with the aid of a jingling hexa-
meter. Wilkins was not an especially interesting man, but
he made our lessons positively exciting.

The other master, Mr. Wheeler, was just the reverse in his
methods but equally effective in his results. I am still conscious of the manner in which he contrived to weave the
interest of literature into the ordinary things of life. For
example, if he had to write me a note it was always in the
form of an amusing little poem. I remember part of one of
these, in which Mr. Wheeler told me the details of a journey
I had to take. It begins :

O, *very little little B.,*
How unhappy should we be
If, by some unhappy fate,
For the train you should be late.
Take, O take, your umbrella ;
Here's one glove—but where's its fella ?

Yes ; for me the memory of the writer will always linger
round many books.

When I went on from Wixenford to Marlborough the
picture was quite different. At my public school I cannot
recall a single master who tried to make my work interesting
to me. It was mainly a continuous grind of grammatical and
mathematical rules, which bored me utterly and kept me at
the bottom of my class. I succeeded only in the subjects in
which I had been interested at home. My favourite subjects

were, however, apparently no more than unimportant side-issues in the eyes of the school authorities.

Dr. James, afterwards the great Headmaster of Rugby, had instituted a prize for English Literature and this I won, since in early boyhood I loved reading and possessed a curiously selective instinct about prose and poetry. History had already become one of my absorbing interests : another was Divinity. In those three directions I think I was more truly alive than most boys ; it seems absurd to me now that no master made me realise that careful study of the classics brought its full reward in a more intimate knowledge of literature and history. Yet at Marlborough no master so much as attempted to do so. They had not grasped the principle on which Sanderson built up the extraordinarily effective educational system of Oundle : the principle that a boy should always see clearly why he is learning anything.

I had the same difficulty with Mathematics, having for my master a hot-tempered, excitable man whom I absolutely infuriated, and for the same reason that my sister complained at home. In Euclid, it was the master's everlasting complaint that I always understood a proposition quicker than any other boy in the class but always left out some of the steps requisite to building up its proof. Yet he absolutely failed to give me cogent reasons for a closer application to my work. Instead, he loaded me with impositions so that one term I accumulated enough of them to last me a year and had practically no time left for recreation or exercise, until the holidays wiped them out.

Marlborough was going through a bad period just then. Long afterwards one of the Eton masters, who had been my contemporary, was most emphatic on the school's short-comings in our day. I fancy the explanation was to be found in the singularly colourless personality of the Headmaster, Dr. Bell. He wandered about with a beard and an amiable expression, beyond which he had no impact on us. We neither liked nor disliked him, and I never subsequently met one of his pupils in whom he had awakened the slightest enthusiasm as a master or a man. Without doubt this had its effect on the masters and their interest in their work as well. I only give this as my personal impression, but I feel it is true. The school had been good under the Headmasterships of Cotton and Bradley, and became very good again after Dr. Bell left, maintaining its prestige up to the present time. I have sometimes wondered whether things can have been better under Dr. Bell's predecessor, Dr. Farrar, whose two famous school stories, *St. Winifred's, or the World of School* and *Eric, or Little by Little*, raise doubts as to their author's understanding of a boy's nature.

While I think these conditions were directly responsible for my public school experience, they were not the sole reason for my failure. I was considered delicate throughout my youth and continually suffered bouts of illness. My ill-health at Marlborough was made far worse by the ridiculous treatment the poor old school doctor prescribed. This consisted of doses of cod-liver oil always administered in cough mixture and my being forbidden to play games or to tire myself physically. As regards the first part of the treatment, the cod-liver oil and cough mixture was of no particular advantage to me, but the second part did me a positive injury. Nothing could have been worse for me, physically, morally or mentally ; I became a loafer, and a very unhappy one at that, deprived of a common life with my schoolfellows whether at work or at play.

I would gladly cut my Marlborough years from my life : I believe that, apart from causing me much unhappiness, they did me a great deal of harm. As my masters insisted that my low position in the school was due to stupidity and idleness, I left with a genuine inferiority complex. My family, not unnaturally, accepted the verdict of the school authorities, with the consequence that " poor Albert " was regarded as being deficient in the upper storey. This may have had its advantages in making intellectual conceit impossible ; and conceit is perhaps the worst of all faults ; but, on the other hand, it discouraged me from making serious intellectual efforts. If

I was so completely unintelligent, what was the use of trying ? I was just on seventeen when my mother, realising the gravity of my position at Marlborough and being afraid that I would have no chance of getting into university, put me into the hands of a tutor.

Mr. Walter Hiley was a first-rate teacher and I was very happy with him. The change from Marlborough was wonderful. Mr. Hiley rented Hyde Hall, a large country house in Essex close to Sawbridgeworth. There were about fifteen or sixteen boys, and though all failures at school, we formed a remarkably congenial crowd and in some cases did very well afterwards. Harry Rawlinson gained distinction as a General ; Martin Hawke, though his fame rested chiefly on cricket, was a grand character and always lived a useful life ; while Graham Robertson, who went in for an artistic career, produced in *Time Was* one of the most delightful books of reminiscences ever written. The remainder of us were just average, rather idle but wholesome-minded boys.

In appearance a happy old gentleman with whiskers, Mr. Hiley ruled us in a remarkable fashion. He had a particularly gentle, kindly way of speaking and a habit of addressing everybody as " dear old boy ". The power of his tremendous sense of humour in making one feel utterly small gave him complete ascendancy over us. An outstanding instance of his power in laughter concerned not us but his butler, who had an absolute mania for carrying immense piles of plates. One day at lunch the butler entered the great dining-room laden as usual to capacity with a new dinner-service, in use for the first time. Suddenly the bottom plate broke and with an appalling crash the rest clattered down in an avalanche of ruin. For a moment there was dead silence and then Mr. Hiley spoke quietly from the end of the table. " Dear old boy! One would have liked to have used them once." I remember another sally when the victim was one of ourselves. One boy with a very flamboyant way of speaking and dressing was invariably late down to breakfast. One morning after everyone else had finished and left the dining-room, Mr. Hiley sat

down in an armchair by the fire to await the other's appearance : I remained talking to him.   At last the boy came hurry-
ing in, full of elaborate apologies.   " Dear old boy," Mr. Hiley
remarked gently, " from the way you behave one might think
you were an important person in this household instead of only
a fraction."   And then, after a moment's pause, he added with
a sniff : " And, indeed, rather a vulgar fraction."

My chief recreation while at Hyde Hall was hunting.
Whenever I could afford it, and sometimes when I could not,
I hired a horse from the Green Man at Harlow and once a
week, either mounted or on foot, I followed the Essex hounds.
I can still remember the weight of the Essex clay on my heels
when, on the less fortunate days, I was running over the fields.
Otherwise we amused ourselves in the various ways that boys
will discover, and altogether had an entirely happy time.

While Mr. Hiley could not make up for the failure of my
schooldays in a few months, he did manage to get me into
Cambridge with credit.   My brief training with him, together
with my almost equally short period at my private school,
were the only times I profited from anything like formal
education.

5

There was a circumstance outside my life at Hyde Hall
which afforded me not a little interest and pleasure.   One of
my mother's cousins, Mrs. Archer Houblon (Aunt Georgie),
lived nearby at Hallingbury.   Aunt Georgie had married a
typical English squire : so typical that all over Essex if anyone
spoke of the Squire it was Mr. Houblon they meant.   He
had inherited his property at the age of nine, and living to
be eighty-nine he became an institution in the country.
While staying with Mr. Hiley, I used to spend a good deal
of my time at Hallingbury.   The house was a great square
eighteenth-century building of red brick, with four corner
turrets.   My chief memory of its interior is one of sweet
scents.   The central hall, with its fine staircase, opened into
a large conservatory, which my aunt kept full of sweet-

smelling flowers; there were bowls of *pot-pourri* on every window-sill and packets of lavender in every cupboard; on the washstand in the bedrooms a great bottle of home-distilled rosewater was always placed. Down to the era of the agricultural depression Mr. Houblon was a very rich man, for in addition to his Essex property he had a large estate in Lincolnshire. At Hallingbury everything was on an opulent scale. The old servants never changed. A model home farm stood across the fields, with a bailiff who dressed in a tall hat, breeches, gaiters and a stock, much as his predecessor would have done a hundred years earlier. A marvellous herd of Guernsey cows grazed in deep pastures near the house and I used to go up to the farm to drink their delicious cream. Next to the park was Takely Forest, private in those days, with a lake and picturesque keepers' cottages, their gardens filled with old-fashioned cabbage roses whose perfume comes back to me still. In the park itself were great elms, and an avenue of cedars planted by the Squire at his coming of age had grown to a considerable size. In the spring there were sheets of daffodils at the feet of the trees and a flourish of May trees on the shores of the lake.

Through the park ran a path of single paving stones, winding for nearly a mile to the church, which is associated in my mind with a delightful family ritual. On Sunday morning, punctual to the minute (for Mr. Houblon was a stickler on punctuality), everyone assembled at the hall door and the procession started. First came my old uncle and aunt, in single file; then the guests; then the butler, the housekeeper, the footmen and the maids—all in due order of precedence. Through the park along the paved path the gathering meandered to the dear little church that my uncle had restored with loving care, considerable expense but unfortunate results. Always, when we arrived inside, there was a bouquet of flowers waiting in my aunt's place. She would take the bouquet up, smell it and then turn, bow and smile to the chief farmer's wife, whose unfailing care it was to provide it every Sunday.

One aisle was filled by my aunt's girls' school in scarlet

Drawn by W. Bartlett

Engraved by H. Wallis

HALLINGBURY PLACE, ESSEX

cloaks with white straw hats and blue ribbons. Under the pulpit sat a group of old men wearing magnificent smock frocks which my uncle provided for them. They occupied that particular spot since, being supposedly deaf, they needed to be near the preacher. The Rector, a half-brother of Mrs. Houblon, was a clever man of a most lugubrious appearance and possessed of a somewhat caustic sense of humour. His sermons, while good, were totally unintelligible to most of his hearers. They would have been useful no doubt at a university but at Hallingbury their only result was that one by one the congregation dropped off to sleep, even my aunt making the most desperate efforts to keep awake with the aid of smelling salts. In my mind's eye I can see now the lime trees through the window beyond the pulpit, catch their scent and hear the buzzing of bees amid their branches. For the singing everyone was fully on the alert. The mixed choir gave voice with the utmost enthusiasm, if with rather modest skill. As for my uncle, he stepped out into the aisle and over-powered the rest with a thunderous bass voice ; as he was very deaf he was quite unconscious of what the choir was doing and frequently at the end of a hymn he was behind, singing the last verse as a solo.

At Hallingbury, where everything went on as it had always done, the all-pervading sense of continuity and order made life supremely peaceful. It was pathetic to see my uncle and aunt struggling, by quite useless and often rather absurd economies, to meet the new circumstances of the agricultural depression. They succeeded only in making themselves extremely uncomfortable.

My old uncle retained to the end of his life, at eighty-nine, immense physical vigour ; whenever he went to London for the day he walked three or four miles to the station at Bishop's Stortford and back again at night. He read prayers every morning in a voice of thunder, so that it seemed as if he were giving the Almighty orders for the day.

Aunt Georgie was very fond of china and had made what was considered one of the most perfect collections of English china in the country. When the Alexandra Palace was opened, the authorities sought permission to show her collection in the exhibition being held to mark the event. Very reluctantly my aunt consented to do this and, together with my uncle, attended on the opening day. As they were showing their tickets at the entrance there was a cry of " Fire ! " and in front of their eyes the building was burnt to the ground. With it went my aunt's china, and while she took the loss very well it was a cruel blow to her.

My uncle had his artistic interests as well. He collected crystals, and there was a cabinet in the drawing-room filled with a number of beautiful specimens. Once every year my aunt and he went to Italy for a holiday and it was there he obtained most of his pieces. He was also very fond of music, singing old-fashioned ballads to the piano in stentorian tones and, in the privacy of his dressing-room, playing upon the flute. During his practice of this last accomplishment nobody was allowed to be present. But my mother, visiting them in later years, was put in the room she had occupied on her first visit as a girl. As this was next to Mr. Houblon's dressing-room she was again able to listen to the flautist at work ; not only did he play the same tunes as he had done thirty years before but he broke down at the self-same places.

The dear old couple were always intensely conservative ; to the end of his days, when other people were introducing electric light, the Squire still spoke of gas as a " nasty new-fangled invention ".

CHAPTER 3

DOCHFOUR

D URING our school holidays each year when we were
away from the Deanery at Westminster, my mother
took us to live with the Drummonds at Megginch
Castle, Errol, or to the Duke and Duchess of Northumberland
at Alnwick.

Megginch was a lovely old Scottish castle. It had a front
that had been added to it by Adam, leaving the rest of the
house unspoilt and providing a fine staircase together with a
really splendid drawing-room and library on the first floor.
The back was as it had always been—presenting the normal
turreted, steep, gabled castle, marked by a strong sixteenth-
century French influence, such as one finds all over Scotland.
It overlooked a magnificent kitchen garden rich in fruit and
flowers, which thrived on the soil of the Carse of Gowrie, said
to be the best in Scotland. Adjoining was a late eighteenth-
century gabled stable-yard, in Strawberry Hill Gothic, with
a dovecote rising in the middle of it. At the side of the house
was a well-planned formal garden, and all round the remaining
sides was a small park with fine old trees which allowed here
and there a tempting glimpse of distant hills.

We kept our ponies at Megginch. These my mother gave
us on condition that we did everything for them apart from
feeding. We cleaned the harness, groomed the animals and
washed the carriages we used. There was a queer old cart in
which we drove four-in-hand, with harness made largely of
rope ; a smart yellow pony-cart my mother had provided, in
which we drove tandem ; and a pony-carriage in which we
drove a pair and took my mother out. In the pony-cart, there
being only two seats, I as youngest sat on the upright board
at the back with my legs dangling, which I found rather a

trial on drives of any distance. We rode our ponies a great deal as well, and altogether we must have kept them pretty busy. Mr. Drummond saw that we learned to shoot, too, himself instilling into us strict discipline with regard to the use of a gun and the manners of shooting. In a word, we had all that boys of that time had in the matter of country amusements and education.

The Drummonds were a branch of the great family of Drummond and their home was filled with all manner of interesting things : pictures, china, relics of every kind that had accumulated through successive generations. There were a number of unusually good family portraits, including several Romneys. Among the mementoes of the various family careers was one of Gordon Drummond who fought in the American War of Independence : it was a little flag reputed to have been the only one captured by the British throughout the campaign. Another great feature of the castle was Stuart the butler, who, although consulted by the family in almost everything, always remained the calmest and most respectful of servants. Before he died he had been seventy-two years in the house. Then there was the footman Charles who turned the stable into a classroom and there taught us to dance the Highland Fling.

Old Mr. Drummond was a model Highland laird. He had been in the Guards as a young man and to the end of his life retained the polish of London Society, although the greater part of his days had been spent in Scotland. He was tall and dressed exactly in the fashion of Sir Walter Scott, in a swallow-tailed coat of grey frieze with shepherd's plaid trousers and a stock. His manners were the most perfect I have ever known ; but while the essence of courtesy and kindness, he could be very firm and even stern when anything earned his disapproval. One inevitably felt, however, that his disapproval was always sadly justifiable. We loved him dearly, and he taught us about country things with infinite patience.

When Sundays came around at Megginch we attended the parish church, which was, of course, Presbyterian. The minister was a dear old man named Dr. Graham, who excited our interest as an astronomer and a fisherman whose strong, dexterous hands fashioned not only his own fishing-rods but his telescopes as well. As a preacher, however, we did not find Dr. Graham exciting and again my mother provided against our restlessness in church by allowing us to follow what was almost a national practice. When the sermon began everybody popped a peppermint into their mouths ; the aroma from the dissolving sweets soon filled the air like incense. We were allowed quite openly to go on Saturdays to buy sweets for the purpose, but they had to be of the hard and not the sticky variety. I can remember one kind that especially attracted me : a large ball of sugar which, as you sucked, yielded layer upon layer of different colours, so that it was an additional pleasure to remove it surreptitiously to see which colour you were getting to. As with our picture-books at Carlsruhe, it is to be noticed that our pepperminting implied no want of reverence. We should never have been permitted to put a sweet into our mouths during the prayers or singing ; it was only during the sermon, as a concession to the limitations of youth.

As we grew older, Dr. Graham's sermons became more interesting to us. In common with all Scottish preaching of that period there was a vividness of description in them which we enjoyed. The old man repeated his discourse at regular intervals so that there was an additional interest and excitement in wondering what particular one we were going to get next. There were certain favourites whose arrival absolutely thrilled us. One was about the young man in the linen garment ; another was afterwards told so often in our family that it became a chestnut. Imagine the dear old man standing up in the pulpit with his bald head overtopping a foam of bushy white whiskers, his corpulent figure enveloped in a voluminous preacher's gown which billowed around him, and in his hand a vast linen handkerchief, so highly starched that if he put it down it stood upright of its own accord in a white, crackling pyramid. In a booming voice he read out the description of the animals eaten in Solomon's household ; the sermon then opened with the following words, spoken with immense solemnity : " A guid dinner is a guid thing. And evidently Solomon thought so." After which came with great emphasis : " He was not what we should call in modern language a vegeta-a-a-arian ! " Yes, indeed ; each time that sermon came round it was a red-letter day. Incidentally, Dr. Graham was the last minister I heard address members of his congregation by their Christian names if they were not paying attention or for any other reason merited rebuke.

When we went to stay with the Duke and Duchess of Northumberland [1] we found a very different home from Megginch. Alnwick was a vast Norman castle remodelled internally on the lines of an Italian palace. When people had remonstrated with the Duke responsible for the transformation, his answer had been that personally he did not care for living with rushes on the floor.

The Castle, with the walls and towers of its *enceinte* covering an immense area, was a great historic building and the home of an historic family. Near the Castle gates was the spot where William the Lion of Scotland was taken prisoner by the English in 1174 ; in the outer wall a gap still spoke of old-time border warfare, and the battle of Otterburn was a living memory.

The old Duke of Northumberland, whom I came to know more intimately in later years, is one of the people I look back upon with most affection and admiration. He was extremely quiet and had no expensive tastes. I learned afterwards of the enormous amount of work of one kind and another that he got through as well as the lavishness of his charities, of which he never spoke. Only gradually was one able to discover that he had a mind stored with a most comprehensive knowledge of French and English literature together with a great understanding of history. But again, he never paraded the fact : it was always in the natural course of conversation

[1] The great-grandparents of the present Duke.

that some question would arise to which he invariably produced the right answer. If outwardly his was rather a mournful manner, underlying it was a most vivid sense of humour and understanding of the young. His brilliant grandson, Warkworth, used to say that while he could never talk to his own father, who was really prejudiced about anything new, he could always go to the old man with new ideas and be met with a comprehending interest and sympathetic attention.

In truth, he did everything in his power to make our young lives enjoyable, even though his wife was an invalid and strangers were apt to think life at the Castle very dull or alarmingly stately. He procured an excellent pony for me on which I learned to hunt, and horses for my two brothers. In company with some young cousins of the Duchess who also spent their Christmas holiday there, we used to have uproarious fun, which the Duke in his quiet way encouraged. Of the Duchess, in view of her indifferent health, we naturally saw very little.

At Alnwick everything was perfectly managed, the servants never changing through all the years we visited there. The old servants were real friends and, if stately and dignified in their general demeanour in keeping with their surroundings, they always unbent to us boys. The Duke's valet was a most amusing character who drifted through life on a stream of malapropisms. I remember once, after the Duchess had been wheeled into the dining-room and dinner was announced, instead of the usual formula : " Her Grace is in the dining-room and dinner is on the table, Your Grace," the valet flung wide the drawing-room doors and proclaimed in his most pompous tones : " Her Grace is on the table, Your Grace ! " On another occasion a violent storm during the night had damaged one of the stone lions' heads that ornamented the springs of the arches of the inner court-yard. At breakfast the next morning the valet made a solemn appearance, bearing on a silver salver a fragment of masonry. " The dog's nose has been blown off, Your Grace," he said.

Thus the story of each year : Westminster, Megginch,

Alnwick—until in 1883 my grandfather died and my eldest brother, James, inherited the property of Dochfour. So it was that in my nineteenth year I came to know a permanent family home. In the years before, in my childhood and adolescence, we had moved from one house to another, never settling for more than a few years. The Deanery at Westminster had filled the place of a home in our lives until my uncle's death in 1881 when my mother moved to a house in South Audley Street. But Dochfour was the birthplace of my father's family and it was here that I first became conscious of a continuous family history and a new spirit of romance and tradition was injected into my young life.

My father came from a family of considerable antiquity. The Lyon King-of-Arms once told me that my descent could indeed be traced back to Lucrecia Borgia, and William the Silent of Orange. The old Lowland Scottish pedigrees claimed the Baillies to be a branch of the great Norman family of Baliol and an ancestor is said to have married a daughter of William Wallace, heiress through her mother to Lamington in the West Country. This ancestor's original property, a group of farms near Haddington, still remains in the hands of the Baillies of Lamington. In the middle of the fifteenth century the three elder sons of the Baillie family quarrelled with their tutor, a priest, and after killing him had to flee the neighbourhood. The eldest took service under his uncle Lord Huntly in the Highlands ; the second went to Ireland, where his descendants are to this day ; the third went to Ar.glesey. The fourth son, being uninvolved, remained at Lamington. After the Battle of Brechin in 1450 Lord Huntly, who had been given the Lordship of Inverness, established the eldest Baillie on lands near Inverness and made him Hereditary Keeper of the Castle and Sheriff of the County.

From 1450 down to the Forty-Five Rebellion, the family story is quite prosaic. We lived as our neighbours lived, and married into the families of the lairds round about. Only one thing affected our fortunes to any great extent. For three successive generations we married into the Clan of

Fraser, our powerful neighbour, with the result that Simon of Lovat, the old scoundrel who was then head of the clan, recognised us as near relations and we took part in the Jacobite conspiracies which preceded the ill-fated rising. At the time of Culloden, 1746, the Laird, Hugh Baillie, was ill and unable to go out to fight, while his three sons were too young. After the battle he was carried up into hiding in the hills and although his property was not confiscated the house was burnt. Very shortly afterwards the Laird died but, curiously enough, out of what appeared to be complete disaster came a great improvement in our family fortunes. The younger brother of the Laird, Baillie of Abriachan, who had become a lawyer and settled in Inverness, managed his cousin Simon of Lovat's affairs and also from boyhood had been the most intimate friend of the son of our neighbour, Forbes of Culloden. That same son, Duncan, at the time of the battle had become President Forbes of Culloden, the most powerful man in Scotland, who did more than anybody to break Prince Charlie's power in the Highlands. I have no doubt it was through him that their uncle, Baillie of Abriachan, was enabled to send the Laird's three sons out into the world, while the sisters remained at home and married neighbouring lairds.

The foregoing period is especially real and vivid to me as the result of several remarkable links with the past. The old fisherman at Dochfour when I was a boy, who with his son and grandson has formed a dynasty of fishermen covering more than a hundred years, used to tell how his aunt, a housemaid at the time of the famous battle, helped to carry the Laird up into the hills. She lived on well into the fisherman's memory. Another curious link with the past is the longest I have ever come across. In 1910 I buried a Mrs. Grant who was over ninety. She was the daughter of my grandfather's grandfather, Evan Baillie, the youngest of the Laird's three sons who were at Dochfour at the time of Culloden. She was born when her father was very old but he lived until she was sixteen. He remembered Simon of Lovat coming over to see the Laird before the battle on the first carriage that they had ever seen, and he told of the awe with which everyone regarded it, as well as how part of the park dykes had to be pulled down, there being no entrance to the place wide enough for the vehicle to pass. But even stranger still, Mrs. Grant's father recalled being taken to see an old lady who had been held up at a window in London to see Charles II ride in at the Restoration. As he was born in 1740 and had known someone who had been six years old in 1660, while his own daughter died in 1910, the three lives covered two hundred and fifty years. But the lives of the father and daughter alone accounted for one hundred and seventy years.

The case of Evan Baillie and his daughter is a noteworthy instance of longevity ; but the Baillies have always been of tough stock. Two of Evan's sons lived to eighty-two and eighty-nine ; his grandson attained eighty-four and his wife eighty-nine ; his granddaughters ninety-two and eighty-nine. My father died before his time in circumstances that I have related, but his three sisters reached eighty-four, eighty-six and ninety-one respectively. My own generation, I must admit, is not quite so good, my two brothers dying comparatively young in their seventies. On the other hand, my sister lived to be eighty-two while I am now eighty-seven, and there was Ernest Noel, my grandfather's eldest sister's son, who died only three months short of a hundred. There would seem, therefore, to be sufficient justification for the local saying at Dochfour that " it takes a hatchet to kill a Baillie ".

The Laird's three sons went to the West Indies and all prospered. It is alleged that Evan, the youngest, who was only six in 1746, was secured a commission in the army almost immediately at that age by an uncle, and that he held it until he was ninety-six ; if this is true, I should think it is a record. The eldest brother, Alexander, returned to England and, after rebuilding the house on a new site at Dochfour, settled down there—though he seems to have had a house at Edinburgh as well. From all accounts he would appear to have been a delightful old gentleman. He came back from abroad with an absolute passion for his old home and kinsfolk and took a new crest and motto—a clump of trees above the words *Mutua Tutela Virent*, by which, I fancy, he meant to illustrate his belief in family connections. Unhappily his son died and as the second brother had settled in England he refused the succession, which went to the youngest brother, Evan.

Before he came into the family property, Evan had founded a great business at Bristol in connection with his West Indian interests. He established the first Bristol bank and his family represented Bristol in Parliament for three generations. But his heart remained in the Highlands, as is shown by the immense amount of land he bought near Dochfour, which at his death left my grandfather one of the largest of Scottish landowners. My grandfather married a daughter of the Duke of Manchester, and was led thereby into the very heart of the great aristocracy of the late Georgian era. For my part, I have sometimes regretted this weakening of our strong Highland tradition ; and that despite the fact that my mother came of pure Scottish blood, while even my paternal grandmother was half a Scotswoman. I have always felt a little like one of my cousins, whose mother was English, and who, having cut his hand as a child, refused to have the cut bound, saying : " Leave it alone—perhaps the English blood will run out."

In a vague fashion, even as a boy, I felt the difference between England and Scotland, but of course as I grew older I was able to see it much more clearly. In England the growth and development of society had its roots in the feudal system, which introduced a certain element of patronage into the relation of the Big House with the ordinary people. It was generally a very kindly relationship, as at Hallingbury, which was typically English. Nevertheless, it was quite distinctly the relation of a superior to an inferior. In Scotland that was not the case. There the feudal system had never swept out the patriarchal system ; indeed, the family remained the essence of the social structure.

To belong to a clan in the Highlands, or to one of the great families such as the Scotts and the Kerrs and the Johnstones in Southern Scotland, was a more important thing than a mere feudal relationship. And just as every Fraser felt he was a member of a great family of whom Lovat was the father, so in the border country every Scott or Kerr believed himself part of the same family as the Duke of Buccleuch or the Duke of Roxburghe. This sense of relationship had been fostered by the constant fighting between clans and families which had continued up to 1745, while the whole tradition was not only kept alive but intensified by the habit of telling old stories and ballads on winter evenings throughout the cottages of the land. Readers of Lockhart will remember how Scott once organised a great football match between the tenants of Buccleuch and the citizens of Selkirk, and how he found that the rivalry so awoke the spirit of ancient feuds that it would have been unwise to repeat the experiment. In the traditional stories and ballads the landlord represented the leader, one who fought alongside of and shared common interests with the humbler members of his clan. During the eighteenth century English tourists laughed when some petty innkeeper claimed to be a gentleman ; but he was a gentleman in the eyes of his fellow countrymen by virtue of the place his forebears had held in the life of the clan or family.

Essentially, therefore, in the Scottish principle of social relationship there was nothing servile. As has often been said, there was to be found in Scotland the most aristocratic democracy and the most democratic aristocracy in the world. I was always conscious of a quality of mutual respect which was quite different from what I was likely to find south of the border. It is, indeed, no small advantage to have the habit of expecting to be able to respect those with whom you come into any sort of contact, and consequently the habit of looking for grounds on which you can base that respect. Liking by itself may be no more than an amiable weakness or, what is far worse, a patronising attitude towards other people ; whereas respect offers a dignified relationship and nearly always draws forth a reciprocal feeling.

It was not the family history alone, or the condition of Scottish society, that made Dochfour a place of romance for me. There was the wild beauty of the spot itself and the magnificence of the west-coast property that ran from Loch Duich to Loch Hourn.

My grandfather was very fond of going to Italy and he believed, quite rightly I think, that Loch Ness and the setting of Dochfour generally were strongly reminiscent of Lake Como. He created, therefore, an Anglo-Italian villa which, if not beautiful externally, is particularly cheerful and comfortable inside and makes an exceedingly pleasant home. But even more than the house itself the Italian gardens my grandfather also made, with their terraces going down to the edge of the lower loch, fit perfectly into the surrounding scene. The view from the house extends away along Loch Ness into the distance for some twenty-six miles, the hills growing in height all the time until everything is merged into the mystery of the great western mountains.

When my brother James succeeded, he and I went up and stayed at Dochfour on our own and proceeded on a tour during which we visited every resident on the property. But it was when we went into the west that the spirit of romance entered into my life and soul. No one will ever again know the western land as it was then. Over long stretches there were no roads and we had to pick our way on horseback amid the grand wonder of the mountains. In my time I have seen many great ranges, much higher than our Scottish ones ; but none of them were able to give me the sense of vast majesty that the mountains of the west did.

During our tour together my brother and I drove over the seventy miles to Glenelg, breaking the journey at Glenmoriston. In those days there was no means of locomotion within the district ; rowing-boats and ponies were the sole means of communication. There were villages in which not a soul could speak a word of English ; nevertheless, there would be the warmest of welcomes for us and the readiest of hospitality—inconveniently ready sometimes, when it involved a consumption of whisky that might have proved serious if we had not had such long distances to travel between the various places.

I have two especially vivid recollections of that time. The first was the occasion of our actual arrival at Loch Hourn. As there was no road from Glenelg, we had to go round by sea in a boat rowed by some hefty Highlanders. The view the whole way was stupendous. On the right hand we had the island of Skye with the serrated line of the Cuillin Hills. In front was the island group of Eigg, Rum and Muck, rising out of the sea. To the left gradually unfolded the entrance to one of the noblest lochs in Scotland, with its great mountainous sides descending sheer to the sea. In our faces the breeze carrying the tang of salt was exhilarating. To my mind came the wonderful story of Prince Charlie's escape and the song " Over the sea to Skye ". I became, indeed, so excited by the whole thing that the boatmen declared I must be *fey*.

The second picture that I have is of a little village on Loch Hourn, about the most isolated spot you could find anywhere. No road ran into it from any direction. As a background to the village there was the sombre outline of Ben Screel, rising almost as steeply as a cliff to nearly 4,000 feet. The arrival of my brother and myself created tremendous excitement, everyone crowding round us and chattering in Gaelic. We found only two persons who could make any pretence at talking English—a shopkeeper and the schoolmaster ; but the latter's speech at best was very intermittent. We finally made our way through into the schoolmaster's house, where he was to entertain us to lunch. But his lack of English made any attempt at conversation next to impossible and in silence we sat devouring a huge dish of the famous Loch Hourn herrings accompanied by a pile of potatoes. Solemnly our host ate his ample meal before delivering himself of his one and only remark. " A fre-esh herring ", he said, " is a very guid thing —especially when she's fre-esh ! "

CHAPTER 4

CAMBRIDGE AND LONDON

A COUSIN of mine who was really not clever had gained a reputation in the family for great wisdom, chiefly as the result of a preternaturally solemn manner of propounding opinions gleaned from *The Times*, which he read sedately, even as a boy. When we were due to go up to the university together our relations took it for granted that my cousin would pass his entrance examination triumphantly and that "poor Albert" would not. When the exact reverse occurred my family was shocked into a belief that I might not be so entirely brainless as they had confidently supposed.

In the lives of the majority of educated men the university period is one in which, as much as anything, they are engaged in finding their feet among their fellows. Where a boy's public school career has been successful, his time at the university represents only the last stage of this process, since he has already learned a great deal before he comes up. In my case, as has been seen, I had no such preliminary preparation. It was true I had had unusual opportunities in knowing very remarkable older people, which had taught me much ; beyond that I had few advantages. I had been brought up practically an only child ; I had been a failure at school, and a failure, too, in that I had been unable to share in the interests or amusements of life with other boys. I went up to the university, therefore, a very lonely boy, and the more so because the inferiority complex I had acquired in childhood made me diffident as to my capacity for achieving friendships, although by nature I was extremely gregarious. In that direction Cambridge was to do for me just what I needed.

I remember very little about my first Cambridge year. I

was at Trinity College and, very fortunately, my Hyde Hall friend, Martin Hawke, got me elected a member of the Pitt Club soon after I went up. By the end of the year I had somehow slipped into a large circle of friends. When I moved from my first very humble rooms overlooking the Market Place into more comfortable ones in Bridge Street, they became quite a social centre and I derived all the benefit that comes from the free intercourse of the young at that stage of their development. My three greatest friends were Willie Bridgeman, Freeman Thomas, and Johnnie Maxwell, a family connection.

Willie and Johnnie and I later shared rooms. There, surrounded by our various possessions, we entertained friends from outside ; living together we came to know one another intimately and established enduring friendships. Freeman Thomas, though not living with us, was an integral part of our circle. We were as most young men training their minds : forever busily seeking solutions to eternal problems ; celebrating our youth in laughter, each of us with

> . . . a light heart still breaking into song :
> Making a mock of life, and all its cares,
> Rich in the glory of our rising suns,
> Lightly we vaulted up four pair of stairs,
> In the brave days when we were twenty-one.

Of these three friends Johnnie was closest to me : besides our family connection we shared a deep interest in art, in which our tastes were sympathetic. Johnnie had a much greater knowledge of art than myself and in later years he was prominently connected with galleries in England and in Scotland. His abilities however were not confined to art alone : he became head of the Forestry Commission ; his collection of rhododendrons at Pollok is said to be one of the finest in Britain and his knowledge of horticulture generally is immense ; he took an active part in Scottish national affairs, with which he was well acquainted, and for his services to Scotland was made a Knight of the Thistle. One of the

Secretaries of State for Scotland once told me that he thought nothing of importance was done in Scotland in which Sir John Stirling Maxwell was not consulted.

Willie Bridgeman and Freeman Thomas were also to carve out distinguished careers. Willie entered Parliament and, created a peer, became First Lord of the Admiralty. Freeman climbed high in the service of the Empire, representing the Crown in Canada and India, and was created Lord Willingdon.

Of the four of us Johnnie and I alone survive. Johnnie is now crippled by ill-health. Each year I visit him in Scotland. We talk a great deal then and I still see the vivacity of those golden early days at Cambridge shine from his eyes and radiate from his smile.

I possessed one special friendship which was right outside my immediate social circle. This was in the person of a quiet man who moved in a small circle of his own but with whom I had shared a study at Marlborough. Soon after he left the University he stepped into the headship of the firm of Debenham & Freebody, already well-known drapers, and together with another Cambridge acquaintance whom he took into partnership, he developed the business into its present vast proportions. Through him I gained two other friendships with men outside my general circle. The first of these was with Debenham's partner, Oliver, who emphasised the danger of our unpreparedness before the first World War in his book *Ordeal by Battle* written in support of Lord Roberts's plea for military training in this country. The other was a famous figure in the political world, Austen Chamberlain, who remained a friend of mine until the end of his life.

There were quite a number of distinguished scholars who were a regular and intimate factor in our existence. Above all, there was Monty James, afterwards Provost of Eton but perhaps better known as a writer of brilliant ghost stories. James was unrivalled in his scholarship but he was also without peer as a social companion. He was a first-rate singer of humorous songs and an admirable actor who played his part to the full in our joyful amateur excursions into the theatre, through the A.D.C., one of the oldest and most famous of amateur dramatic clubs.

The A.D.C., while we were at Cambridge, had one excellent rule : nobody could be elected simply on account of his histrionic capacity ; they had to be eligible for their personal qualities as friends and companions. It remained, therefore, an essentially jolly, cheerful club and the intervals of action were immense fun. Although I was notoriously the worst actor in Europe (and probably for the purposes of this comparison I might, as Sydney Smith said, extend my geographical limits), I became President. One of our committee was my friend Johnnie Maxwell, and another, Sir Aubrey Smith, who flourished as a popular favourite on the films with an unquenchable youthfulness, until his recent death. But there was a personality beloved by many generations of Cambridge men with whom the A.D.C. brought us into contact. This was J. W. Clarke, a man I believe of great learning. Fired with a delightfully humorous enthusiasm for the stage, and especially the French stage, he was our guide, philosopher and friend in all matters appertaining to our acting and always attended our committee lunch on Sundays.

Outside the A.D.C. I was once asked to act in a Greek play. I pointed out that as my Greek was extremely elementary, I must be given a part in which I had nothing to say. Accordingly I was allotted the part of Hermes and walked through the role in a beautiful classical dress consisting chiefly of wings on my head and at my heels. The most amusing feature of this experience, however, lay in the quite violent quarrels that the play's three directors used to have. J. W. Clarke was responsible for the direction of the acting, Professor Waldstein directed the classical correctness of the piece and Stanford wrote and conducted the music. As they were all men of hot temper and decided opinions, they addressed one another with the utmost frankness and provided the rest of us with the most diverting by-play. This first modest connection with the stage gave me a love for the art of acting and its exponents which has remained with me through life.

Having been forbidden to play games all though my youth, I naturally did not do so at this period. While a large number of my friends were athletes—Willie and Freeman played cricket for the University—my only athletic accomplishment was riding, of which I was passionately fond. Not being very rich, and without horses, I was only able to go with the Drag occasionally. When, at the beginning of my last year, a vacancy occurred in the mastership I was offered it and was forced very reluctantly to refuse, being unable to afford a mount. Lancelot Lowther, now Lord Lonsdale, was then offered the mastership and stipulated that he would only accept it if I would be his whip. I explained to him that this was impossible, but he insisted and offered to keep a horse for me. Such generosity I could not graciously decline and we had an extremely happy season. I may say that Lancelot has been throughout my life one of my most loyal and affectionate friends, in spite of our interests and occupations being so different as to prevent our meeting very frequently. But I do now have an occasional chance of visiting him, and I fancy any stranger would be entertained to see two old gentlemen, both over eighty, sitting laughing and chaffing one another just as they used to do sixty years earlier at Cambridge.

My tutor, a kindly, absent-minded mathematician, never addressed a word to me about my work during the whole time that I was nominally under his care. Indeed, I never saw him except on the occasions when I went to him for the signing of an Exeat. Nor, for that matter, did anyone else inquire as to the work I was doing. Two or three years after I had gone down, when I visited Cambridge and called on my tutor, he solemnly told me that he had considered my character very carefully on my first coming up and had come to the conclusion that I was one of those people who were much better left to their own devices. I did not take his statement very seriously. As far as the authorities were concerned, I might have been absolutely idle during the whole of my university career.

The fact that I passed my Little-Go without difficulty was a tribute to the soundness of Mr. Hiley's teaching. I then entered myself for the History Tripos and began my reading. I never had a coach for my work until towards the eve of the examination and, though I used often to analyse my books in the margin, I took no notes. But I was acquainted with one celebrated historian, owing I think to family connections. This was Professor Seeley, a most delightful man, who used to ask me to dine with him but never, that I can recollect, made any inquiry about my work. On one occasion around his dinner table there was an extremely learned party among which I was the only undergraduate. Creighton, afterwards Bishop of London, and Robertson Smith, whose learning was a thing spoken of with awe, were among those present. Between these two a rather heated argument arose as to the number of hours an undergraduate ought to read, which in view of my position struck me as unpleasantly personal. Robertson Smith firmly stated that all undergraduates ought to read, as he himself had done, at least thirteen hours daily. Creighton replied that any ordinary man who did such a thing would become an idiot; his contention being that no more than six hours was the requisite amount. In the end they most unfairly asked me my opinion. I disclaimed any opinion but ventured to say something as to a student's need of exercise; whereupon they both fell on me, declaring that when you were working your brain, exercise was quite unnecessary if not actually detrimental !

Still, I did read a certain amount. I had already developed a habit of rising very early in the morning, somewhere about six o'clock, and I would read steadily until Cambridge woke up and friends began to come in. I read all the set books, many of them several times, and I read many others as well. But I read easily, as I should have done with a novel or a biography, not with the self-conscious application of a student, though I gained a very fair general knowledge of the subject. History to me was not the bare study of facts but the study of people; the facts were only the setting of the people they concerned. I think this is a sound method, but it is not the best method of preparing for a history examination.

During the next three years I read most mornings for at least three hours, but by ten o'clock when my friends began to look in, I put my books aside for the day. In the last year, however, on the eve of my Tripos, I did read again between tea and dinner. When I went in for the final examination I had no expectations of achieving anything above a Third Class. This was partly because my conviction that I was stupid had prevented me from aiming high in my work, inclining me to absorb just as much as I found interesting in my reading. That I managed to obtain a Second was by accident and quite undeserved.

A day or two before the examination I dined with Professor Seeley and the question of whether history could be treated as a science was discussed. My host elaborated his views with the lucidity and point for which he was justly famous, and my joy can be imagined when on sitting down to my set essay in the examination hall I found that very subject had been given us. I proceeded to write down diluted Seeley with the greatest enthusiasm. In due course I was sent for by the examiners and told I had produced the equal best essay of the year, my only rival being by far the best historian competing. I must now confess that my Second Class in my History Tripos has always been a source of some shame to me. But I may also admit that I did not tell the examiners the true facts of the case.

As regards the real object of education, the power of reasoning, I was completely uneducated. I could not think for myself; if I was called on to make a little speech at one of our dinners I was unable to put two or three sentences together intelligently. My education had served simply to store my mind and memory with a certain amount of knowledge, but I had missed the necessary training showing me how to use it. Thus was proved once again the pointlessness of formal education where I was the pupil. I was fortunate, however, in meeting during these last months at Cambridge a man who was to exercise a lasting influence on my mind. When the results of the examinations in which I had gained a Second were published, he wrote :

My dear Albert,

I have not the remotest idea where you are, but I have just seen in the evening paper the name of Baillie, of Trinity, and must say how pleased I am—so pleased that I am quite prepared to pay the five pounds that Bridges told me he should win from you if you got your Second Class. Seriously, I am very glad indeed : it will please you ; it will please your mother, and it will confirm you in your desires to go on reading. It is the best news I have seen for many a long day. . . .

I first saw the writer one night in the Green Room of the Cambridge local theatre, during the performance of the Greek play already mentioned. I imagined him to be a good deal older than he actually was, his clothes being reminiscent of the days of the dandies and, as a rule, to be found only among the elderly who affected the dress of their youth. He was of medium height and sturdy build ; he wore a brown frock-coat with a velvet collar and his tall hat had the curl of the brim that one sees in the hats worn by D'Orsay and his friends ; he had whiskers, a moustache and an imperial, also in the same earlier fashion. He was talking to Stanford the musician, who presently introduced me to him. I found him a witty and most entertaining talker, and invited him to a supper party in my rooms after the play, to which many of the actors were coming.

So began my intimate friendship with Mowbray Morris, which lasted over twenty years until he died in my house at Rugby. By the time I first met him he had won a considerable name for himself and was Editor of *Macmillan's Magazine*, in connection with which he did great work in helping and advising young authors. Among them was Kipling, of whom he wrote :—" I hope you read the ballad of the King's Mercy in my last number, and thought it good ; if you did not, you will never come to any. The writer is a young fellow by name of Rudyard Kipling—queer name is it not ? . . . He is a most amusing companion, full of life and fun, very shrewd withal, and I think not likely to be spoiled." Morris sent a monthly letter to the Indian paper in which Kipling's work had appeared and this had led to Kipling being given a letter of introduction to him.

My greatest debt to Mowbray Morris was that he educated my love for literature. But this he could hardly help doing because literature was the absorbing interest of his life. It was a constant grief to him that the pressure of pot-boiling never allowed him the time to write anything of importance ; nevertheless, he was always meticulous in whatever writing he had to do, irrespective of the time limit set upon the work. His sense of literary form extended even to a careful approach to his work. Like Sir Walter Scott he would not write so much as a letter until he was fully dressed. In his eyes it would have been a disrespect to literature to be careless in either his clothes or his shaving when he sat down and took up his pen. His judgment of literature was remarkable. After his death Fred Macmillan told me he could say of Morris what he did not suppose a publisher had ever been able to say of a reader, that during all the years he had read for the firm they had never published a book on his recommendation which had failed, nor published one against his advice which had succeeded. Which encomium was the more remarkable in that, in ordinary talk, Morris seemed full of prejudices with regard to books and authors, and you might easily have been led to suppose he often judged on very superficial lines. But his exaggerated expression of prejudice was largely due to a sense of fun. If he gave a serious judgment it was invariably balanced ; and he would carefully consider all books even though written by men at whose work he girded in conversation or whom he happened to dislike personally.

I have said that my association with Morris cultivated my love of literature to an extraordinary degree, yet it was the fun of his companionship which I enjoyed most. Not only was he full of wit but he could fool with the most enchanting abandonment, and inspired fooling is one of the rarest of gifts.

Morris possessed an astonishing memory and always had an apposite quotation ready to hand ; he also often garbled a quotation with delicious effect. During my later time at Rugby he frequently made long visits to the Rectory and though his health had broken down he loved to drive round, specially to see the hounds, and was familiar with all the historic runs and the names of the villages round about. On Sunday nights, when my curates were in, he used to make himself the centre of the most wonderful talk. I recollect one night the talk had been running on poetry and something had been said about how extraordinarily prosaic Wordsworth could be. " Yes," Morris remarked, " don't you remember the line ' Smith, with this spade I spank thy lowly tail ' ? " Ever afterwards he used to chaff one of the curates who, he declared, had taken him in all seriousness and spent the greater part of the night searching through Wordsworth's works for the words he had used. Certainly I owe an immeasurable debt to Morris, for the pleasure he brought into my life no less than the benefit he conferred on my mind.

2

During those Cambridge years I gained some little insight into London society, dominated still by the great ladies of the old order. It was, of course, very near its last days, but no one seems to have suspected the change which was to come so rapidly. During the winter and spring vacations I was at Dochfour engaged in the usual country pursuits, but I used to visit London in the middle of June, at the beginning of the Long Vacation, and stay at my mother's house in South Audley Street until the end of July, when we went to Scotland. As soon as I arrived in town I would find myself flooded with invitations, since a large proportion of the prominent hostesses counted cousins with me and asked me automatically. I was continually being presented to old ladies who began the conversation with the words " Of course, we're cousins, you know . . .". And there was in society in those days a general family feeling.

During the Season the London of the 'eighties was a delightful place. The West End was free from marauding commerce. No lorries or omnibuses were allowed either in Mayfair or Belgravia and only private carriages were permitted to enter Hyde Park. The streets within these areas looked very gay, almost every house possessing window-boxes brilliant with flowers from top to bottom. There were hosts of striped sunblinds shading the windows. The carriages, also, were a very pretty sight ; infinitely more attractive than motor cars. Sitting up in a carriage ladies used to display their beauty perfectly ; in a motor car everybody looks alike.

It was then still the habit of some of the older men to do their afternoon calling on horseback, and there were boy crossing-sweepers ready to hold the horses, as may be seen in Leech's drawings in the contemporary numbers of *Punch*. The habit died out, along with crossing-sweepers, with the introduction of wood pavement, which was too clean to need the sweepers and too slippery for horses. Nevertheless, riding remained quite a common thing and I used to ride down to garden parties at the Duke of Northumberland's place at Syon, through Hammersmith, Chiswick and Brentford over what was then a pleasant macadamised road, without much traffic except at Brentford.

For a young man London society was very much easier then than now. The life was regular and clearly defined. A large proportion of people rode in the Park, either before breakfast or at twelve o'clock, and the Row, filled with fine horses, was a sight to behold. Others walked or sat at the side of the Row, so that the whole thing was not unlike a vast private garden party. Then there were luncheon parties ; some people kept open house for their friends and the porter would advise any callers whether or not there was still room available. After tea everyone sat out on chairs between the Achilles Statue and the Marble Arch. You would almost certainly be able to find there all your partners for that night's balls and so settle to which you would be going. At other times there were dinners or plays to attend of an evening.

At the time of which I am speaking young men could not entertain ladies. Indeed there were no facilities that made such entertainment practicable. There were the Café Royal and small Italian restaurants in Soho which young men frequented, but anywhere to which ladies might be taken did not exist. A young man was always entertained in private houses or went to his club. All this made it possible for him to go into society at very small expense. To the young people of today it may sound dull, but we did not find it so. We enjoyed ourselves thoroughly.

I am glad that I knew the London social scene of those days. It was a time of great beauties, of great men and of a galaxy of eccentric figures who now move across the tapestry of English social history like people from another world. Of the eccentrics Oscar Wilde is the most notorious. I saw a certain amount of him both in London and at Cambridge before the debacle occasioned by his trial and before people generally suspected him of the vice that led to his imprisonment in Reading Gaol.

Wilde was not very highly thought of by the world at large. He had never penetrated into very good society and he was not a man whom people were inclined to take into their homes. Brilliantly amusing and therefore acceptable to a great extent in masculine company, he was seldom very much liked since he was such a blatant poseur and one in whose sincerity nobody believed. Personally, I was repelled by him and by his strenuous efforts to be on terms of friendship with me. Still, although I did not like him he was so incredibly amusing that it was impossible not to laugh when he talked, and since you cannot very well laugh at and snub a person in the same breath I avoided him in so far as I could.

When Wilde first came to London, Mowbray Morris and Archie Wortley, the artist with whom he shared a house, invited Wilde frequently to see them. When finally they realised that he was not really trying to do good work but only using his immense powers to obtain notoriety, they stopped asking him. Morris, however, continued to know him right to the end. If he had chosen seriously to do good work, Wilde might have achieved very great things. As it was, he never got beyond doing merely clever things and none of his productions serve as a measure of his potential genius.

Of the great beauties, none wore a mask of make-up to conceal those lovely changes and harmonies of colour that are among the sex's greatest attributes. There are certain compensations, perhaps ; the plain have now a better chance. Today, very few women look positively plain, although I think very few look beautiful either. It may be, however, that on the whole this average comeliness which has been achieved is pleasanter.

When I began at eighteen to move about in London, my mother helped me to find my feet in a way that was particularly her own. She never gave me advice or warnings, but she liked me every morning to come and sit on her bed and tell her all I had seen and done the evening before. She saw the fun of everything almost more than I did and made me feel the greatest pleasure was being able to describe it to her. This, of course, whether consciously or unconsciously, gave me the sense that there must be nothing I did which I could not share with her afterwards. But then that was so essentially her ; she always understood, she always trusted, she always took for granted that one was doing right. And I could not help trying to live up to her faith. Even to this day I cannot hear an amusing story or experience anything of note without wishing I could pass it on to her and see the laughter and interest dancing in her eyes.

Till the end of her days people used to express admiration for her beauty. I remember once King Edward VII remarked to me : " You know, I knew your mother before she married " ; adding, after a pause, in his most guttural tones : " she was ver-r-ry pretty." Now, according to the most commonly accepted standards, she was not in the least beautiful. Her features were far from good, and her face was too square. She had attractive hair and a remarkably fine complexion, but that was all. Why, then, did everyone consider her pretty, right up to the time she was an old woman? I think the answer is that people *looked* at her face but *saw* nothing but her eyes. Grey in colour and of moderate size, they were not really fine eyes, but they seemed to possess the power of speech! I have never known another example of this. If my mother was indignant her eyes flashed, if she was amused they danced, and always when she was listening to you there was an intense sympathy in their expression that made you feel her whole soul was going out to you. Whoever you might be and whatever you might be saying, you invariably felt that she was giving you her attention preeminently, with an absolutely absorbed interest.

Because of this immense sympathy people were drawn to confide in her and share with her things which affected them most personally and intimately. I remember when she died her doctor telling me that after the funeral he walked away with Sir George Grove, the great historian of music, who said to him : " The last person has gone to whom I could go in a difficulty, absolutely certain of getting good advice." And yet I doubt if she ever gave advice. That was not her way. Her's was far too humble a spirit ; but she listened so sympathetically that it cleared your own mind and gave you light by which to guide your own decisions.

It was only natural that she should make a wonderful hostess. While I was at Cambridge she once brought the great American preacher, Phillips Brooks, who was staying with her, down to see me. To meet them I collected the most interesting men I could think of among my friends and acquaintances, including the historian Seeley and J. W. Clarke. Altogether, as I recollect, it was a rather heterogeneous party but from the start it was an entire success. Everybody gave of themselves freely, and my mother was the centre of it all. Not that she said much herself ; it was, rather, the interest with which she met every remark that drew out of those present their best. I am sure our guests left saying what a wonderful talker she was.

Another side of her great quality of sympathetic interest in people was the breadth of its operation and effect. At my friend Johnnie Maxwell's coming of age, she opened the Ball with the leading tenant of the Pollok estate, a dour old Scotsman. Afterwards they sat down together and it was entrancing to watch the interest they found in one another. The old farmer told her everything he could think of and at the end of the evening, long after she had gone to bed, he came up to me and confided enthusiastically : " Your mither's a gra-a-and woman ! "

My mother could never bear to hear us saying that anyone bored us. "If you find anyone uninteresting," she once declared to me, " you may be sure that it is because you are too stupid to find out what is interesting in them." And she herself certainly lived up to that principle.

During my father's lifetime my mother had the reputation of being wonderfully well-dressed. Now, to anyone who knew her later, such a thing would have seemed little short of comic, since clothes did not preoccupy her to the smallest degree. But when she and her sister Augusta had been girls in Paris, a young Englishman came over and started a dressmaking business in the French capital. The two girls, being intensely patriotic, were among the new dressmaker's first customers. He continued to make my mother's clothes until my father died, keeping his charges low. The young man was Worth, who, after the marriage of Napoleon III, became arbiter of fashion for the whole of Europe, through the patronage of the Empress Eugénie. As he took a personal interest in my mother she was remarkably well turned out, but I am sure she never took the slightest interest in the matter herself. After my father's death she had only two day dresses : a stuff one for week-days and a silk one for Sundays ; and two evening dresses : of silk for ordinary occasions and of satin for best. Moreover, when these wore out they were replaced by facsimiles. In one respect only was she fastidious about her clothes—everything she wore had to be absolutely clean.

Being a year senior to all my most intimate friends at Cambridge I naturally wished to stay on for another year after taking my degree. If I did so, however, there arose the question as to what my work should be ; accordingly I let it be known that I wished to be ordained. I had never deliberately concealed this, but somehow I had happened not to mention it. As I had been very much to the fore in the gaieties of life, my friends had never suspected my intention. I am glad that nobody seemed to consider the idea unsuitable, though most people were surprised. I liked to feel this meant I had won their respect as a man.

My mother, of course, had known the direction towards which my thoughts were shaping, but, characteristically, she had never pressed the matter : her only concern was whether I was equal to so high a calling. She was certainly very glad when I made my decision. Curiously enough there had never been any doubt in my own mind ; I took it for granted that I should be a clergyman. This was remarkable in view of how completely detached my existence had been from ecclesiastical things. It was true my uncle, Arthur Stanley, was a clergyman and that I saw a good many clergy at his house ; but, except at Hallingbury, I had never seen a parochial clergyman at work. It is not easy to explain, but undoubtedly my ignorance of the workaday world of a clergyman was responsible for my having no real affinity with the ecclesiastical mind all through my life. A tendency which has its good as well as its bad side.

The Cambridge authorities suggested I should give my extra year at the University to the study of Hebrew. This was an entirely fatuous suggestion : I had never properly learned either Greek or Latin or shown any aptitude for languages ; in any case Greek and Latin were of much greater value to a clergyman. I did begin reading Theology, however, and also made some very amateurish efforts at learning

The Author at Cambridge (*centre*) standing at the entrance to P Old Court, Trinity

On author's left, W. C. Bridgeman, and on his right, Sir John Stirling Maxwell. The servants, from the left, are Bridgeman's College gyp, Mrs. Smith and Mrs. Gayler, bedmakers, Sir John's servant, Edwin, and seated, centre, the author's servant, Bertie.

parish work by teaching in a Sunday school and night school. Meantime I was conscious of no visible change in my relationship to my friends. My tutor, against all ordinary rules, allowed me to live in College and, moreover, arranged for Willie Bridgeman, Johnnie Maxwell and myself to have rooms on staircase P in Old Court. I had a small third room in which we used to have our meals. We were extremely well looked after : Johnnie had a servant who remained with him afterwards a great many years ; I continued under the care of the son of my old landlord in Bridge Street, while Willie had one of the College gyps. We were blessed, too, with two most excellent bedmakers, both resembling the type of charlady that George Belcher was later to draw so inimitably. Mrs. Gayler was stout and masterful, Mrs. Martin thin and submissive. Between them they provided a working team which could not have been bettered.

We lived an altogether congenial life during those final Cambridge months, entertaining a great many of our friends and maintaining our common interest in the A.D.C. Our tastes, none the less, were by no means wholly frivolous. Willie was a scholar and sincerely religious ; Johnnie had an extraordinary variety of interests ; the majority of our mutual friends brought an intelligent and liberal mental activity into the already delightful harmony of our personal fellowship. It was at this stage that I became Whip of the Drag, so that this was, I think, the happiest period in my Cambridge career. But I grew increasingly conscious that I ought to devote myself more completely to my preparation for Orders. To this purpose I knew I would do better to terminate my somewhat distracting way of life. Accordingly, at the end of my second term, I firmly made my decision and left.

CHAPTER 5

PREPARATION FOR ORDERS

FROM Cambridge I went to Dochfour where I spent the summer alone with my second brother, Augustus, who was managing the property. It was the year of the first Jubilee, which gave us several months of glorious weather, through summer into early autumn. My brother was busy with his work and I enjoyed complete leisure. I rode a great deal and wandered about, soaking in the glorious beauty of the country and thinking of my next step towards ordination.

There was much enthusiasm among young men for taking Orders at that time, both in England and Scotland. My special interest just then was a study of the Established Church of Scotland. I had long had a great admiration for that body and the stir of disestablishment in the air excited my desire for further knowledge of it. I read, therefore, everything about this Church I could get hold of. Because of my early training I could never have become a Presbyterian. Since it was the Church in which Scottish character had been formed, however, I loved it and admired the wonderful virility of its thought. But, if it was impossible for me to find a place in the Scottish Established Church, the Scottish Episcopal Church seemed so alien to the main stream of Scottish life that it had many of the characteristics of a sect, and I should have been even more unhappy taking Orders in it. I was left, therefore, with no other alternative than to enter the English Church, my love for Scotland notwithstanding. I still retain a deep affection for the Church of Scotland, while I have since grown to a fuller understanding of the Episcopal Church and its history.

I dreamed on throughout that summer at Dochfour in a confused and muddle-headed fashion ; always at the back of my mind there was the knowledge that with the autumn I must be ready to take the final step. I knew of two people who were training young men for Orders : Dr. Vaughan, the Master of the Temple, and Bishop Lightfoot of Durham. As they were both great personalities it would have been an immense advantage to be with either of them. Dr. Vaughan, an old family connection, invited me to go to him. My final decision, however, was influenced by Bishop (later Arch-bishop) Maclagan, a life-long friend of my family to whom I paid occasional visits during this time. They were remark-able visits, which helped me considerably ; partly because of the intimacy I developed with the Bishop's chaplain, Arthur Winnington-Ingram, afterwards Bishop of London, whose fellowship was an inspiration to me in my unsettled state ; mainly because Bishop Maclagan had a profound admiration for Bishop Lightfoot and urged me strongly to make him my choice. In reply to a letter from Maclagan on my behalf, Lightfoot answered that his love and admiration for Dean Stanley were such that he would regard it as no less than a privilege to take his nephew into his care. So began the most important influence in my life next to that of my mother.

2

At Bishop Auckland, a moderate-sized mining town, I passed through the great gateway in the market place leading to the Bishop's park and palace. Auckland Castle, Bishop Light-foot's residence, was large and ancient, rich in associations which thrilled my deeply rooted historical sense. The old chapel had been destroyed during the Commonwealth and in its place the beautiful hall of Antony Bek, the famous fighting bishop of the late thirteenth century, had been converted to that purpose, providing a building through which a wealth of memories came to cluster in my heart.

At Auckland I entered into an entirely new world ; a world which to this day means as much to me as anything I have ever known. The hub, the axis, the very core of everything was Bishop Lightfoot himself. He was the greatest, the best man I have ever encountered, and I say this deliberately after the experience of many years. At first sight he was startlingly ugly : a stout little man with grotesque features and a squint. In a day or two one's consciousness of his outward shortcomings vanished and his face appeared the most beautiful and lovable thing imaginable. He had no popular social gifts, being shy, silent and awkward in general company. When he was entertaining strangers there was a childlike helplessness about him that was comic, but few men can have been capable of making people love and understand him so quickly or so completely. He was without even the ordinary gifts of oratory and yet, through love, he succeeded in bringing to life a diocese that had sunk into apathy and dullness. Whoever they might be, pitman or peer, they all spoke of him with a tender affection and reverence which it was his especial characteristic to evoke.

When I arrived, however, I knew nothing about Bishop Lightfoot except that he was a man of great learning, of whom people like Bishop Maclagan held the highest opinion, and that he used to take some half a dozen pupils at a time to train them for Orders. I found myself in a new world, a purely ecclesiastical atmosphere in which I at first felt very much at sea. Everything was strange to me. My fellow students were of other types than any of the young men I had been associated with before, with other interests and ideas. All this soon passed away, and I found myself making friends and entering joyously into my novel environment. We students had our rooms, in which we did most of our work, in a long wing of the Castle, named Scotland as it was said the Scottish prisoners were lodged there after one of the great border battles. Beyond an assumption that we would be present at meals and in chapel, there were practically no rules.

We lived an essentially happy, friendly communal life. Our relationship with Bishop Lightfoot was like that of sons, which he called us. He made no attempt whatever to dominate us. He accepted our ecclesiastical points of view without trying to alter them. He did not teach us himself at all ; I do not think he lectured to us once during the whole of my time ; and he preached only once a year, at the annual reunion celebration, though his sermon then was always momentous. The actual teaching was in the hands of the Bishop's two domestic chaplains : Harmer, afterwards Bishop of Rochester, and Welch, afterwards Vicar of Wakefield. Both men were very able, though Harmer was to have the more distinguished career.

The essence of Lightfoot's power lay, I believe, in the fact that love moulded his character and inspired his every thought and act. All of us felt that love. There was nothing senti-mental about it ; it was that emotion based on respect which St. Paul describes, no mere undiscriminating amiability. There were, of course, men for whom he felt a special affection, just as Our Lord felt a special affection for St. John. But Our Lord's love for St. John did not make the other Apostles jealous ; and so it was in our case. I think we should all have said that Edgar Lambert was the disciple who Lightfoot loved in that particular sense, and we who knew Lambert at all well would certainly have agreed that such a regard was natural.

There grew up around Lightfoot the Brotherhood of his disciples. There were a good many of these already when I joined their number, as he had been taking pupils for the past six years, and they were out in the world and working, mainly in the diocese. His heartfelt admiration for them and their doings made of them heroic figures in our younger eyes. There were among them some of the men he had chosen as chaplains and examining chaplains from Cambridge, when he went to Durham, and who became part of the Brotherhood. They were men of considerable intellect, like Armitage Robinson, afterwards Dean of Westminster, George Eden, afterwards Bishop of Wakefield, and Savage, afterwards Dean of Lichfield. There was also Tommy Strong, afterwards Bishop of Oxford, chosen to represent the sister university. But there were others who, if not of special intellectual power, were none the less possessed of great force of character and therefore cast in no less heroic mould. Edgar Lambert was one of these. And who that knew him could forget the saintliness of Sim, who died in the mission field ; or the great Macdonald, the " Long Mac " of our affections, who threw into his work the most tremendous atmosphere of joy. Among my own contemporaries was Cecil Boutflower, of whom I shall have much more to say.

The older Brothers came back constantly to visit us at the Castle, relating stories of their experiences and generally combining to give us the feeling that our work was a great and splendid adventure. Even today, although a vast number of the Brotherhood's members have died, there are yet enough remaining to meet periodically and revive in each other the immortal spirit that unites them. For it is a remarkable fact that with the death of its founder, the Brotherhood lived on. Both of Bishop Lightfoot's successors, Bishops Westcott and Moule, not only provided fresh members with the pupils they trained themselves, but they kept alive reverence for Lightfoot and the spirit of his influence. The body remained Lightfoot's Brotherhood, and that is perhaps the greatest witness to Lightfoot's greatness, since each of the succeeding Bishops had a personality strong, distinctive and totally different from that of their predecessor. It would have been perfectly natural for them to have had their own disciples, but with wonderful self-abnegation they merged their followers within the older fellowship.

In the carrying on of Bishop Lightfoot's work the two Bishops had an invaluable assistant in Cecil Boutflower. He was Westcott's chaplain right through his Episcopate and there was nothing into which he threw his great powers and lovable character with more enthusiasm than the welding into the Brotherhood of Westcott's disciples. He continued the same course after he had left Auckland and Bishop Moule had succeeded at Westcott's death. Only the other day one of Moule's pupils said to me : " The trouble that Boutflower took with all of us was astonishing " ; and, in my own case, he never forgot to write to me on my birthday through all the years until he died. I doubt whether the two Bishops could have welded their own pupils with those of the original band without Boutflower's help.

The first and foremost characteristic of the Brotherhood was its prevalent atmosphere of joyousness. In illustration of this I recall one year, when I was Dean of Windsor, inviting the members to come to me for the annual gathering. After Bishop Westcott's death, when they ceased to be held at Auckland, not more than thirty attended such reunions and I made my calculations accordingly. It was something of a shock when I received no less than ninety acceptances. I managed to get my neighbours at Windsor and Eton to provide the necessary beds and we had our meals at long tables in the Cloisters. Although most of us were becoming elderly men, the gaiety of the company was more like that of under-graduates. At our solemn service, which used to mean so much to us when Lightfoot and Westcott preached, Cecil Boutflower was chosen to give the sermon, his long period as chaplain to Westcott making him the natural link between the older and younger generations. He fulfilled his task magnificently. As there were eleven bishops among us, we decided on a cricket match between them and a pick-up of the rest. It proved a first-rate match and the bishops wiped the floor with the others, the Metropolitan of India showing especial prowess. Thank goodness we were always too happy among ourselves to be the least pompous.

Second, we were none of us ever able to sink into a purely professional view of our work. To us, in some measure at least, the priest's life must always remain an adventure.

Third, no Brother could ever, I think, become a contro-versialist moved by party spirit. Certainly I never knew of one who did. Naturally we had our differences of view, and held to them strongly ; but we respected one another's views, and though we might discuss them freely it was never in the spirit of partisanship.

Fourth, I do not think that a Brother could ever give way

to artificiality or pose, or to self-advertisement. One had only to think of Lightfoot and the other Brothers to make such a thing impossible.

Fifth, behind everything our founder left us with the spirit of devotion as the background of life ; often unworthily lived up to, perhaps, but never quite forgotten.

Sixth, a Brother could never be a pessimist or lose heart when things looked rather hopeless.

Quite recently, after our gathering, the then ninety-year-old Edgar Lambert wrote to me, expressing his pleasure at our renewal of friendship. The letter closed with the words : " I see the coming of the Kingdom with power. God marches on." That was, indeed, the very spirit of Lightfoot speaking from the experience of a long life in times which induce despondency in many people.

It was while I was at Bishop Auckland that I began an acquaintance with Lord and Lady Boyne and their family which led ultimately to my marriage. They lived not far off at Brancepeth, another of those great border castles which lend such interest to Durham and Northumberland. The Battle of Neville's Cross was fought nearby and I like to remember that an ancestor of mine, according to tradition, was captured there and imprisoned, probably at Brancepeth.

My greatest friend throughout my Auckland training was Cecil Boutflower, and when the question of my finding a title arose I sought permission to go as a voluntary curate to Tyne Dock, whither Boutflower had gone three months before. I had already been offered Chester-le-Street, which was con- sidered the plum among curacies, and of course dear old Bishop Lightfoot, who always put the best construction on everything we did, was loud in his appreciation of what he called my " unselfishness " in choice. But it was not unselfish- ness : I thought I should like it better working with Cecil. After my ordination I at last set hopefully out for Tyne Dock, upon the first step of my great adventure.

It is of importance at this stage to draw attention to certain predominant features of the world in which, as a clergyman, I was going to work. The 'eighties and 'nineties were years of revolution in almost everything. In this respect the literary changes that grew out of that period seem the only changes to have been carefully studied ; nowhere better than in Holbrook Jackson's *The Eighteen-Nineties*. Nevertheless, that revolution was equally marked in other spheres.

I was ordained in the year 1888, just after Queen Victoria's first Jubilee. That event was the outward manifestation of the climax of a civilisation as great as any known to history. In the achievements and benefits of that civilisation the rest of Europe, our Dominions and the subject races that came within our Empire had their share. The European interests involved were shown by the impressive bodyguard of Princes who rode in Jubilee procession beside the carriage of the Queen. There was the splendid figure of Frederick, heir to the newly created German Empire, no more than a generation old ; there was the Crown Prince of Italy, also a new kingdom welding into a single strong monarchy the many little states which had rent Italy into warring factions during centuries of misgovernment and misery ; there were the representatives of the Balkan States and Greece, torn at last from Turkish rule and restored to their ancient independence. Each and all of those countries had felt something of the vital force that had brought the latest world civilisation to its splendid culminating point, in which position of general stability and welfare it seemed permanently to be established.

But it seems to be a law of History that when a civilisation reaches its peak it begins to decay. This law asserted itself in Europe. In England during the next ten years, and before the second Jubilee came round, the process of disintegration had started. The framework of society on which the established order of things rested was no longer capable of preserving itself ; standards of life and of morality were changing, and before the poor old Queen died she saw that unfortunate South African War which seemed the negation of much that the first Jubilee had meant. After the Queen's death the process of dissolution continued steadily, and continues visibly today, the two Great Wars wiping out the last clinging vestiges of the old civilisation. The tremendous prestige throughout the world, to which the first Jubilee testified, has vanished and little races, because they believe England to be weak, are yapping insolently at her heels. Nor is it only England that has suffered—all Europe is in chaos.

But at the time of my ordination, when the great transition at home was just beginning, it was reflected within the body of the Church itself. There was never a period when enthusiasm for taking Orders was so earnest and widespread. However, the ideal that was pressed upon us during our training of what a clergyman's work ought to be was something quite new. Organisation, and the influence it was capable of exerting on men, formed the subject of every lecture and every talk which we were given. What we ought to teach, and how best to teach it, was stressed comparatively lightly. We were given all manner of theories and commentaries to study, while it was taken for granted that the Gospel was something we all knew.

Was there any common foundation in the change brought about by the new line of thought that in those days began to affect society ? I have been pondering the question ever since I retired into my present peaceful life and the conclusions to which I have come are these :

The change, I am convinced, was caused by two things. The first is summed up in St. Paul's words : " Professing themselves wise they become fools." The success of the British Empire built up during those fifty years of a queen's progressively glorious reign made us enormously conceited. It was the old story of Nebuchadnezzar looking round upon the greatness of Babylon and boasting about what he had made. It astonishes me now when I recall the cocksureness with which everyone used to talk about our splendour and take for granted that it must last. It was, of course, the greatest civilisation since that of Rome ; but even as Rome fell we ourselves were bound to fall, and such will always be the fate of any civilisation regarded by its citizens as primarily their own work.

The other revolutionary factor, I think, lay in the effect on men's minds of a tremendous advance in science and a conceit of the capacity of the human intellect that went with it.

The Church in England during the nineteenth century made a great mistake. It knew that spiritual truth could not be learned by the intellect, but it turned aside to attack the scientists on their proven discoveries as to the structure of the world. The churchmen founded their attack upon an absurd theory as to the nature of the authority of the Bible, in doing which they gave away their real case. Yet though in theory they denied the place the intellect was accorded by scientists, in effect they accepted the conception of the intellect as the only faculty we possess for learning all sides of Truth. If they had taken their stand on the claim that spiritual truth was outside the scope of the human brain, they would have been unanswerable.

For there are many things that we learn through other faculties than that of the intellect, even in the case of material things. All that is sensory, for instance, our intellect alone can never explain. Intellectually we can neither bring home to anyone the scent of a rose or the peculiar satisfaction it gives us. And, above all, intellect cannot enable us to know another person. The cleverest among us is not capable of knowing other people more easily than someone who is comparatively stupid. They may, indeed, know a great deal about a person ; but they need quite another faculty to know them in the truest and fullest sense of the word—the faculty which the Bible calls love. Love is a word one hardly dares employ today, it has been so grossly vulgarised and misused. But in its real meaning, as implied by Our Lord and by St. Paul, it is the only medium through which we can learn truly to comprehend our fellow-men.

Nevertheless, it has become our cardinal fault that instead of denying the claim of the unique supremacy of the human intellect we have bowed to it and sought to prove the truth of revealed religion by means of intellectual arguments and definitions. I must confess that since realising this fact a few years ago very few of the sermons I have heard, or of those I have preached, had any aim apart from convincing the intellect of the hearers and the hope that through intellectual conviction would come faith. It is remarkable that at the turn of the present century a scientist declared that faith was not merely credulity but a separate faculty for acquiring the knowledge of certain sides of truth, and it is even more remarkable that such a tremendous admission had no more than an ephemeral effect and was very soon forgotten.

PART II

YEARS OF EXPERIENCE

CHAPTER 6

TYNE DOCK

TYNE DOCK was not an attractive place : it had sprung up almost accidentally in the derelict riverside district between Jarrow and South Shields. On the rising ground by the station was a colony of grimy brick houses, tenanted by pitmen and other workers. That was our respectable quarter. About half a mile off, on the low ground by the river, another group of houses clustered round the square in front of the dock gates ; shabby and tumble-down, they marked the end of South Shields's slum area. The police classed it as a criminal slum, into which they would not venture by night except in pairs. That was my district.

Cecil Boutflower had the more respectable neighbourhood, where the station and the church stood and where we both lived. Our rooms were close to the station : two little square sitting-rooms, and two tiny triangular bedrooms in which, when the saucer-bath had been pulled from under the bed, it was very difficult to move. Our windows overlooked a narrow lane at the opposite side of which a high embankment carried the railway line. Every twenty-four hours two hundred and forty trains drew past their open trucks of coal, on a level with our windows. Consequently inside and outside the house was thick with coal dust. The very water absorbed it, so that washing failed to make us really clean. When we went away it always took us a day or two to get back to our normal colour. Nearby a chemical works created a pall of smoke that overhung the whole district and killed all vegetation except a few anæmic elder bushes. Once Mowbray Morris came to stay with me when Cecil was away and occupied his room. He never came again, declaring that sleeping in a room where his head was on the railway

75

line and his feet in the sitting-room was more than he could stand.

Coming from a life in which my surroundings had been always attractive, Tyne Dock might easily have been depressing. Happily, it was nothing of the sort. Bishop Auckland had instilled in us the sense that we were engaged on a romantic adventure, and the experience ahead of me possessed the excitement and appeal of novelty.

I was to share my adventure with a man for whom I had the profoundest admiration and affection. Cecil Boutflower was tall, spare and ascetic in appearance. When he moved it was with the sudden rapidity of a released spring. He had a brain, and it had been highly cultivated. At Oxford he had been expected to take a First in Greats and, though he just missed it, was acknowledged as a man of unusual intellectual power and force of character. One remarkable thing about him was that all the leading theological dons at Oxford, of every school of thought, admitted him to friendship. I remember some years later meeting one of them, and when Cecil was mentioned the don remarked : " Yes, when he was an undergraduate we all said that living with Boutflower was like living with the law of nature."

Cecil had come from a clerical home suffused with a deep Evangelical piety. There he had absorbed the devotional spirit which was the dominant background to his life, though himself not an Evangelical. Neither was he a High Churchman or a Broad Churchman. No one could claim him as a partisan, but men of all schools accepted him as a friend. On intimate terms with Liddon and Scott Holland and the other leading High Churchmen, he was equally intimate with Chavasse, leader of the Evangelicals, who one day invited him to become Vice-President of Wyclyffe Hall. Cecil admired and loved Chavasse so much that his offer was a great temptation ; on the other hand, Wyclyffe Hall was a definitely party Evangelical place and he doubted if he would have been happy there. It was characteristic that the person he consulted in the matter was Liddon, who said : " It would be a great privilege to work with Chavasse; I'll tell you what I always feel about him. If we differ about anything my first impulse is to feel that I must be wrong." But Liddon agreed that Cecil would not be at home in the atmosphere of the College. Incidentally, it would have been just as natural and probable for the opposite school of thought to have offered him a post of the same kind; for the same reason he could not have taken it. His Christianity was bigger than any partisan organisation.

In spite of an exceptional sureness of taste in his use of words, and a great facility in writing verse (I think he won the Newdigate), Cecil never deliberately sought new fiction as a recreation. This, I fancy, must have been due to the influence of his Evangelical upbringing. The feeling general in such homes was that all literature not directly religious or purposely moral was a dissipation. Cecil was free from such prejudice, and when introduced to any new books he almost invariably enjoyed them.

The dissimilarity of our interests and abilities was one of the influences that made our intercourse so stimulating. My friend's greatest gift lay in his humour, which was similar to that of Dickens. He saw the comic in people through a medium of love, as Dickens did. Every day, when he returned from work, he would be bubbling over about the people he had encountered. We took our meals in Cecil's sitting-room seated at a round table in two horse-hair armchairs, which we christened the Chair of Philosophy and the Chair of History.

Another person who vitalised my life at Tyne Dock and who played a great part in forming my mind and character, was our Vicar, Robert Vaughan. The son of a Birmingham artisan, he started life as a brass-finisher, possessed of an overpowering thirst for knowledge. In order to read the Greek Testament he taught himself that language, walking to and from work each day. Though he never became a great scholar he gained an accurate knowledge of the Greek Testament. His ultimate proficiency in the language opened the door to his study of theology and philosophy, which became his absorbing interests. He never took any thought at second hand. I was about to say that he had never been a disciple of any great thinker, but I must except Swedenborg, whom he had studied profoundly and for whom he had a deep admiration. Yet even there he could not properly be described as a disciple, since he accepted none of Swedenborg's ideas without first analysing them, digesting them and making them his own. I once asked him whether I should study Swedenborg, and he answered : " If you are prepared to give seven years exclusively to the study of his writings it would be well worth your while, but if not I should leave him alone." I left him alone.

In consequence of the independence of his thought, Vaughan's ideas were extraordinarily vital and interesting. He had been brought up as a Congregationalist and, although he was entirely self-educated, he was accepted for the Congregational Ministry, in which he gained a considerable standing, holding an important chapel and enjoying a substantial income. He married exactly the right wife, who never attempted to enter into his intellectual interests but built around him a joyous, happy home, meeting all the changes and chances of life with an imperturbable spirit. When eventually he became dissatisfied with the Congregational theology (though to the end of his days he retained an immense respect for the Congregationalists as a body), the course he took was typical of him. For a year he closed every book except the Greek Testament, at which he worked with tremendous concentration, and when the year was over he announced : " I'm joining the Church of England." He scarcely knew a single clergyman ; but he had a great respect for Lightfoot, in spite of having never seen him, and went to him to prepare for ordination. It never seemed to strike him, or his wife, that the question of giving up a settled home and a good income to live as a curate on a hundred and fifty pounds a year was a matter of the least moment. After a few years the Bishop gave him the living of Tyne

Dock, which, though not one of the plums, was adequate for their simple needs.

I have never known anyone to inspire enthusiasm for abstract thought like Vaughan. The young clergy from round about flocked to hear him when he lectured on the Greek Testament. I can see him now on Sunday evenings, his wife laughing and joking as she cleared away supper, sitting in a straight, high-backed chair ; as he talked his eyes sparkled in his lean ascetic face and his beard, black to match his hair, bobbed about with the movement of his bottom jaw. When Mrs. Vaughan had finished and he had settled down with his pipe, Cecil or I used to propound to him a thesis. For example, one of us might say : " Now, Mr. Vaughan, tell us about original sin." Whereupon, without hesitation, he would begin to talk and for the remainder of the evening absorb our attention. He never laid down the law, and was quite ready for questions or interruptions, but he sincerely propounded what he believed on every subject. We called him Socrates.

With the Vicar and Cecil Boutflower as my constant companions, I was inspired to learn how to think. In parish work my position was altogether different and I was taught nothing.

The parish at Tyne Dock was a fallow field ; it had had for twenty-five years a singularly disreputable Vicar who stayed just within the law. There was no tradition, no machinery, no organisation and no real body of church workers ; this was especially true in my district. Cecil, who understood parish work and had had three months' start before I came, managed his district admirably, but in my district nothing whatever had been done. Mr. Vaughan himself had no idea of what the organisation of a parish meant, and I do not think he saw much advantage in it. His view was that you had to preach the truth and if people would not come to listen that was their misfortune. But of the endless varieties of influence which may be brought to bear through carefully organised effort, he had neither knowledge nor understanding. Not that he was a cipher in the parish, far from it. His personality had impressed the people and was most valuable as a background to any work that we might do. But he was simply unaware of what that work might be. Consequently, when on the first day I walked past the chemical works into the valley and saw my district, I was embarking upon a quite uncharted sea. I was absolutely without experience or training to help me. I could rely only on a genuine interest in my fellow creatures, telling myself that all those grimy little houses in front of me contained living people whom I sincerely desired to know.

The mentality of a slum in those days was vastly different from now. The slum dwellers of sixty years ago were entirely unself-conscious; they took themselves and their slum for granted. They had not yet been affected by the incessant stream of talk with which philanthropists, politicians and theorists were later to flood their minds, making them sour and sorry for themselves. Before that avalanche of self-pity fell on them, there was less unhappiness among the people of the slums, though today there is more opportunity for recreation, more comfort and a better average standard of health.

While my parish district at Tyne Dock was very squalid, it was not poor. Wages were high and very few people were out of work. I was surprised, therefore, when during my rounds of visits I discovered signs of the most abject poverty. I remember the miserable home of one family I came to know through the father's illness. There were no carpets, no curtains and no furniture deserving the name. The family sat on packing-cases for want of chairs; the beds were covered with old clothes instead of proper bed-clothes. The high wages earned by father and son were dissipated in drink and gambling, leaving no money for housekeeping. The worry of maintaining her home under these conditions crushed all hope out of the mother. When I won her confidence I learned that she had come from better circumstances and the squalor of her life had eaten into her soul. As she did not drink she could not even share the

BISHOP LIGHTFOOT (READING) AT BOURNEMOUTH

With three of his old students: J. R. Harmer (chaplain), afterwards Bishop of Rochester; A. F. Sim, who later died in the Mission Field; and Cecil Boutflower, later Bishop of South Tokio. Bishop Lightfoot, after his health collapsed, stayed for a time in Bournemouth, where a chaplain and two of his old students took turns in looking after him.

false excitement that kept the other two going; instead she simply lost interest in everything. She was very worried because she was in debt and I offered to lend her the money to clear her. It was quite a small sum which I told her she could pay back gradually, hoping in this way to restore her self-respect and courage. She became quite excited at the idea of repayment, telling me repeatedly how she was getting on and how soon she hoped to clear her debt to me. Her interest in life was returning and my experiment seemed hopeful. And then one day I found her sunk back into complete hopelessness. Her husband had found the little store of money she had been saving to pay me, and he had stolen it. With that she succumbed to a despair from which I was never again able to rouse her.

In another squalid home a man was dying. On going in one evening I found him delirious. His wife, dead drunk and still fully clothed, lay stertorously asleep by his side. I sat on a packing-case beside the bed and counted the hours till morning, when the man's life ran out. It was a grim night; the only sounds, the babbling of the dying man and the woman's snores.

But drunkenness, waste and squalor were not exclusively the conditions of life at Tyne Dock, for I met there the holiest and happiest woman I ever knew. She was poor, as her elderly husband was unable to earn much; and, being bedridden, she lay alone throughout the day until the evening, when her husband returned and did all he could for her. Whenever I visited her I never failed to find the old lady radiantly happy. She was invariably full of some new discovery, for ever realising something to be thankful for, knowledge of which she was anxious always to share with others. The other inmates of the little court in which she lived were the roughest of drunken navvies, and yet these men were always sneaking up, one at a time, just to sit by her bed and listen to her talk.

In one of a line of old houses tenanted by pitmen, lived a family for whom I developed a great affection. It was

an astonishing household. There were two rooms downstairs, and whatever could be squeezed under the slope of
the roof above. In all the building held twelve people : the
father and mother, a married daughter with her husband
and baby, two grown-up sons, two lads and two girls between
sixteen and twenty, and a lodger. I still do not know how
the house contained them. The men were unusually well
paid, according to the scale of those days, some as pitmen
and some as trimmers, and the amount of money coming
into the home was considerable ; since none of them either
gambled or drank, they remained comparatively well-off.
As far as food was concerned they lived extremely well.
Their teas were such as you only get in the north of England.
In the sitting-room burned a huge fire which the mother
used proudly to say had never been out in all the thirty years
of her married life, an occasional bucket of water teemed
down the chimney keeping it clean. The men of the household had their hip-baths in front of this fire when they came
in from work. I can recall sitting down to tea with the
family while the father sat in his bath by the fire, being
scrubbed by his fat, jolly wife who talked volubly throughout.
This scrubbing had to be carefully done, because of an ancient
tradition that there was a triangle at the base of the spine
which water must never touch, for fear of weakening the
man. In spite of the public use of the bath the utmost care
was taken with regard to decency. They were a model
family, always happy and cheerful.

Occasionally, when returning home from visits in my
district, the activity in the streets through which I passed
revealed to me—more than even the houses—the conditions
of life in Tyne Dock. Late one night, when everybody was
in bed, I encountered a man so drunk that he was much more
troubled by the width than the length of the road. As he
was in uproariously good spirits I went up to him and said:
" You're finding it a bit difficult to get along, shall I give you
an arm ? " He accepted my help but at intervals he stopped
to express his intense amusement at the idea of walking with

a parson. His home was right at the end of our long river-side street, about two miles off, and my companion continued to shout and laugh until we arrived there. He told me he had to go to work at six. I thought if I could catch him when he was feeling the after effects of his evening out I might be able to talk to him with profit. As it was then two or three o'clock in the morning and it was hardly worth while my going to bed during the interval, I passed the time with men who were loading coal barges, on night shift. As I might have expected, my convivial friend overslept himself and failed to appear at six.

One result of the unself-consciousness of slum dwellers in those days was a curious quality of childishness. They seldom had any obvious discipline of mind. They could be very violent and they could equally be tender and kind ; they could be criminals and they could be like naughty children. On going down to the district one afternoon, I entered the square by the dockyard gates to find a crowd assembled and a fight in progress. With the enthusiasm of youth I pushed my way through, succeeded in separating the fighters and gave all present a talking to. The fighters and the crowd then dispersed while I went about my business in the neighbouring streets. But on my return some half an hour later I saw the crowd had recollected and the fight had been resumed. At sight of me someone called out "Here's Mr. Baillie !" and before I reached the spot most of the gathering had again melted away. As for those few that remained, they met me like naughty children, pretending to have been doing nothing at all.

Sometimes, of course, men who were drink-maddened were dangerous. One day when I went to visit such a case I fortunately had another man with me. The fellow I was visiting was so inflamed by drink that he went for me with a knife. If I had been alone I do not know what might have happened, whereas two of us were well able to deal with him. The poor chap did actually commit a murder some time after I left the parish, and was hanged.

At one period I was acting as chaplain to a reformatory ship on the Tyne. On Sunday afternoons I met a boat which took me to the ship, at a jetty half-way down the riverside street. Just by the jetty was an empty allotment where a house had fallen down, leaving behind it a pile of rubbish and old, crumbling bricks. As I went past this spot I always saw a group of fifteen or twenty lads, from sixteen to twenty years of age, sitting there gambling. The police told me they were the lowest kind of hooligans, who were constantly appearing in the Police Court. I considered I ought to do something about it and the following Sunday I went up to the lads. I was very shy and had not the slightest notion of the reception I might get, but I braced myself and said, " You know, this is a rotten way of spending Sunday afternoon." They answered, " Oh, nobody cares what we do." I retorted, " That's nonsense, because I care. Now I have to come here every Sunday afternoon to get my boat, if I come early will you let me talk to you ? " My suggestion was accepted and the next week I went down wondering what would happen. I found that out of the old bricks lying about the lads had built a sort of room, no more than four feet high, and there we all had to squat on our hunkers, as Tynesiders always do. There was a fire burning in an old much-punctured bucket and, in the confined space, the atmosphere was simply awful. Fortunately my place was by the entrance, so I was able to manage fairly well. I continued my visits every Sunday, until I had found a room nearby which I turned into a Club. Not long afterwards I had to leave the district and there was nobody, alas, to whom I could hand on the work. I wonder what happened to those lads ? I always hope that I succeeded in lighting some little spark in one or two of them.

My reader will remember my reaction to the countryside around my family home of Dochfour ; it was mainly a romantic one and reflected that element in my character. It is possibly because of this romanticism that I cherish one memory of an old woman and her grandson at Tyne Dock above all others. The grandmother was tall and stately, though dirty and untidy, and indeed looked like an old witch. She faced the world with fierce pride but lavished passionate love on her grandson, a poor consumptive lad of sixteen.

Her husband had been a sea captain and in her younger days she had seen better things. Once the captain brought home an ebony and ivory walking-stick from India, which became a sort of fetish to her. No poverty had ever induced her to part with it ; it lay in a drawer, wrapped in tissue paper, and to be shown it was like solemn admission to a sanctuary. Her grandson kept two doves in a cage ; the stick, the birds and their mutual affection were all the woman and the boy had. Being young and cheerful I gained their confidence and used to drop in for tea to cheer them up. I was, however, too ignorant to teach them anything and she was far too proud to have accepted charity. But I think she must have grown fond of me because I brought a little brightness into her desolate life. On the day I left the parish the boy visited me, bringing me a farewell present. In one hand he carried the walking-stick, in the other the cage of doves.

So ended my two happy years of initiation. Mr. Vaughan moved on to another living and Cecil Boutflower went off as chaplain to Dr. Westcott, when the latter became Bishop of Durham. I then accepted an offer from Edgar Lambert to work with him at the Mission for Seamen at Sunderland, but the few months I spent there count for little in my life, as I was in very bad health and they were terminated by a serious illness.

While at Sunderland I had an opportunity of understanding what the Merchant Service means and what fine fellows merchant seamen are. One incident made a deep impression on me. I went one day to visit the men on board a small collier. After I had been chatting with them they said : " You ought to go and see our captain. He's a wonderful chap. He used to make the ship absolute hell with his temper, but he's quite changed now and you couldn't serve under a better man." I saw the captain and told him what I had heard, asking how the change had come about. "Well," he answered, "some little time ago I was walking back to the ship one night and passed the door of a Mission. A service was going on and a man was preaching. I don't know why, as I wasn't given to attending services, but I went inside. Well, what the preacher said got hold of me and as I thought it all over I felt it was up to me to take myself in hand. So I started with my temper. I was fortunate because I had my cabin to go to, and whenever I felt my temper giving way I ran down below and prayed about it and at last I mastered it. . . ."

During my illness a letter arrived from Randall Davidson, who was Dean of Windsor, asking me to go to him as chaplain as he had just been made Bishop of Rochester. I refused because all of us of the Auckland Brotherhood felt we owed it to Bishop Lightfoot to stick to our own diocese. As it was obvious that I should not be able to continue at the Mission, however, Bishop Westcott kindly invited me to work with Cecil in the capacity of his second chaplain. The offer was a tempting one but, great as was my admiration for Westcott, I never felt quite happy with him. He seemed so detached and aloof from life. While my whole nature had been warmed by the knowledge that Lightfoot loved me as an individual, I had always a feeling that Westcott's interest in a man was as a specimen of the human race. I dare say I was quite wrong in that, but the feeling made me hesitate in accepting his offer.

In the end the doctors solved my difficulty for me by saying that I must go south. I wrote Davidson that if his chaplaincy was still vacant, I was free to come. It was vacant, and, after a visit to the Deanery at Windsor, the second chapter of my ministry experience began.

CHAPTER 7

RANDALL DAVIDSON

THERE is no education like close association with a great character, and Randall Davidson was a great character. First among his qualities were immense simplicity and directness. There was not a shadow of pose about him. Seen standing among ordinary people in ordinary dress he could have been mistaken for a typical Lowland Scots farmer—shrewd, strong-minded and with a characteristic pawky sense of humour. He talked little about religion and was free from all ecclesiastical conventionalities, but the power of his sincere faith was far-reaching and impressive. He had achieved no special distinction in his university career and, until Rochester, his work had been of a kind which had not revealed him at all to the rank and file of churchmen. Chaplain to Archbishop Tait and, while remarkably young, Dean of Windsor, he was generally classed as a second-rate man who had gained prominence through Court favour : High Churchmen had an idea that he was a Latitudinarian and treated him with suspicion.

Shortly after Davidson was enthroned Bishop of Rochester, he had a serious illness which lasted for many months. His nearest neighbour among the clergy, the leading Anglo-Catholic parish priest, Canon Brook, became a constant visitor during that time and got to know him intimately. Ecclesiastically they were at opposite poles of thought, but three or four years later, when Davidson was translated to Winchester, Canon Brook, entering a room where his curates were assembled, said : " I've a terrible piece of news for you. We are losing our Bishop who is certainly the greatest saint the Church of England has produced since the Reformation,

87

and perhaps in all time." And as he said this his eyes were full of tears. So it was that all men who came into close touch with Davidson, notwithstanding their views, recognised his greatness.

The influence of Davidson's piety cannot be divorced from the character of his wife, a daughter of Archbishop Tait. She was his perfect helpmeet. Whenever he was inclined to take himself too seriously she could, by a delicate touch of humour, bring his feet to the ground ; and she created in the home an atmosphere of intense spirituality, leavened with cheerfulness and gaiety of heart.

The second great quality in Davidson was his fairness and love of justice. He would have preferred to lose any case rather than twist a piece of evidence in the slightest degree. His fairness laid him open to the accusation of being indifferent to the truth, whereas the exact opposite was the case ; he cared too much about the truth to use it, or misuse it, in the enforcement of his own opinions. His absolute impartiality gave him a remarkable judicial capacity. I remember being greatly impressed by his hearing of a quarrel between a Chaplain of a Mission for Seamen and his Committee. Davidson summoned the Committee to his house and put them through a cross-examination which no lawyer could have excelled, gradually disentangling the personal elements of the dispute from the real facts. That done, he dictated in the presence of the Committee the real facts into a statement, the truth of which they could not deny, and got them to sign it. He next summoned the Chaplain, subjected him to a similar cross-examination and took his statement. After that he saw both parties together and gave them the true facts of their quarrel so clearly and impartially that they could not possibly evade the issue, nor either side consider themselves unfairly used. At the end he pronounced his judgment with such sympathy and kindness that the parties gratefully accepted his decision.

There were many smaller things at Rochester that taught me a great deal. Every morning I opened the Bishop's mail. He had an average of fifty letters a day and it was not difficult to extract, without reading them, the ones which were of a personal nature. There were others which, although not personal, I still felt must be submitted to him. A great many, on the other hand, involved matters of pure routine and these I dealt with myself. Among them were letters concerning ordination candidates, in which I was deeply interested. I made every effort to get to know the candidates and with the aid of my consequent knowledge of them I was enabled to help the Bishop and sometimes the men themselves. This work prepared an atmosphere of friendliness for the times of the ordination, in which men found themselves already known and cordially received as individuals. My experience was of later value to me in choosing my own curates.

No one ever knew how to economise time and carry business through with such perfection as did Davidson. He never wasted or frittered away a single minute, and yet was always able to detach himself for any fresh call on his attention. An unconscionable number of important people consulted him on, as it often seemed to me, matters which hardly justified the demand made upon his time, since they had no connection with his work as a bishop. The person who naturally consulted him most was Archbishop Benson. Hardly a day passed without a letter, or a chaplain, or the Archbishop himself coming from Lambeth to seek advice. It is to be remembered that apart from his clear mind, which made him a wonderful adviser, Davidson had had an unusual training. As the confidential chaplain of Archbishop Tait he had learned to understand ecclesiastical questions and the work of a great administrator. (For, however much people may disagree with Archbishop Tait's views, he was unquestionably a great administrator.) Additionally, during his time at Windsor, Davidson had studied in detail almost every side of the Church's work, serving on the Committees of all the big Church Societies and restudying the life and work of Tait by writing his biography.

He went, therefore, to his work at Rochester with an unrivalled knowledge of the Church's life. For me, watching him and working for him over a period of two years was truly a marvellous education.

I was entirely untrained and unfitted by temperament to be a good secretary and, to the end of his time, Davidson always introduced me to people as his "first and worst Chaplain". Fortunately my inadequacy in this position did not matter, as he had a lay secretary, Arthur Shephard ; a saintly man as near perfection as is humanly possible. A reporter on the Windsor newspaper and employed by Davidson before he became his secretary, Shephard was not only technically efficient but had an astonishing memory. The Bishop might be dictating a long letter on some question that had been under deliberation for a considerable time, when Shephard would interrupt him, saying : "I think, my lord, you forget that in June of last year you wrote so-and-so." He was invariably right.

My value to the Bishop lay in quite another direction. He said I had a remarkable capacity for getting rid of tiresome people who came to see him, without giving them offence ; an important help to such a busy man, whose house in Kennington Park Road was so accessible. He also found me useful in getting to know the diocese. I went either with or for Bishop Davidson to almost every parish, thus learning at first hand of the work each parish was doing and of the kind of men their clergy were.

It was through this period of activity that I was given a training in dealing with constantly increasing populations, the problem of which was to be the most pressing in all the parishes I later held. To a certain degree the Church had at that moment awakened to the urgent necessity of extending and adapting the parochial system to the tremendous growth of population that was taking place. Rochester, which had South London foisted on to it, probably suffered more acutely from this difficulty than any other diocese. Its vast population had no centres and no landmarks, or rather the old centres and landmarks had been submerged in the vast areas covered by a migratory population : how migratory it was showed in the district in which the Bishop's house then stood, whose whole population changed in the course of three years. The only influence which tended to settle people was a church to which they became attached. But there was an absurdly inadequate number of churches and the whole parochial system had virtually broken down. This was a new problem for Davidson, and he had not been prepared for it either by training or disposition. Bishop Thorold, Davidson's immediate predecessor, had, on the other hand, been ideally suited to tackle the problem. With characteristic humility, Davidson set himself first to study and then to build up his predecessor's work. Inevitably I had to enter into the same study and consequently came to know intimately Thorold and Canon Grundy, the man who most helped him in his work. Both men were striking personalities—in many ways eccentric—possessed of singular concentration of purpose and power to induce great enthusiasm in their people for the cause for which they were working.

Superficially, Thorold was a rather ridiculous person. He was an ugly little man, with a small spare body and a rigidly upright carriage. No guardsman on parade could have been better set-up. It was difficult not to laugh at the sight of his stiff little figure, moving like an automaton and with great pomp. He had the manner of a person several times his size, and the effect was comic. He would drive up to a church even in the worst slum in South London, in a dignified carriage and pair. His servant preceded him into the vestry with his bag and laid out on a table all the appliances for his toilet : a looking-glass, ivory-backed hairbrushes, a bottle of scent, a clean pocket handkerchief and lavender kid gloves. It had been the custom of all bishops forty years before to wear lavender kid gloves with their robes but, except in Thorold's case, the practice had died out. Thorold was then carefully robed, his few remaining hairs meticulously brushed and his pocket handkerchief scented. Once the service had begun, there was a complete change and you entirely forgot his little peculiarities. He became a gentle pastor.

Polished though Thorold's sermons were, they were never above anybody's head and showed a deep understanding of the problems of human character. They were, in fact, the foundation of his great influence as a bishop. He possessed other gifts, of course. He had the mind of a statesman; he saw the problems of South London as a whole and applied to their solution a wonderful wisdom and vision in which I never knew his superior. Even my own Bishop Davidson could not have dealt with the problems in their early stages in the way Thorold did. Finally, Thorold was an excellent judge of men and knew how to pick the right person for the right job.

It was one of Thorold's peculiarities that he replied to every letter he received by return of post and in his own hand. As his letters must have amounted on an average to fifty a day, for most men this would have been an impossibility. But he had an epigrammatic gift which in my experience was unique. His replies never covered more than a couple of lines, sometimes taking the form of a text from the Bible or simply a reference to the text. Nevertheless, the problem was always adequately dealt with and the question answered. One day the minister of our Walworth Mission, whose name was Chapman, wrote to Thorold asking for his support in some wild scheme or other. The Bishop answered: "Dear Chapman, you may be a sky rocket, I don't intend to be the stick. Yours faithfully . . ." The certainty of receiving an answer by return, in the Bishop's own hand, produced a general feeling that his eye was on everything and his attention ready to be given to all that concerned the diocese. His absurdities were in small things; in the big things of life he was great.

With his amazing capacity for choosing the right person, Thorold had selected Canon Grundy, who held the living of a well-to-do parish on Blackheath, to raise the necessary funds and organise the Church Extension Society. Grundy was a little cock-sparrow of a man, with a lisp and an astonishing sense of humour. On one occasion a friend of mine lunched with him at the St. James's Restaurant. There was a bar and over it what was in those days called a *masher* was leaning, flirting with the barmaid and making himself generally conspicuous. At last, in a loud voice, the masher was heard to exclaim : " I'll be damned ! ", whereupon, jumping to his feet, little Grundy observed in tones that penetrated the whole hall : " My dear good sir, you are probably right as to your ultimate destination but I don't see that it's anything to swagger about in public ! " At the sally there was a roar of laughter from everybody present and the unfortunate young man slunk out.

Grundy had an astonishing hold over his great parish. His church, for example, was so popular that he not only had no need to pay the choir but no man could be a member of it without paying a subscription of three guineas a year. Believing his young people to be extremely stupid in their selection of husbands and wives, he operated a matrimonial agency which ran with great success for many years. More often than not his church notices were so amusing that one could not possibly forget them. He would announce : " Such and such a meeting will be held at seven o'clock on Tuesday evening " ; then he would pause and, gazing round at his congregation, he would add : " Now don't, when I meet you on Wednesday morning, say that you are sorry you weren't there because you thought it was at eight o'clock on Thursday."

Grundy never for one minute lost sight of his purpose and he could make people consecrate their lives to that purpose whether by their gifts or their service, in a way I have never seen equalled. As a result he raised an annual £25,000 for the Diocesan Society, year after year. He did more important work still. Pointing out to Bishop Thorold that the East End had captured Oxford, so that the Oxford House and all the Oxford College Missions represented a considerable power, he asked, " Why don't we capture Cambridge ? " Thorold's answer was, " Go and try ", and Grundy did it. I once saw him address a meeting of undergraduates crammed to the doors in the great hall of Trinity. His audience were rocking with laughter one minute and almost in tears the next. By the time Davidson and I were there the Cambridge College Missions, as well as many school Missions for which Grundy was also responsible, were among the outstanding features of the work of the diocese.

Two of these Missions I knew most intimately : the Charterhouse Mission and the St. John's College Mission.

The Charterhouse Mission was situated in the blackest part of the Borough slum quarter. Both men running it were outstanding. Waggitt, the first of the two, was extremely clever and very witty, while his preaching was outstanding. His companion Vyvyan, who afterwards became a bishop in Africa, was the type of man developed by the Oxford Movement. He was cultivated, refined, spiritually-minded and consecrated to his work. Together these two workers had gained a strong hold on the district. Whenever I was able I attended their service, spending the evening with them afterwards. That service was unique, with the Mission Room packed with real slum people. It was the ordinary Prayer Book service, entirely read except for the hymns, and yet it was positively exciting because of the fashion in which the responses, especially the Psalms, were rendered. Few people can easily read the alternate verses in the Psalms as some of them are long, consequently at the Charterhouse hall they read them in half-verses. The people's half invariably came with an absolute roar. I have never felt such a sense of enthusiasm anywhere else. The evenings I spent with Waggitt and Vyvyan were delightful ; we were all three of us full of the adventure and excitement of youth.

The St. John's College Mission was quite different. Phillips, the missioner there, had a real church of considerable size and his population, while also a slum population, was that of not quite such a bad slum as the Borough. He did not have a packed congregation, but what he did have was very impressive. When he was visiting in his district, people often said to him, "We must come and see you at the Church", which was a common phrase at that time. To this his answer was always : "You can't do that. Attending a service is not a thing you can do without preparation. It is too important. But if you like to come to the ante-chapel I will instruct you." Consequently if you went to a service of Phillips's you found not only a good congregation in the church itself, but a large number of people in the ante-chapel. They could see and hear the service through the west doors but were not allowed to take part until they had been prepared. The result was that everybody in the church gave you the feeling of being tremendously in earnest, of doing a thing which seemed to them of the first importance. It was not enthusiasm such as was shown in the Charterhouse hall, but instead an intense earnestness. Again, the service was read throughout, with the exception of the hymns, and every response was made with powerful sincerity. Missions such as these were of enormous importance.

Though most of my activities during this time were confined to South London, Bishop Davidson and I occasionally went to Rochester, which was still part of the diocese, where we stayed with Dean Hole. Witty and amusing, almost senti-mentally sympathetic by nature, physically vigorous and energetic, the Dean was one of the most engaging personalities I ever met. Besides being a popular mission preacher and a devoted priest, he was a great hunting man and one of the most famous rose-growers in England. Our Rochester visits were always a great joy to me.

While staying with Dean Hole there was one parish that we visited which afforded a complete contrast to those we knew in South London. This was in the Hundred of Hoo, and while I do not know what it may be like today, the dis-trict was then the abomination of desolation and the clergy marooned in it only too liable to become eccentric, if not mad. I accompanied Davidson to a parish in this district, where the clergyman in charge met us with great *empressement* and remarked : " You must come and see my pictures. I've only taken to painting lately, but I've done a lot of work." He then took us round the house and showed us a series of immense daubs that were like nothing in heaven above, or in the earth beneath, or in the waters about the earth, but in each and every case provided with a splendid frame. At the end he announced : " And now we are coming to my greatest work. This picture I painted from a little print in a newspaper ! " The thing was staggering, but the artist told us serenely : " Bishop Thorold admired it very much." Davidson, of course, knew that this was quite impossible ; at the same time he knew his predecessor, Bishop Thorold, and he inquired exactly what the Bishop had said. " Oh," replied the painter, " after I had brought him here, he fetched a chair " (Davidson and I could well imagine little Thorold fetching a chair with great pomposity), " sat down in front of the picture and, after gazing for some time in silence, he turned to me and said, " Mr. Blank, you don't mean to say you painted that ! "

The Bishop thought that I should have some direct parochial work, side by side with the work he needed from me, and I had charge of a big Mission hall in the Surrey Gardens. The Mission added very little to my training; indeed, I think having two independent interests was bad for me, as what I really needed to develop at this stage was the power to concentrate fully on a single purpose. The experience of a divided responsibility did not assist me in gaining this power.

2

During this time with Bishop Davidson was renewed my link with the Royal Family.

From that close intimacy which my Aunt Augusta had had with Queen Victoria and her children, and which my mother shared as soon as she grew up, the Queen had stood as my godmother. That meant that my first thoughts of her were of a kind old lady who was interested in me, the idea of her being Queen having no special significance. As a boy I was annually taken to Windsor, and presents of toys would arrive at Carlsruhe; I remember particularly a magnificent pair of tin carriage horses, to which I was deeply attached. When I started school, my Windsor visits were more intermittent and the presents came to an end. Meanwhile my sister had become a Maid of Honour, and my mother corresponded with the Queen. At special times, such as that of my Aunt Augusta's death, the Queen entered prominently into all our lives. As I grew older, my godmother's regal side counted more with me, and by the time of the first Jubilee she had become a tremendous person. But somehow the godmother always meant more to me than the Queen.

When I went to Davidson, who was one of the Queen's most intimate advisers and friends, her attention was drawn to me again and I suddenly received a summons to spend a week-end at Osborne and preach. It was an awe-inspiring prospect for a young curate, but, with her usual thoughtfulness, the Queen chose a time when my sister was in attendance to make it easier for me.

At Osborne a room had been converted into a chapel by the insertion of a pulpit and altar, with a small choir at the back. In this chapel no congregation were present except the Queen and her daughter, with two ladies and one gentleman. At the end of the service the gentleman said to me: "I've seen a lot of life, but I do not think a man could face a more awful ordeal than preaching here." Matters were not made any easier by the fact that, anxious to comply with all the rules, I used the surplice provided for me—one of the old-fashioned kind, with endless yards of thick, highly starched linen that billowed and crackled with my every movement, and when I knelt almost supported me on all sides like a scaffolding. But after I had finished the Queen was transformed into a kindly godmother once more, talking to me easily and naturally about the sermon and about my work. As I left, she pressed into my hand a small packet, which she said was a little remembrance. It was her Jubilee Medal.

Preaching to the Queen became an annual affair and soon lost its worst terrors for me.

My last visit in Queen Victoria's reign was made to her at Windsor. The Duke of Portland, who was there at the time, in recording it in his memoirs makes two mistakes which are worth correcting. In the first place the idea that she had summoned me to preach because she was considering me for some post is quite absurd; at my age she would not have considered me for any position. She asked me simply because I was a godson and my mother's son. The second mistake, which is a more interesting one, is that I was warned not to preach for more than ten minutes. The exact opposite was the fact; both the Archbishop of Canterbury and the Master of the Household telling me on no account to take less than twenty minutes, as the Queen considered a short sermon disrespectful to the subject and to herself. That would naturally have been the view of any older person of that generation.

When I became engaged to be married, the Queen received the news most warmly and showed a truly godmotherly concern over every detail connected with the event. Not only did she make me a very handsome present, but she expressed her intention of being godmother again if I should have a son. Unhappily, however, my first child was stillborn and by the time the second arrived she was dead. Her regard for me, therefore, was in every respect a human regard and her interest a personal one begotten by an old family connection.

I saw another side of the Queen's character. After the Prince Consort's death she ceased dining with the Household, and on the Sunday night when I was visiting her at Windsor I was included in the small party she had asked to dine with her in the Oak Room, where she took her meals. Among the other guests was Lord Salisbury (then, I think, Prime Minister) and the Queen's secretary, afterwards Lord Stamfordham. As we sat down the Queen inquired of Lord Salisbury: "You got my message this afternoon?" "No, ma'am," Lord Salisbury replied. Turning to her secretary, and in her most

rasping tones, she said : " You sent my message ? " " Yes,"
he answered, " and I had it acknowledged from Arlington
Street." I cannot remember what followed, except that the
air seemed to turn blue. At last with the words " It must
never occur again " the Queen put the matter from her and,
clearing her face, was gracious and charming for the remainder
of the evening.[1]

Though I saw this flash of the awe-inspiring side of her
character and realised her very solemn appearance throughout
the more serious part of her life, those who had the opportunity of seeing her in her more relaxed and domestic life,
as I did, could not help observing an almost rollicking sense
of fun which burst out when she was amused by a story or
when some comic incident struck her attention. On those
occasions, and they came often, throwing back her head and
opening her mouth wide she abandoned herself to laughter
of a kind that suggested her descent from her Guelph uncles.

That so dominant a personality should have been combined
with great kindness of heart, charming courtesy and consideration was not so surprising. But the Queen possessed
another quality which at first struck one as astonishing. When
Lytton Strachey's book came out I asked Princess Beatrice,
who had lived with her mother all her life, whether she had
read it. " Yes," she said. " But you can't expect me to
like it ; it is not written in a tone one likes to hear used
about one's mother. But there was one thing that surprised
me. He left out what I always felt to be her strongest quality,
which was her personal humility." The Queen considered
that hers was essentially a great office, and just as she believed
England to be the greatest of countries she believed that as

[1] The day following this incident I met Pom Macdonnel, Lord Salisbury's
secretary, in London and said to him : "I heard your chief catch it last
night !" "And he thoroughly deserved it," he answered. "He hates
telephones and though we wrote out the message and put it on his desk,
advising him it was from the Queen, he would not read it because it came
by telephone." An interesting instance of the robust individualism of the
great Victorians.

Queen she carried a tremendous responsibility. For that very reason she kept continually before her the fact that it was but a weak, fallible woman who bore that glorious burden.

The figure of the great Queen provides a seemingly inexhaustible source of historical study and comment, and much has been written extolling her gifts of moral courage, sincerity and capacity for truth. For my own part I knew all these things in the simpler being who was my kind and lovable godmother ; it was no more than a fortuitous circumstance that that same personality set up a new and splendid pattern for kings and princes.

3

During my two years with Randall Davidson I continued to study, at first hand, what might be termed the statesmanship of Church Extension. I was daily able to watch him continue the work Thorold had begun in developing the Church to meet the needs of the people. There was no move that was haphazard ; everything was planned. But after my second year drew to a close, Davidson said to me, " I have made up my mind to send you to the most church-forsaken spot in the British Isles." When I learned that I was to start a Mission which the Diocesan Society was founding in one of the two vast parishes into which Plumstead was divided, I knew he was not exaggerating.

CHAPTER 8

PLUMSTEAD

THE year of 1894, during my Plumstead time, opened with the marriage of my elder brother to Nellie Bass, the only daughter of Lord and Lady Burton. This was a truly wonderful event; for it brought into the family one who for fifty years and more was to be the model of all that a sister-in-law could possibly be, and ensured Dochfour continuing to have the atmosphere of home for my brother Augustus and myself. But 1894 was also a sad year : after a very long illness my mother died.

In all respects the greatness of her wonderful character had impressed itself on my life. Every step I had taken till then had been with her knowledge and almost every thought had been shared with her. From the time I had gone up to Cambridge we had written to each other every day. With the beginning of her last illness that chapter of my life was closed, although her influence ever afterwards pervaded all my thoughts.

The loss of my mother meant a great change in the circumstances of my life. I had no longer anywhere that was properly a home. Dochfour was too far off for me to manage more than an annual visit. I was especially at a loss when the doctors ordered me away after periodical bouts of illness, the nature of which made essential the freedom of home surroundings. It was then that Lord and Lady Burton adopted me, throwing open to me their houses in London, the country and Scotland. I became very fond of them and was deeply touched when Lady Burton told me that during his last illness her husband had said that he had counted me his greatest friend throughout the last years. Up to the time of my marriage, and to a lesser degree even then, the Burtons' houses were my regular convalescent homes.

Another and quite different benefit I derived from my association with the Burtons was the opportunity it gave me of observing a curious phase in our social evolution. Towards the close of the century the old aristocracy began to fall from its high estate primarily because of the agricultural depression. In place of this aristocracy an artificial society emerged, which attempted to win acceptance as the aristocracy of England. This new body was called sometimes the *smart set* and sometimes the *Prince of Wales's set*.

Both Lord and Lady Burton possessed a genius for hospitality. They had been accepted in the highest stratum of the old society but they were unavoidably captured by the new. Now, an aristocracy must be a real class ; that is, a definable body of people. It must have some corporate consciousness and believe that it occupies an important place in national life, with definite duties to perform. It must also have a code of moral characteristics which it accepts as necessary for the fulfilment of its responsibilities. The old aristocracy had those qualities ; but the newcomers of the 'nineties had not. Among the latter there were neither corporate moral standards nor a corporate sense of responsibility. Some of the new aristocracy's individual members were people of the highest character who fulfilled a number of valuable duties in life. Their order of society taken as a whole was, however, quite without significance. It was no more than a set of rich people who made life pleasant for each other, by means of a luxury the old society had never attempted or dreamed of approaching. Money by itself came to be the social touchstone of the period.

Going three or four times a year to stay with the Burtons, I might find them alone, or nearly alone, which was what I really enjoyed. But only too often I was in a house full of the new society, which to me was not of great interest. Above all else, it was comparatively lacking in culture. I remember Lady Burton, who had a kind of cynical realism in her outlook, once saying to me : " I never allow conversation with these people, it bores them."

Several other differences there were between the old order and the new which astonished me profoundly in their absolute variance from what I had previously accepted as qualities essentially characteristic of true ladies and gentlemen. For one thing, it was always the price and not the merit of a purchase that was constantly discussed. If Lord Burton, or anyone else, had bought a new picture, the primary interest was in how much he had paid for it. Money was the *leitmotif* running through every phase of existence. Again, I was quite bewildered to hear land talked of as a speculation. Land had always been to me a basis of a family's life and the primary field for the exercise of its responsibilities. I thought it splendid when people made really great sacrifices, as they often did, in order to redeem the family property from debt. The idea of speaking of land as no more than a speculation seemed to me utterly, painfully vulgar. It was the same over the scale of remuneration, which had become a young man's first consideration in choosing a profession. I was shocked to hear the meagreness of the pay of the clergy put forward as a reason for not taking Orders.

People sometimes speak as if the new society was merely an evolution out of the society preceding it. Actually it was a complete revolution, the means of sweeping away the old life. One significant indication of its uncultivated character was provided by the emergence of a little group known as *the Souls*. This association had as its leaders some of the most brilliant of the younger people, headed by Arthur Balfour, and avowedly existed to make social life more intellectual and finely tempered. It was, of course, too self-conscious a thing to exercise any considerable or lasting influence and its members were generally regarded as being affected or, simply, as downright cranks. But *the Souls* amounted to something more, as was proved by the astonishing brilliance of many of its members' sons. The two Grenfell brothers afforded examples of that ; if unfortunately the first

World War had not swept them both away, there can be no question but that they would have had an outstanding contribution to make to the social history of England.

I must make it clear that I did not dislike all the people I encountered at the Burtons ; nor was I wholly averse to the luxury, which had about it a distinct appeal. Everybody I met was extremely civil to me. I was, however, always there as a convalescent and in the happy position of being able largely to follow my own inclinations during the week of each party. Still, such intercourse as I had with the so-called *smart set* of the time was quite sufficient for me to feel that it injected into English life the virus that was not only to revolutionise but to destroy the great pattern of English aristocracy.

2

My first day in Plumstead was a bewildering one. The district had originally been a huge country parish, stretching from the borders of Woolwich eastwards. With the coming of the Crimean war the Arsenal and Dockyard were so developed that Woolwich overflowed, turning the part of Plumstead adjoining it into a densely populated working-class district. The vicar of that time, apparently a man of energy, realised that the little country church outside the area covered by the new population was an impossible centre for the parish in its new conditions. Accordingly he built a large church in the centre of this new population, making it the parish church. He also built schools and bought an excellent eighteenth-century house as a vicarage. On his death he was succeeded by a man named McAllister, who was incumbent when I arrived there.

McAllister, a dour north Irishman, was so extreme a Calvinist that he declared nobody between him and London Bridge preached the Gospel. As this involved ten miles of solid population and many hundreds of parishes, it was a large claim. He had been trained by MacNeil of Liverpool, and had acquired the strikingly dramatic style of reading and preaching for which his master was famous. Throughout his long career at Plumstead McAllister invariably collected a congregation and, equally invariably, quarrelled with it. His Calvinistic teaching resulted in the majority of people becoming Plymouth Brethren. After a time the population spread eastward to cover almost the whole of Plumstead and he divided the parish into two, making the old parish church the centre of the new parish. In this he placed his brother, a less brilliant but equally dour and quarrelsome personality. Together, the brothers excited such virulent hatred among the people that they lost all influence. This was partly due to their dabbling in the speculative building that followed the sudden increase in population. They were not accused of dishonesty, but speculative builders are never popular, and the church people resented the vicar entering their ranks. Through his preaching the elder brother continued to have a certain following, but the younger one became completely alienated from his parish. He had about twenty-five thousand people at the time of my arrival and a little old church seating a bare three hundred, without even a vestry attached to it. His new vicarage had been built a long way from the church and people, close to the site of my new Mission. It is not exaggerating to say that there were not a dozen houses in his parish he could have entered without the probability of being insulted. One grim story gave some measure of local feeling. A dying man was said to have sent for the two brothers and, on their inquiring why he had summoned them both, answered that it was because he wanted to know what it felt like to die between two thieves. The whole vast population thereabouts had come, as Bishop Davidson had said, to be really church-forsaken.

Plumstead Common stretched along the ridge from Woolwich almost as far as Abbey Wood, the populated part lying on the north slope which went down to the river flats. The west half of the Common had been made into something like a park, while the east half, an immense gravel flat, was left to the Artillery as a practice ground. At the extreme south-east end of the Common was a little group of streets, practically a slum. At the south corner of this slum there were some old school buildings which had been acquired by the Diocesan Society as the centre of the Mission to which I was appointed. A new site was also acquired on the other side of a ravine which cut across the Common, dividing the parish into two, where a church was to be built which would be convenient for the population. The little school buildings were wretched jerry-built affairs of two long rooms and two small ones. Beyond the buildings was a cottage, which previously had been the schoolmaster's house and was now to become mine. There were two rooms downstairs and two up, with a kitchen at the back. There was also a room for a servant, in which I installed a retired marine and his wife. He was a great character and she was very efficient. They were to stay with me until after I was married. One day when Mowbray Morris came to see me and asked my marine how he was keeping, he was answered : " Very well. I eats well, I drinks well, I sleeps well, and I'm eighteen inches round the neck. What more can you want ? "

Plumstead Common was about as exposed as any spot in Europe ; there was nothing between my house and the Arctic Circle. The north and east winds whistled unchecked across the great gravel flat used by the Artillery, blowing directly on to us. As the walls of the house seemed to be only a single brick in thickness, the resulting cold can be imagined. I started, too, with the worst winter I had ever known. Practically from Christmas to Easter the frost and snow continued, as it did in 1947. In the morning, after the fire had died down in my bedroom, the jug of water on the washstand by the fireplace was frozen hard.

On my first day in the Mission I found myself with an almost blank sheet on which to work, having very little experience to guide me. In the one-time school premises were five faithful people, two men and three women, who had struggled on with a little Sunday school of twenty-five children and who proved loyal and enthusiastic workers all

MOWBRAY MORRIS
As seen by Harper Pennington

through my time. We fitted up one room as a church and, as one of my five recruits could play the harmonium, we decided to begin the services the following Sunday. My helpers undertook to visit as much of the district as they could and invite people to attend.

It was like putting a match to a fire. In a population of that sort there were, of course, a great many people who had been accustomed to church life elsewhere, and they were thirsting for something of a similar kind. Consequently, everything grew like a mushroom. Within six months we had over six hundred children in the Sunday school with a full staff of teachers, and more communicants than we could get into the church for a single service. I claim no personal credit for this; it would have happened with any man of energy who had undertaken the work. But it was immensely exciting. Everybody who came felt the enthusiasm of the new life in the air, while the Rector of Woolwich said he felt the repercussions of it even in his parish.

At the end of those six months was started a work which contributed greatly to our sense of unity and common purpose. I suggested that a squad of men be formed to dig the foundations and fence the site of the new church. This was no easy task as the ground had not been disturbed since the Flood and was as hard as concrete. However, about forty men used to meet me at five in the morning and we toiled away at the job until it was time to prepare for our regular day's work. Our efforts later inspired the neighbouring district to go one better; they built their church entirely—the architect, clerk of works, bricklayers, carpenters and the rest giving their labour for nothing. But that came after my day. I remember one Sunday night, at the end of the service, giving out the notices and finishing with the words : " The squad will meet on the site tomorrow morning at five o'clock." After that I announced the opening words of the hymn, which chanced to be " Christians seek not yet repose ". Whereupon, I am afraid, we one and all burst out into joyous and uproarious laughter.

It was a wonderfully exhilarating time. At Tyne Dock I had had a pure slum to deal with ; at Walworth the monotony of a fluctuating population, with a great deal of poverty. Now there was a big population of workers, all employed at the Woolwich Arsenal, with a small mixture of elementary school teachers and one or two doctors and lawyers. This purely artisan population proved a very happy one to work with. If they undertook anything in connection with the church, they carried it out with extraordinary dependableness and loyalty. I think I have always been happiest when working with such people.

The younger McAllister, in whose parish the Mission operated, violently resented my intrusion and regarded me with the darkest suspicion. His house was close to the Mission and, in spite of his resentment, he always invited me to have supper with him on Sunday nights. Each week he would meet me with mistrust and antagonism, but by persistently keeping off dangerous topics and remaining invariably cheerful I managed to leave him in a better frame of mind by the end of the evening. At the close of the next week, however, the clouds had descended again. After some months I almost lost hope. Nevertheless, I held on, convinced that, for his own sake as well as that of the parish, it was important to encourage him into a happier frame of mind. Besides, in a curious way, I had grown fond of the old man. The struggle went on for quite a year and then, suddenly, one Sunday evening I found him friendly and reasonable, just as I had left him the Sunday before. From that day forward his confidence in me, and I think his affection for me, never wavered and he became a gentler and happier man. I have always been very thankful that I persevered.

In my second year at the Mission I found that I must have help, and Robert Hutchinson came as my curate. He was a man whose generous proportions physically were matched by those of his spirit and mind. A very solid and conscientious worker as well as a most lovable man, he did admirably in his career after he left me. In regard to women's work, which was needed very badly, we were faced with a serious difficulty. Obviously it was awkward for two young bachelors like Hutchinson and myself to have young unmarried women, while elderly case-hardened female parish workers would have been liable to attempt to dominate us. In desperation we advertised in the *Church Times* for two young widows. Although our advertisement created some amusement, through it we discovered two excellent sisters, both of whom had been married to clergy and widowed after a short married life. They were strangely different in character and temperament. One was a quiet and devout woman, whom we felt would never marry again but consecrate the remainder of her life to religious work ; the other was gay and active. Somewhat irreverently, Hutchinson and I christened them the Widow in Deed and the Widow in Word. Our name-giving turned out to be prophetic. Within a few months he was engaged to the Widow in Word.

Although it was a most successful marriage, and Mrs. Hutchinson was the greatest help to her husband in all his subsequent work, it was nothing less than disastrous to us at the time. For it is a curious fact, to which I have known no exception, that parishes always resent the engagement of one of their clergy to anyone in the parish. Even if my leaving the Mission for other reasons had not necessitated Hutchinson's removal, I am sure he would have had to go. As it was, with the death of the elder McAllister the patron offered me the vicarage of Plumstead Parish Church. This, on the enthusiastic advice of Bishop Davidson, I accepted.

3

The vicarage at Plumstead presented me with an entirely new set of problems, though it involved exactly the same artisan population.

Up till then I had, in one sense, always been alone in my work, having never been under a vicar who trained his curates, and having always had a virtually independent responsibility in running my own Mission. Moreover, never having

been more than two years in any one place, I had not had
to adjust my effort to the sustained parish work of an
incumbent. So far I had only been learning and experi-
menting.

So I came to tackle a parish with a tradition and a great
responsibility attached to it. In the Mission there was no
reason to think of anyone outside one's own district, nor was
there any of the responsibility towards the general population
of a large neighbourhood that inevitably falls on the vicar
of a big town parish. My one advantage lay in having
grasped the principles underlying Bishop Thorold's work in
Church Extension.

A tradition behind a parish is either helpful and inspiring
or extremely depressing. There was nothing inspiring in the
history of Plumstead Parish Church. There were two things
which I had immediately to consider : the first, what would
be my relationship with the people in the church I inherited
from McAllister ; the second, the study of the social condition
of the population in whose midst I was set to live.

My relationship with my parishioners was bound to be
conditioned by McAllister's continual teaching, over a great
number of years, of the extremest form of Calvinism. I
expected the people to have become bigoted Calvinists who
would regard any change with the fiercest suspicion. And
yet I was compelled to change practically everything ; I
could not possibly teach on my predecessor's lines or work
as he had done. Considering the question very carefully in
relation to the church, which was of course to be the nucleus
of my work and effort, I announced on the first Sunday that
instead of a sermon I would try to explain what alterations
I felt were necessary in the conduct of the services. I said quite
frankly that I disagreed fundamentally with Mr. McAllister's
religious position, and that while I was very reluctant to
upset the religious habits of the congregation by sudden
changes, nobody could deny that as members of the Church
of England we were bound to follow the directions of the
Prayer Book. I read them the rubrics which I considered

we were violating, telling the congregation what steps I thought necessary to bring us into obedience to them. Of course it was also an opportunity, of which I took advantage, for explaining that the essentially important thing was reverence and worship. My frankness and moderation, combined probably with the reputation I brought from the Mission, were completely successful and I did not have, then or afterwards, the smallest trouble or complaint about the changes made.

There was, however, one discord amid the general harmony that followed. We had a large mixed choir who were eaten up with conceit. They said quite openly that the only thing for which people came to church was the beauty of their music. For my part I considered their music both florid and vulgar, but that was not the point. During those parts of the service when they were not singing they trooped down a little staircase leading from the gallery in which they sat into the porch, remaining outside smoking and talking until they were needed again. Such conduct was intolerable. For some weeks I did my utmost to make them see the need of a spirit of proper reverence, but they only treated me with what amounted to contempt. Accordingly, I drew up a short set of rules which I sent to each of the choristers, requiring them either to agree to the rules or to leave the choir. I was as courteous as possible, but firm.

In the belief that I should be unable to do without them, they then attempted to force my hand. Quite late in the week, with the exception of a small nucleus which was really religious-minded, the choir wrote to me individually to say that they would not be singing on the following Sunday. The organist threw in his lot with them. I accepted the challenge and without any great difficulty I found in the parish enough people to help me out. They practised on the Saturday with a voluntary organist and on Sunday morning, when the recalcitrant members of the choir appeared in church hoping to see my downfall, the service was held just as usual. Indeed, it was better than usual; for from habit the old choir sang in the congregation, giving a fullness and volume which the singing had not formerly possessed. An additional touch was that the rebels had the mortification of hearing, as they came out of church, the comments of the congregation on the unusual excellence of the music. After that my opponents climbed down completely and wanted to return ; but, with the exception of the small nucleus that had remained loyal, I refused unconditionally to have any of them back. The incident established my authority in the church.

With regard to the social condition of the parish, I found that our artisan population lacked leaders and was entirely without corporate feeling or corporate conscience. They simply failed to realise themselves as a body. We had no local paper of our own or any other sign of corporate life. This incoherent social character was further aggravated by one essential weakness. The Arsenal was Government-run and it is curious how many people, absolutely honest in their personal dealings, will be quite dishonest in their dealings with public funds. As they realised that no one individually would be affected, most of the Arsenal workers had no scruples in using all kinds of small graft to feather their own nests. Retired foremen would confide to one with a chuckle the diverse little devices whereby this could be done. Municipally we still had only the Parish Vestry, a most unsatisfactory body to which I belonged *ex officio*, the members of which were not above participating in fundamentally dishonest schemes for their own ends. It was very difficult, of course, to pin any such transactions down. For instance, when the line of a new road was under discussion, one knew quite well that the matter had already been privately discussed by the people affected, while the line they advocated was really governed by the extent to which it would benefit a particular vestryman's building land, or something of that sort. Nobody saw any harm in this quiet graft ; they simply thought that it was a legitimate and clever way of doing themselves good. There used to be a saying that boards were screens, with neither a body to be kicked nor a soul to be saved ; and public money has always behind it a kind of impersonal board. Yet while I perceived all this around me I had too little knowledge and too little experience to know how to attack it.

Another thing that lowered our moral standard was the condition of our political life. Our Member of Parliament was a very astute lawyer, of whom I did not have a high opinion. He had built up an astonishing organisation by which he controlled the votes of the whole population and there was nobody to raise public opinion against him. His method was quite simple. He was ready to do any small job for anyone who supported him politically, but was equally determined to do nothing for those who did not. I remember one instance of a man going to him on some perfectly legitimate business ; after inquiring the caller's name the Member consulted a ledger and said : " I see you have never voted for me. Why should I do anything for you ? Good morning."

There again handicapped by my youth and inexperience, the most I was able to do was to try and inculcate a higher conception of moral principles among those with whom I was directly concerned. Looking back, however, I realise that I missed a great opportunity ; there was one man who could have helped me. Grinling, the man in question, had been ordained deacon but, becoming a Socialist and determining to follow another line, he never went on to the priesthood and practically renounced his Orders. Socialism in those days was no more than an academic theory of a reconstructed society, and had not yet hardened into a political programme. Grinling, after coming to live in Plumstead, resolved with his wife to devote their lives to improving local social conditions. For at least fifty years he laboured with the most unselfish devotion to fulfil his purpose. There was nothing to prevent my working with him as the work he was doing was not in the least political. Together we should have made a really strong team, starting as we did

with the friendliest of relations and never quite losing sight
of one another. I regret very much that I failed there to
see my chance, as I believe Plumstead offered a rare opportunity for showing how a big population could be led into
working in unison for the uplift of the entire community.

My experience with Bishop Davidson made me realise that
I had other responsibilities towards the 50,000 people of
Plumstead, which number was always increasing. I set myself
to discover strategic points that might serve as the centre
of future parishes, sometimes in still undeveloped parts of the
district, and to secure sites for churches and schools and a
parsonage. In this the Diocesan Society assisted me with the
necessary funds. Our old schools were immensely inferior,
as regards buildings and equipment, to the great board schools
nearby, and yet they were always crowded. If you asked
any parent, even those who had no connection with the
church at all, why they sent their children to us and not
to board school, their answer was always the same : " Oh,
you teach the children manners." We did not, directly,
teach them any more than the board school, but in the board
schools there was a complete divorce from all other influences
connected with children's lives. In the church schools, the
home and the church were closely associated with the school,
and when a child went to school he remained under the
influence of the home and the church. I believe the moral
effect of that to be tremendous.

During this time I first had a staff of curates. There were
three young men, a priest and two deacons, who remained
among my most loyal friends throughout their lives. They
lived in the Vicarage at Plumstead with me and later came
as my curates to Rugby. I was not much older than they
were, so my connection with them was not that of an experienced rector training a staff but simply of one young man
trying the experiment of clerical life in their company. And
a very jolly experiment it turned out to be.

One arrangement I made proved most effective. It was
a preaching school, in which the younger clergy of the neigh-

bourhood, from Woolwich and round about, joined us. As I was so very little older than the others, I did not set out to teach them but invited them to learn with me. The method I proposed was as follows :

Each in turn wrote a sermon and made an analysis of it. We then provided copies of the analysis, putting at the head the main points of the sermon, if possible in a single word, but at least in not more than one sentence. As I felt then, and feel still, the weakness of so many sermons is that they are diffused over a multitude of points and lack the necessary unity to leave a definite impression on the hearers. Further, I insisted that each sermon should be regarded as an address to help us in the spiritual difficulties of life, thus preventing them from becoming a mere intellectual exercise. Finally, on a fixed day, we would meet in church and each man had to preach his sermon extempore from his own analysis, copies of which we had before us. At the end we discussed what we had heard. We gained enormously from the whole practice.

My normal duties continued and gradually I grew to understand more fully the daily business of parish life. After some time I was asked to take over a fever hospital, which stood some distance outside Plumstead. I happen to have a strange immunity from infection, having never had an infectious disease apart from a slight attack of German measles. In the hospital I used to have tea with crowds of little boys in the most infectious stages of scarlet fever and other complaints, without it affecting me at all. But my visits to the hospital were responsible for something much more important to me personally. With the addition of this call to an already considerable round of visits, it became essential that I should have some means of locomotion. My brother James, therefore, gave me a pony and I purchased a trap. I was looking for somebody to take care of these, when George Dawson, a boy of nineteen, presented himself at the Vicarage door. He came from a farm in the country and had been sent along to me to see if I could find him work. I was out at the time but my housekeeper offered him the job of looking after the pony, which he accepted. That was the beginning of an association which has made an enormous difference to my life and still, after fifty years, helps my old age.

On the social side I had one very pleasant outlet at Plumstead. I lived quite near the Artillery Barracks with their great Mess. All the young officers at the Barracks had come from homes very similar to mine and, our ages and tastes generally coinciding, I found a number of friends among them. One achievement that won me an especial reputation with the very young ones was my ability to drive four-in-hand, having done so since boyhood. There was only one officer similarly proficient and, being a great friend of his, I occasionally drove the officers' coach when he was otherwise engaged. My chief popularity at the Barracks, however, resulted from an exciting escapade.

It was known I had been Whip of the Drag at Cambridge and the officers were persistently urging me to go out with their drag. I always refused, thinking it unsuitable, until one day the Master, Major Paget, offered to mount me, absolutely insisting on my turning out. I yielded to the temptation. The drag was in the marshes, with tremendous dykes to be jumped. My horse was a large, gaunt animal with a string halt; a perfect drag horse, but one that could never have been hunted, Paget normally using him for his brougham. The meet was in a field in the marshes, and as no one wanted a jump straight from the meet, a bridge had been built across the nearest dyke. My mount was very fidgety; as I knew that I should have little or no control over him, I decided it would be safer to face the jump instead of crowding over the bridge with the rest. My decision proved momentous. Since nobody had yet seen me ride, one of the best men had been told off to look after me. Thinking it his duty to follow where I led he promptly took the jump and fell into the dyke: I saw him no more. In this way my horse established a lead which he never lost. He did not actually run away, but I was totally unable to stop or turn him. I suppose Paget, who knew him well, could manage him, but for my part I found the bit worse than useless and resigned myself to letting him gallop and jump, both of which he did magnificently. Then there came an awful moment. I heard shouts at my back and saw the dyke I was fast approaching had two strands of barbed wire loosely stretched along the top. My only chance lay in speed and, driving home my spurs, we breasted the wires. Now barbed wire is safer than ordinary wire as, under sudden strain, the barbs act as nippers. In this case the strands snapped and I landed with wire wound round and round my horse. If the beast had struggled anything might have happened. Mercifully he stood like a rock and allowed me to dismount. After I had removed the wire and remounted, he started off again as if nothing had happened and once more assumed complete control. We ended by finishing first, the rest of the field having made a wide detour. The *éclat* I gained among the younger officers as the result of my little adventure was so tremendous that I refused to go out again. I felt that my reputation should not be endangered.

I also gained at the Barracks one very pleasant link with an older man. General Maurice, who commanded there, used very kindly to lend me a horse so that I could ride with him before breakfast. He was an interesting man, with only one drawback : a fervent belief in the Baconian theory about the authorship of Shakespeare's works. Whenever he started on that I was done for. None the less, both he and his family did much to add to the happiness of my life during that time. On one of my early morning rides, I had a serious accident. I had bicycled over to ride with a young subaltern friend of mine, who said to me : "I wish you would ride my new horse. He is rather a handful and I feel like a quiet ride today." I raised no objection and we started out. It was a bright, crisp morning with hoar frost on the ground. As we turned on to some grass at the side of the road, my horse bolted. I was not worried, however, since at the end of the road was the Common, with a long upward slope.

But going round a bend my mount's forelegs slipped under him and he came down a tremendous crash on his side. I was hurled on to the ground and if I had hit my head first I should certainly have been killed. As it was, I fell on my shoulder, smashing my collarbone and scraping the skin off the whole of one side of my face. My ankle was badly sprained and on one side my elbow, hip and knee were abraded deep into the flesh; the scars still remain. I was, of course, unconscious. Some neighbouring soldiers brought a stretcher and I was carried into the Barracks. Later my friend told me that the men were deeply impressed because each time they moved me I murmured, "Thank you." In the afternoon, when the doctors had dealt with me, I was still unconscious, so I was put into an ambulance and taken home. I was unable to move and my three curates, standing in a row with their hands under me, used to lift me about while I remained quite rigid. But as I always heal very quickly, my convalescence was rapid. One day Hankey, the subaltern whose horse I had been riding, as he was leaving after paying me a visit, met one of my women parishioners. She asked him how I was and after he had told her she burst out feelingly: "I only wish I could get hold of the man who lent him that horse." Poor Hankey fled.

The parish was very excited by my accident, especially as my godmother, having been told of the mishap, sent every day for news of my progress. In those days Queen Victoria was a mysterious figure and any form of direct contact with her produced a sense almost of awe.

After Easter, in the year 1898, the curates and I felt in need of a holiday. As we could not all be away at once, two of us settled to start on Easter Monday and return in time for the others to go the following week. One of them, named Bennett, and I were both going into the Midlands. We took the first week, planning to bicycle to Rugby, sleep there and go on to our respective destinations next morning. But we missed our proper route at Dunchurch and had to ride nearly to Coventry and back, making our journey over a hundred miles. As it was raining for the last twenty miles, we reached Rugby very wet and tired. After a good night's rest and a good breakfast we were quite fresh again and started out to have a look at the town. My first impression was distinctly unfavourable. There was hardly a house that was fifty years old ; the church had been rebuilt ; Rugby School, at the end of the main street, was a collection of buildings architecturally uninspiring to a degree. "By the way," I remarked to Bennett, as we wandered about, "I think a cousin of mine is patron of the living here." "Oh," he replied with interest, "if it becomes vacant do you think he will offer it to you ?" "Not the least likely," I assured him, "and if he did I certainly shouldn't take it."

I was going on to stay with Lord and Lady Burton at Rangemore in Staffordshire, and when I arrived there that same day I found a telegram for me on the hall table. I took it into the drawing-room where everyone was at tea and, reading it, cried : "Ah, I've been offered the living of Rugby." Amid some excitement the development was then discussed, and in the face of my very definite inclination to decline the offer, Lord Burton begged me to give the matter further consideration. I did not want to leave Plumstead, and I had not been attracted to Rugby during my visit. Nevertheless, my host persuaded me to go with him and investigate the place again the next day.

At Rugby, Lord Burton and I saw the old Rector. His resignation was not to take effect until the autumn and so I agreed to consult Bishop Davidson and one or two other people before making my decision. Everybody I consulted was unanimous that I ought to accept. Finally I took the general advice, but I looked forward still to my last summer at Plumstead.

PART III

LIFE'S WORK

CHAPTER 9

RUGBY: FOURTEEN YEARS

ON August the 9th, 1898, I married Constance Elizabeth, third daughter of Gustavus, 8th Viscount Boyne and his wife, daughter of the Earl of Eldon. I never fell in love in the poet's sense of the word, but very soon after meeting Constance, when I was at Auckland ten years earlier, I realised that I had found the only woman I should like to marry. I do not think her beauty had anything to do with it. Indeed, I always hesitated as to whether she or her sister Maud were the most beautiful. They were alike and yet different. Both had the luxuriant hair which belonged to the family ; in their case fair and curly ; but there was a difference : Maud's hair had a touch of red in it, Constance's a sheen of gold. Her complexion was warm and rich and she had magnificent eyes, but what made her so striking was that with all this colouring she had coal-black eyebrows and long eyelashes. You could not help noticing Constance ; there was a quality in her beauty which I think was wonderfully expressed in a verse from an Italian love poem translated by Rossetti, which Canon Alexander Nairn wrote under her photograph when she died :

> Even as the moon amid the stars doth shed
> Her lovelier splendour of exceeding light—
> Even so my lady seems the queen and head
> Among all other ladies in my sight.
>
> Her human visage, like an angel's made,
> Is glorious even to beauty's perfect height ;
> And with her simple bearing soft and staid
> All secret modesties of soul unite.

For ten years I waited. I told nobody except my mother

of my hopes. I knew that there were always a great many men wanting to marry Constance, and yet I waited because I did not see my way financially to offer her a home. Throughout those years I visited the Boynes a great deal and was adopted into the family circle. A singularly gay and happy family it was, and their cordial affection has remained with me through the years, especially that of the two unmarried sisters.

When I accepted Rugby I saw my way to marriage. On July 9th I decided to attend a garden party at Syon, where I knew Constance would be, and ask her if she would marry me. When we met there I took her wandering in the great grounds, and when we reached a willow tree beside the lake —I can see it vividly now—I asked her. I do not think anyone who saw us would have noticed that anything was happening. We were neither of us given to emotional expression, but we knew that it was the crisis of both our lives. She said *yes*.

I had driven down in my pony cart and her mother allowed me to drive her home to London. As we knew each other so intimately there was no reason to wait and there was an opportunity of fitting in a longish holiday between my leaving Plumstead and my going to Rugby. It was hectic getting the arrangements made in a month, but we managed it, and on August the 9th we were married in Westminster Abbey. It had been the familiar home of all my younger days and was full of memories. The Dean agreed to our marriage there on the ground that I was a child of the Abbey. As we knew that there would be a considerable crowd we were not married in Henry VII's Chapel, but at the High Altar. Randall Davidson and Cecil Boutflower took the service. The Abbey was represented by the presence of Canon Gore who, when he became Bishop of Worcester, became one of our greatest friends. The choir was occupied by relations and friends, many hundreds of them, and the two transepts were full of people who had come from Plumstead. When the service finished we turned to walk the aisle to the west end, where the registers were to be signed, and found a double aisle of

THE AUTHOR WITH MRS. BAILLIE ON THEIR HONEYMOON

Plumstead people stretching the whole length of the vast nave. It was a very moving beginning to our new life.

Ours was a grand honeymoon. After resting for a few days at a house in Sussex, we travelled to Perth, with Dawson, the boy who had first come to me in Plumstead, in attendance. There our two ponies awaited us, with light luggage in saddle-bags, and we rode off on a wonderful tour of the Highlands, visiting endless houses of friends and soaking in the beauty of my native land, which meant so much to me and was new and exciting to her. Dawson, proceeding by train with our heavier luggage, met us from point to point along our route till we reached Dochfour, where we stayed for several days before turning to ride south again, to Rugby.

When finally my wife and I reached Rugby I felt as I had on first seeing the town with my curate, Bennett. On first sight it was not impressive. The oldest School buildings, very early Victorian Gothic, were in a degree dignified, but their effect was lost in the incongruity of the buildings grouped around them. These were the work of Butterfield, designed and built in his curious style of Gothic with variegated brick-work. A common Saying at the School was that Butterfield had built a library in which you could not see, a rackets court in which you could not play, a swimming bath in which you could not swim, a chapel in which you could not hear, and a school hall which would not hold the boys. This was a slight exaggeration; nevertheless, the buildings as a whole were unsatisfactory and undignified, producing the general effect of a jumble. Only when one had penetrated the surface did the town and school reveal their striking and individual personalities.

There were two outside elements which widened the interest of Rugby parish. One was, of course, that of the School. Many of the tradesmen and residents had been educated there, and almost everyone, in one way or another, had been con-nected with it. The masters permeated local society, intro-ducing an intellectual element not usually found in a country town.

The second outside influence was sport. For years Rugby had been a well-known hunting centre and great numbers of people took houses or rooms there for the winter. This practice largely died out in our time, since, being situated right in one corner of the county, three packs were required to hunt to any extent, which made it expensive. Our situation also meant that we were some distance from all the kennels, making the hounds draw away from Rugby at night and giving hunters a long ride home. But one person there was who continued to attract to the town a great deal of hunting society, keeping us fully in touch with the hunting world : this was Captain Beatty, father of the famous admiral. An Irish squire with real Irish charm, the Captain was one of the most important horse-dealers in England and his house, then opposite the church but since swept away, was a constant rendezvous for hunting society.

The old Captain and his family became great friends of ours ; especially David, the admiral son, who remained a much-loved friend till the end of his life, and the only daughter (who married Miles Courage), who, with her family, remained on intimate terms of friendship until her recent death.

In the Rugby days David, then a young naval captain and more or less a contemporary of mine, spent a lot of time at my house when on leave. During the 1914–18 War, on the evening following the Battle of Jutland he wrote me eight or nine quarto pages about the engagement and his own reactions to it. His hopes had been bitterly frustrated and, while I can take no part in the controversy as to where should lie responsibility for what took place, I can record that the action was a crushing blow to him. In addition, during the course of the battle his greatest friend had been killed before his eyes. His letter was of absorbing interest, but of so confidential a nature that I showed it to nobody and at once locked it up in what I considered a safe place. Shortly afterwards I moved from Coventry to Windsor. One of my first concerns when the time for packing arrived was for my letter which, apart from its personal value, I knew to be of historical importance. To my astonishment when I went to fetch it the letter was gone. It has never reappeared. I can only suppose someone stole it, though how that could have happened remains a mystery.

Besides hunting there was also polo. An old Cambridge friend, Ted Miller, had established a great polo centre to which many people came. For exercise I frequently helped to train the polo ponies, whose stud groom soon came to regard me with approval. Ted Miller's brother was away during the first few months of my appearance and on his return the groom said to him : " Very nice gentleman the new Rector —a good rider, with fine hands " ; adding, quite by way of an afterthought : " And a good preacher, too." (It was very touching when I went recently to preach in my old surroundings, to hear that one of the old polo grooms, who had long retired from active work, observed : " I've not been going to church lately, but I must go and hear Mr. Baillie.")

But while the interests of hunting and polo appreciably affected the town and tended to make it more alive, they were quite outside the organic life of the parish ; this sprang from the inter-relationship of three classes—the aristocracy, the tradespeople and the railway workers.

The nucleus of what I call the town's aristocracy consisted of a body of old ladies of exceptional individuality and character, such as are perfectly portrayed in the pages of Mrs. Gaskell's *Cranford*. The difference between fact and fiction is that Mrs. Gaskell leaves out the important part played by the ladies in the religious and philanthropic business of the town. The history of the Rugby ladies was very characteristic of the locality. Down to the 'seventies the local residents had an enormous advantage as regards the education of their sons, who were automatically admitted to Rugby School. People of standing, country gentlemen and the like of not very large means, came to settle in the town because of the educational advantages they gained. When in the 'seventies the town's privileges were swept away this ceased, but the existing families remained. The sons went out into the world, the parents died, and only the unmarried daughters were left behind.

These unmarried daughters were the social arbiters of the community. Sincerely religious, they provided the chief church workers of the town. They lived in very small houses on very small means. There was one dear old lady who had become an invalid. During her youth she had been very active but when I came to know her she lay on a sofa with a soft woolly shawl over her cap, surrounded by family relics. There were water-colour portraits, old fans and miniatures, snuff boxes and bits of china ; the very essence of the refinements of an earlier time. She was not, however, a pathetic figure. You could feel that she was of strong and almost stern character, but with delightful humour she could vividly describe the life of her youth. She told of days when as children they went to parties in a sedan chair which was kept at the local inn ; of a day, a special school holiday, when with the rest of the population they went to see the first train that ever passed through Rugby ; of days when the Waverley novels were still coming out, when Arnold was headmaster and Moultrie was Rector, so that the town was in touch with the most active intellectual life of the time. She used to play with the headmaster's children and described with peals of laughter Matthew Arnold's ungainly efforts at the dancing class. She also told how she had knelt next to him in the school chapel, when they were confirmed by Arnold's great friend, Archbishop Whateley. Listening to her, indeed, was like stepping back across the threshold of the past. At the same time she was no dreamer. The present was extremely real to her, and her voice and words were vigorous, not to say trenchant, in relation to passing events or living persons.

Another old lady was Miss Dulcie Radcliffe, as exquisitely sweet as her name, who lived with her sisters in a little house filled like all the others with relics of an earlier period, among them a perfect little library of the best books of her youth in beautiful bindings.

It was from these old ladies that most of my district visitors were drawn at the beginning of my Rectorship. A cousin of mine who saw them arrive at the Rectory for a meeting one day frivolously remarked that it was a gathering of the maimed, the halt and the blind. Appearances can be very deceptive. They did their work with immense energy, and did it well because they were bound to the people they visited by all manner of ties and associations. However, it must not be for one moment imagined that our relationship was a constantly smooth stream of beautiful, sentimental perfection. They were very human, with vigorous prejudices and opinions and with tongues only too capable of expressing them, not always with a sufficient care and restraint. We had our rows and difficulties often enough. Even so, my chief memory of them still is one of great grace and beauty.

About the old ladies as a nucleus there were the masters of Rugby School, the lawyers and doctors and so on, who made up the upper stratum of local society. After fifty years, one of the lawyers still stands out for me as a man whose influence has steadily grown throughout a long life to make him the wisest and surest guide in the life of the church and diocese. I recently mentioned his name to the new Bishop of Coventry, who said, " Oh, yes, Fred Harris is the most useful man we have ; I don't know what we would do without him." I am glad to think he is little changed, still going on conscientiously and with a calm dignity in his enormous work.

Our next class, centring on the tradesmen, was far better educated than that then found in a country town. Many of its members had benefited, as residents' sons, from receiving their education at the School. They came mostly from large families with ramifications all over the countryside, names of whose members could be found in all the neighbouring parish registers—as churchwardens, overseers and the like—as far back as the seventeenth century.

Railwaymen comprised the third class. They too had very definite grounds for self-respect : they believed in their railway. In their eyes it was the greatest and best railway in the world, and I am by no means sure they were not right. They knew that they could work for it during the rest of their working life and that a pension was waiting for them after that. In a word, they regarded their place in the railway as a dignified and honourable one.

In the Rugby of those years the relation between the three classes was at once intimate and respectful. To see one of the old ladies going shopping was a pleasant sight. The shop-keeper addressed her as Miss Mary or Miss Jane, and would ask after Master Harry or Master John, who had probably been away in the Civil Service in India for the last thirty years, but was still a boy in the shopkeeper's eyes. Then the ladies wanted to hear all about the shopkeeper's family on their side. When one of the railwaymen was in any difficulty with his children, or any other family concern, there was sure to be one of the old ladies to whom he went as a matter of course. In all probability she had taught him in Sunday school. She would know all about his children and it would be quite natural to go to her. But even then such things were beginning to die, echoing sadly like the notes of an old song. The shadow of the new twentieth-century industrialism, which, bit by bit, was irrevocably to sweep away that kind of world, already overhung the scene.

The focal point of all this Rugby life was unquestionably the church, no doubt because of two Rectors whose working lives covered a period of seventy-five years in the town's history. Rectors of Rugby before that had been long-lived; there were only four of them between 1674 and 1874, with an average of fifty years' service each.

The last of these four Rectors, John Moultrie, who was appointed in 1824, was a remarkable man. He had been one of the circle of outstanding young men, including Macaulay and Praed, united by a close friendship at Cambridge. Nor was Moultrie regarded as being the least among this group, having gained some distinction through his poetry. He wrote delightful occasional verses; among them an autobiography in verse, which is one of the most attractive things I know. When he went down from Cambridge he took a mastership at Eton and was ordained, henceforth firmly resolving to write no more poetry. It was impossible, he said, to do two things requiring the consecration of a man's whole life. Under the evil custom of the time he then accepted the living of Rugby from Lord Craven on condition that if Lord Craven's second son should be ordained on growing up, Moultrie would resign the living. Happily the son was not ordained and Moultrie continued as Rector for fifty years. It was remarkable that a quarter of a century later when I went to Rugby, his name still retained a sweet savour in the place, faces softening into smiles the moment it was mentioned.

Moultrie was a tall, thin, absent-minded man, with a sense of humour and a habit of walking about with his head in the clouds, noticing nobody. He was universally beloved. The gift by which he was most widely known was that of reading, people coming to Rugby church from far and wide merely to hear him read the Lessons. He used also to give readings of Shakespeare's plays to gatherings at private houses—in connection with which, a characteristic story : an Irish squire, lately come to settle in Rugby on account of his sons' education, was rather a flamboyant person quite devoid of literary tastes or culture. Somewhat inadvisedly he was asked to one of these readings. The play chosen was *Romeo and Juliet*, and Moultrie's reading so moved everyone that at the end there was a dead silence. The Irishman, thinking it a poor way of showing appreciation, bounced to his feet and, standing before the fire with his arms tucked under his coat-tails, announced in his heartiest manner : " Clever man, Shakespeare ! "

A devoted parish priest, John Moultrie died at the age of eighty-five of smallpox, caught when visiting a servant girl. His doctor told me that Moultrie was probably a unique case, having had smallpox five times in the course of his long life : once in his youth, when he was inoculated ; after a third attack he was vaccinated ; and contracting it for the fifth and last time, the doctor said it killed him like a dose of poison.

Ecclesiastically, Moultrie was one of the small body of pre-Tractarian High Churchmen who did remarkable work which, being later overshadowed by the Oxford Movement, was almost forgotten. In his earlier days the Evangelical Revival was at its height and the Evangelicals did not approve of him. One of their ladies, once encountering him in the street, went up to him and said, " Mr. Moultrie, I have sat under your ministry for the last five or six years and I feel that I have gained no good from it." Moultrie looked down at her for several moments in silence, before briefly responding, " I perceive it, Madam", and passing on. He agreed, however, to the Evangelicals having a church of their own, and St. Matthew's Church at Rugby was built.

John Murray, who succeeded Moultrie as Rector, was singularly unlike him. I first met him during my visit to Rugby with Lord Burton, to inquire into the conditions of the living. He was sitting in his study, smoking a pipe and with a large cup of tea beside him. That cup was always there, full of tea which he never drank till it was cold. I thought him quite one of the oldest men that I had ever seen. He was short and square, with an unkempt grey beard ; when he spoke you felt him to be a man of power. If we had visited him a few months earlier Murray would without doubt have electrified us (as he never failed to do with all strangers who came to see him) by saying, " Now we will go and see my mother." At his age one could scarcely conceive of his mother being alive. Yet up to the time of her death two years before, his mother, a neat brisk little old lady, at ninety-five had looked considerably younger than her seventy-five-year-old son.

One of the early Tractarians, Murray worked his parish with that meticulous attention to detail characteristic of his kind. He was a stern disciplinarian and insisted on everything connected with the services being done with accuracy and thoroughness. One lady who undertook to look after the altar linen had folded it a little carelessly and Murray, entering the vestry, noticed this. He sent for her, waiting in the vestry for a long time till she could be found. When she arrived he gave her a talking to which she never forgot. I believe—as I mentioned in the instance of my old nurse—

that this insistence on care in relation to everything connected with God's service is a wonderful method of instruction. Certainly the fruits of Murray's ministry were obvious in the parish, and his was probably the best training that could have been given after Moultrie's work. The town was definitely afraid of him, as he was a man of strong will and hot temper, but, though I do not think he was as much beloved as his predecessor, they respected him deeply. It was the life and work of these two men which made the name of Rector of Rugby a considerable one.

2

In my new job my wife and I soon discovered that we were faced with some serious problems. The first was a violent party spirit in the church. Mr. Murray had been a strong man, who expected obedience and got it, but as he grew old he failed to realise quite what was going on behind the scenes. He was a Tractarian; his curates, without his appreciating it, were mostly Anglo-Catholics. This division into parties within the church itself led the curates into attracting little caves who followed them about wherever they preached, firmly believing they were receiving instruction in, and correctly observing, the real religion. This, of course, caused great partisanship and controversy, and when I came the caves were much perturbed. All the curates save one were leaving and the followers of each felt all the more that they must keep the flag flying. Now, it has always been my belief that party spirit is one of the worst dangers to religious life. It was so in the early Church when there was one party who claimed Apollos, another Paul, another Christ, as their leader. In tackling the problem at Rugby, however, I determined not to fight my opponents but to win them. By that I do not mean bringing them over to my way of thought, but bringing them into a way of religion through which they could realise that a true faith was bigger than their own little *ism*. Only thus could we achieve unity and fellowship in spite of difference about many things.

In achieving this unity I believe I succeeded. To my infinite joy I recently obtained evidence to support my belief, after an interval of thirty-five years. There was a very saintly woman and a great church worker who, in spite of the fact that I did not at all represent her way of thought, worked loyally for the church throughout my time. On recently re-visiting Rugby, I learned that she was blind and deaf and permanently confined to her room. She had been in the habit of attending Communion every day, and when she was no longer able to do this, the Rector offered to take the Communion to her once a week. "No," was the reply, " Canon Baillie used to say that we mustn't be selfish and ask too much of our clergy, as there are many others who need them. Besides, I know the service by heart and all the Collects, Epistles and Gospels, so I can say them quietly by myself while you are taking the service in church." I visited her and, in spite of being unable to see me, she showed the greatest pleasure at our reunion. After a little time had passed, she said : " There's something I have wanted to see you for. Sitting here unable to read, I naturally think over the past. I wanted to tell you I'm convinced your successors couldn't have done the great work they did but for your preparation. You found us torn in pieces by divisions of party spirit. You left us a happy united place by treating us all impartially with patience and love." So often when people speak of one's good work, they speak from a desire to be kind, and little more, but I knew that she meant what she said, and I was very thankful. Of all things, the one I have most desired is to encourage unity of spirit and the bond of peace. If I succeeded in doing that at Rugby, I achieved something really worth achieving, whatever my shortcomings and imperfections in other directions.

Another problem we had to face was that the whole social structure of Rugby was threatened by the coming of the first big works, in whose wake a new type of urban population came flooding in. Both day-school and church accommodation threatened very soon to be hopelessly inadequate. Once again I benefited from my knowledge of Thorold's methods of church extension. It matters very much where new churches and schools are placed, so I set myself to try and find the strategically right situations.

After studying the parish, I thought out very carefully what policy to pursue. The need of extending church machinery to meet new populations had to begin by considering what we already had. Moultrie had met the growth of the town with a big new church, meant to replace the old parish church. This last was small and had been architecturally ruined by very bad additions and alterations, and the new church was built almost next to it, in the churchyard. It was a fine church by the standards of the day, but mechanical and uninteresting in its architecture, as churches of that period were. When it came to pulling down the parish church, however, there was at once a chorus of protest and resentment from the old people ; accordingly Moultrie allowed the two churches to stand. The result was that the new church became the fashionable church and was crowded, while the congregation in the old church became thin. When Murray succeeded Moultrie he accepted the position. He was determined, however, to rebuild the old church and eventually, with Butterfield's help, he raised a large, rather majestic edifice with all the characteristics of Butterfield's work. Immediately that became the fashionable church, and Moultrie's church was deserted, or nearly so. Besides these two churches there was just one small mission.

Having decided that, as soon as feasible, a church should be built on the outskirts of the parish where the population was growing, I started a mission there in preparation for it. I determined also that we must have two more missions at the bottom of the hill, so that we should have three churches along the ridge and three missions in the valley. Though in the end we attained our goal, it took us the whole of fourteen years to do so.

The need for schools could not be allowed to wait. Moultrie and Murray had built schools, but it was quite clear that before long we should need a considerable number of new buildings. All these activities required money, and when it came to a point of raising sufficient funds to cover our plans I came up against a completely defeatist spirit. I was told that the two previous Rectors had built their churches and schools through the generosity of three rich old men who were all dead, and, since there was no one else who had any money, it would be quite impossible to raise what was needed. I knew that this was nonsense. Twenty shillings are better than a pound as they show that twenty people instead of one are interested. If we could excite sufficient enthusiasm to obtain a multitude of small gifts, we should not only get our money but create a healthier spirit in the parish. We succeeded : the new church and the new missions were built, mainly from weekly contributions of working people. Moreover, everyone that subscribed was proud of the church and liked to share in its activities. I have never been in favour of things being done for a parish by single rich donors ; it is bad for the spirit of the place. Rich men can, however, give you a valuable start, so preventing people being disheartened by the task lying ahead of them.

During my fourteen years the balance of the population at Rugby was steadily changing, hastened by the building of a second and still bigger industrial plant. We were turned, in fact, into an industrial town. For my part I really enjoyed the transition, Plumstead having given me an immense affection for an industrial population. But the poor old Rugbyans did not share my feelings. The aristocracy looked down their noses at the possibility of social intercourse with the men at the works ; the tradespeople felt rightly that it was the end of their day and that multiple stores would soon overwhelm them ; even the railwaymen did not much care about the newcomers. In fact, everybody was thoroughly uncomfortable. The first reaction on the part of old Rugby was to ostracise the newcomers. My experience made me see there a very serious danger which at all costs must be faced. If possible the unity and fellowship of the town must be preserved, and obviously my wife and I were the only people who could do it. We were without a Mayor, and there was no one else who could take the lead. Our basic difficulty consisted in first getting the people—old and new—to know and understand one another.

My wife and I started by making friends with the new people ourselves, making them feel that we wanted, as indeed we did, cordial relations with them. When that was done, and it did not take long, we tried an experiment : we gave an evening party in the Town Hall. To it we invited the old order and the new, as well as the members of the Town Council. Things were distinctly difficult at first. Several of the old ladies wandered about with their noses very much in the air and one of them, with her hands folded in front of her, her elbows tucked well into her sides, her lips pursed, came up to me and observed : " You seem to have some very queer people here tonight ! " I laughed and answered : " I'm sorry you think so, but they all happen to be friends of ours." Still, it was touch and go, and if the party had ended without achieving its object it would have done a great deal of harm. But my wife and I were determined to make it a success. Bit by bit we got the new class introduced to such members of the old as we felt sure would play up, until conversation was set going and any strangeness between the guests had ceased to be apparent. In the end we could really say that the affair had been a pleasant occasion. After that, things were much easier, and in a comparatively short time the whole question of difference had been forgotten and everyone shook down together on their own merits.

There soon followed another plan to unify the people. We gave a party in our garden once a week during the summer. They were big parties of from two to four hundred, all guests being invited for some especial reason, thus avoiding the question of social distinctions. One week, for example, all the Sunday school teachers in the Rural Deanery came ; another week all the churchwardens, sidesmen and the like, with whom we included our Councillors. Such parties mixed all classes quite easily on the ground of common occupation. Then we asked what I may call the public servants—the cabmen, postmen, policemen of the town, with of course their wives ; and with them there would be a few of our own friends who used to come and help get up games and amusements. Among these friends was one old lady who was a very tower of strength. She had a considerable position in the town and was quite remarkably generous. People thought her rich because of the generous gifts she made, but she was not. She was, however, a careful businesswoman and employed her income wisely, managing always to have a surplus for kindly gifts. Possessing a gorgeous sense of humour, she was ready to help in everything. At the end of one party, when we had had an uproarious game of bumps (one of the best remedies for stiffness in the world !), she came up to me bubbling with amusement, saying, " I'm sure I've sat in the lap of every cabman, postman and policeman in the town ! "

After people had met each other and had fun together, little prejudices faded out and finally we became a friendly community. I need hardly say that we managed to weave in the Nonconformists just as much as the church people, which not only induced a happy feeling but, from the point of view of my work, had the advantage of meaning that almost everybody in the place came into contact with me in a pleasant way. It is true you cannot break down human separations and prejudices without constant effort ; and effort which is not recognised as such—as, for instance, contriving to show a person to whom you are talking the merits of someone you know quite well he is prejudiced against. Hundreds of little things of this sort presented themselves every day in our efforts to promote harmony and friendliness, producing in time the desired result. If you take for granted that people want to be friendly, and show them that you take it for granted, eventually they become friendly.

The two main problems, then—first, of killing party spirit in the church ; second, of producing goodwill and fellowship in the town—had been recognised by us as vitally important almost from the moment of our arrival. To their solution we gave a great deal of attention all through the fourteen years we spent at Rugby, until at the end there was hardly an association of people for any object whatever in which we had not an interest and a share. I was greatly amused when, not long before we left, I was asked to become President of the Singing Birds Association.

3

My wife and I were assisted in all this parish work by my staff of curates.

The theory in those days (and, I think, a right one) was that, to bring the influence of the church to bear fully and adequately on the population, there must be one priest to every two thousand people. That is an ideal which is now almost impossible to live up to. At Rugby we began with four curates and ended with nine. I had one great advantage in increasing my staff. The income of the parish when I arrived was only a moderate one, which I succeeded in raising through the sale of a piece of glebe, right in the middle of the town. I had made strenuous efforts to prevent this ground being built upon as it was hoed for allotments, which I felt were of incalculable physical and moral value to an urban population. The town authorities were constantly urging me to let the glebe go for building, and at last I did so, determined, however, to turn the land as far as possible to the benefit of the parish. Having private means, I was able to lay the property out on my own account. When everything had been done, I put the plots into which the ground was divided on to the market and in a single day they were all sold, at astonishing prices. The income from the invested proceeds of the sale soon became very large, and, after discussion with my churchwardens, a substantial sum was set aside for a curate fund while the residue went to make provision for any Rector who should be appointed and be without private means.

The experience I had gained with the ordination candidates in the Rochester diocese stood me in good stead when selecting new curates. I always went to the Theological College where the candidate was being trained so as to get to know him. My aim was to find men of strong individuality. I did not mind to what school of thought they belonged, so long as they were real men who were prepared to throw themselves fully into the work of the parish because they believed in it.

The parish was divided into six districts, each one centring on some particular church or mission. Each of the big districts had two men attached to it, a priest and a deacon ; the rest had one. There were, therefore, six centres. As I believe that differences of view in the Church are not grounds for separation, but only differences of emphasis which make different men give special value to particular sides of the truth, and which only become dangerous when an atmosphere of controversy arises, I necessarily felt in Rugby that the Church ought to provide places for services and teaching in harmony with all views. St. Matthew's relieved me of the need of having a definitely Evangelical church ; the parish church represented the early Tractarian point of view in its services ; Holy Trinity was more advanced, Cambridge Street still more so ; while St. Peter's and St. Phillip's were more or less the same type as the parish church. I put my men to work in the church where they would find themselves in harmony with the general atmosphere. This system was liable to have created caves with disastrous party feeling, as had in some degree happened in Mr. Murray's later years. I met this danger in two ways : first, I kept in close touch with all the centres, encouraging the man-in-charge to bring his proposals to me, to which I listened sympathetically without interfering with his full authority. Additionally I made the people feel my sympathy with them by going regularly to all the centres in turn. Secondly, I worked to develop a sense of fellowship among the clergy.

On Sunday night the majority of the curates—that is to say, all the unmarried ones—used to come to the Rectory for supper. I allowed them to bring any young laymen with whom they had made friends, deliberately cultivating conversation among them but, instead of talking much myself, giving sympathetic attention to whatever they said. The evenings were always gay and interesting, all sorts of subjects coming up for quite free discussion. Finding me ready to work with them, and discuss any point on any subject, gave to the importance of their individual opinions a greater sense of proportion. Their minds were widened, their sympathies enlarged, and they became as happy and united a band as you could wish to find. Moreover, the constant chaff that went on was particularly wholesome for any young man who showed symptoms of priggishness.

On Monday mornings we again met, to discuss questions in connection with the parish. We began by arranging the services, meetings and so forth for the week. Then we read over the list of the sick, each one reporting on the cases he was visiting and very often inviting discussion on problems connected with them which were worrying him. Everyone took part in those discussions, though we never tried to override the opinions of the man-in-charge. Finally, general questions came up, often leading to tremendous exchanges, sometimes heated and sometimes resulting in uproarious laughter. Thus, while maintaining their individual positions and tenets, the curates learned to understand the viewpoints of other people. Their work could not but gain in value through such unity. Weak members derived moral support from belonging to a much respected body ; strong members carried the weak, making their work far more effective by their unconscious support ; while my influence was strengthened through their wholehearted loyalty to me.

In my own case nothing could have been of greater worth than these meetings. The young naturally have a background which is quite different from that of the previous generation, and living with them and hearing their discussions kept me in vital sympathy with them and helped me to understand their thought.

Although, after the very intimate association that existed between my curates and myself, any specific references or descriptions would be a breach of confidence, I cannot resist writing about Studdert-Kennedy, or *K.* as we called him.

K. was one of the strangest characters I ever knew. An Irishman, with brains, he had infinite charm, complete devotion to his work and a fine sense of humour, but mentally he was incredibly undisciplined. At least once a week he dashed into my room with some new idea. They were sometimes quite preposterous, but they were always held by him for the moment with burning earnestness. If one argued with him gravely about them, he was quite clever enough to have defended his position with success, when the result would only have been to harden his beliefs. But his new idea always had a humorous side due to its very exaggeration, and an appeal to that brought him down on his feet again. In his earlier days he preached a sermon in the heat of the moment in which I felt he had gone more than a little too far. After church I took him for a walk alone in the Rectory garden and, with apparent gravity, I said : " You know, I think you exaggerated when you said that there had been no one between St. Paul and yourself who had understood the Gospel." At once he burst into a shout of uproarious laughter and he had learnt his lesson. I always told him that he must not come to me with more than one new heresy a week, as after that it became a bore. After he left me, people were so dazzled by the amazing force of his eloquence that they took him seriously, which did him a great deal of harm.

As a man, *K.* had no sort of discipline about small things. Whatever he had in his pocket he gave away, until his landlady took charge of his money and rationed him with it. It was the same with his clothes. He gave them all away and walked about almost in rags, wearing a cassock to conceal the fact. What he might have turned into I cannot pretend to know, but his want of mental discipline might have had serious consequences. As it was, his complete sincerity, his passionate belief and astonishing eloquence made him a great power for good in my Rugby parish.

We had one small district that was practically a slum, and K., whose nickname of Woodbine Willie became a household word among our armies in France during the first world struggle, gravitated there, getting me to buy a derelict Nonconformist chapel as the centre for his work. His work was very useful. One of his activities was to wander in and out of the public houses and talk to the men. His personality made it easy, and the men would welcome him even in the worst and lowest places.

In the years that followed, whenever I came into contact with Rugby people, though they spoke with great warmth of my successors,[1] they always said : " We've never had such good curates as yours." I am sure this is quite false, and that individually the curates were every bit as good, but possibly the fellowship among my own men, and the fashion in which they brought their influence to bear as one body, did make their work much more effective.

Among the personnel who played so large a part in bringing to fulfilment my aims and efforts at this time, there is one name to which I must pay a separate tribute. Shortly after I went to Rugby, William Sudworth, the son of one of our engine drivers, came to me as secretary. His character was a great influence on my family and all of us clergy, and with his delightful, happy and humorous nature he was the means of smoothing out many of our troubles. The twenty years that he was with me would have lost an indispensable element without him, and it was a sad day when ultimately he had to leave me because my work at Windsor allowed no room for the services of a full-time secretary. I have missed him enormously ever since.

[1] All of my successors were remarkable men, becoming in turn the Bishops of Peterborough, Truro, Bury St. Edmunds and Singapore.

CHAPTER 10

RUGBY: SUMMARY AND CONCLUSION

AT the time of my ordination there was a disturbing atmosphere within the Church which was a reflection of the spirit of unrest pervading society and the world. Though the first reaction of the Church had been rigidly to oppose all questions that suggested mistakes of any sort in the Bible, there was a growing band of scholars who criticised the Scriptures, especially the Old Testament, on a scientific level. The controversies to which this gave rise left me entirely confused as to what I could believe and what I ought not to believe in the Old Testament, and even to some extent in the New. Indeed, after I was ordained I found myself unable to read my Bible with confidence or comfort, though I still read and used in preaching the Biblical stories illustrating human character in relation to God. Always, however, there was a latent fear that what I read might be mere invention. I was not disposed to believe that it could be so ; on the other hand, I did not feel strong enough to contradict the overwhelming company of scholars who had questioned it. This attitude of mind remained with me up to the time I went to Rugby. Nevertheless, I never lost the feeling that I would regain my confidence ; my fundamental faith, which in itself remained perfectly unshaken, had been born entirely of the Bible, as my mother had introduced me to it.

Bishop Maclagan once told me how, in his young days as a Scottish Presbyterian, he had always considered the habit of expounding the Scriptures in addition to the sermon, one of the most impressive parts of the Scottish service. (I have been sorry to notice, on the few occasions I have been able to attend a Presbyterian service in Scotland of latter years, that the habit has apparently been dropped.) The Bishop also told me how, as Vicar of Kensington, he experimented along similar lines, one night a week giving expositions from the Bible. He did not expect to attract many people, especially as the time he 'fixed conflicted with many people's dinner hour. To his astonishment, however, he found the enormous church absolutely packed the very first night and it continued to be so until the end of the series. Exposition consists simply of reading the actual words of the Bible, with only such comment as is necessary to clear away obscurities.

Soon after my arrival at Rugby I recalled my talk with the Bishop and decided to try something of the same kind. As I felt more confidence in the New Testament than the Old, I began with St. Paul's Epistles, supplying just as much of the setting in which they were written as was necessary, but otherwise reading them exactly as if they had been letters. I gave them as lectures to men, at three o'clock on Sunday afternoons, and the attendance being large, I continued during the eight winter months for two years. At the end I discovered that the Epistles had acquired an altogether new value for me, while St. Paul himself had become an excitingly vivid personality. "But," I then said to myself, "you're a coward. You know how much you owe to the Old Testament and how much it meant to Christian people in your young days. It's pure cowardice to shirk it," and announced that I would begin the next course of readings with the first chapter of Genesis.

To begin with I used all the latest commentaries, but I found that instead of helping they only confused me. Accordingly, I dropped the commentaries, and with that began to discover the extraordinary interest of the Pentateuch. Abraham and Moses became real people to me, just as St. Paul had emerged as a real man through the reading of the Epistles. I came to see the sort of man Abraham was, being led into a firm course of action by the truth that he found in his Bible, which consisted of those allegories that we have in the early chapters of Genesis. I passed on to Moses and was able to envisage his mother, while she was still his nurse, teaching him Abraham's Bible and adding to it the stories of the Patriarchs. The actions of those great Old Testament figures become far clearer and more compelling if one realises the limits of their religious knowledge.

Before very long I found it ridiculous to suppose that the Bible was uninspired. Other nations had had allegories on the same plane of thought as those of Abraham, but they died, while Abraham's Bible had remained the basis of religious knowledge ever since. Whether we have it in its original form or rewritten later no more affects the question of its validity than it would that of the *Canterbury Tales* were they translated into modern English. The completeness and convincing reality of the story of Abraham and Moses made a petty insistence on details of composition absurd.

Though my curates at Rugby said, "It's all very well but people won't come when you pass on to Leviticus and Numbers," that did not prove to be the case. I think my hearers were even more interested in the later books than they had been in the earlier. I had four hundred men who came to hear the Pentateuch read to them for eight months of each year over a period of eight years. Indirectly, moreover, I had a larger audience still. Many of those who came on Sundays were men in various local industrial jobs. I was constantly told that the first thing to happen to them on Monday morning in the workshops was to be asked the subject of my reading on the previous day, which often continued to be the subject of general discussion throughout the week.

The supreme importance to me personally of the whole thing was, of course, that thereby I came to have the Bible again, with all its old force and meaning. I was not very much interested in the victory of the critics over the idea of verbal inspiration. I had never been taught that view of inspiration; but I had once believed, and now believed again, that what the Bible conveys as to God's relation to Man and Man's relation to God is unshakable.

2

In addition to solving the special problems that confronted us at Rugby, the curates and I were carrying on the ordinary parochial work to the best of our powers, and as far as one could judge by statistics, we were very successful. The numbers that attended church were extremely large ; the Sunday schools were packed ; we had innumerable church workers. The number of communicants was also astonishing ; I have never known any parish with so high a percentage of them. But the most remarkable thing was that though the population was growing fast, and growing entirely by the influx of working people from industrial towns, the proportion of communicants to the population was increasing more than in proportion to the growth of the population.

Not only was our influence in the ascendant within Rugby, but we were extending it outside the town. As Rural Dean I was conscious of the feeling of isolation common in country parishes, depressing to parish and clergy alike. At first I puzzled what to do for the best. I knew it was essential for the unity of the deanery to encourage some form of regular intercourse between the town and the country districts surrounding it. As we had a very large staff of clergy and church workers there was no room for lay readers in the parish. But we had a considerable number of men qualified to do lay readers' work. I therefore suggested to the country clergy that if they would like it we would send out lay readers in pairs to take services and, where convenient, organise Sunday schools in the outlying hamlets of their parishes. The clergy accepted gratefully, so we organised a body of twelve lay readers, whom I made responsible for the work. The arrangement proved most successful, forming the required link between us and the country by showing, as it did, our interest in them.

In some instances we had men who, while competent as

speakers, were unable to undertake regular work. When, therefore, as not infrequently occurred, any question arose which was interesting to the Church at large, we got the country parishes to arrange meetings and two of these extra laymen, after very careful preparation, took the meetings and explained the question to the people. This also helped to make the people in the villages feel themselves part of a bigger life and so mitigate their sense of isolation. The weekly garden parties I have described were also used for this purpose.

Because of the wide knowledge of the parishes I gained through these activities the patrons took to consulting me in their appointments of new men ; not without advantage, I think, as besides knowing the parishes intimately I had a very much larger knowledge than they of available men. All of which made our ruridecanal conferences very vital and active events. The Bishop used to hold what he called Bishop's weeks in the rural deaneries, during which he came with a body of clergy and held a Mission in all the parishes. He told me that both he and the men who accompanied him had been immensely impressed with the vital life of our deanery, appreciably different to the life they found in other places.

I risk being accused of egotism and conceit in saying all this about our work, but I have done so quite deliberately because our success failed to satisfy me. I had a feeling that somehow it was not producing in the people the kind of personal religion evident among the best Christians in my younger days. It certainly raised morality ; it certainly turned people to Christian observances ; it certainly made a great many people do what is called Christian work ; it certainly made immense numbers listen to instruction. But were we giving our people the real thing and developing within them the power of true Christianity ? So deeply was I concerned about this that after I had been at Rugby for ten years, although everything seemed in a most satisfactory condition, I went to Bishop Gore, who was then my bishop and an intimate friend. Having laid the case before him, I told him I thought I should resign as I felt that I had done all I could and it needed a man of deeper spiritual understanding to build on to it. The Bishop did not consider I had sufficient grounds for resignation ; instead he suggested I make an especial effort to deepen my own spiritual grasp of religion. My feeling is that we were both right. The weakness of which I was aware was not purely due to my individual faults—it was part of the weakness of the contemporary Church. I believe that the majority of the clergy were suffering from the same limitation as myself. We of the priesthood believed in the influence that can be brought to bear through organisation. We believed that a right theology was a very important thing, and that we must instruct the people in theology ; we studied and acted accordingly. We believed in the education of the young in a high standard of morality, and we tried to give them this education. The Church was behind us in each of these respects. I am quite certain there has never been a period in which the clergy were more conscientious and hard-working, and yet I felt there was something wanting with us all. However, what it was we missed I was unable exactly to discern, and it saddened me a good deal.

My problem was by no means a new one. I had felt it at Plumstead, and indeed in all my work. But at Rugby I had far greater opportunities for testing all the means I knew of for impressing Christianity ; the effect on me was far greater when I felt that all those means had failed. I do not mean to imply that we did not achieve any good, for that would be absurd. Nor do I mean there were not people who had the vital religion which it seemed to me that our work lacked. It was, rather, that I felt such people derived it either from home influences or from the teaching of my predecessors instead of from us.

3

The years I spent in Warwickshire, first at Rugby and then at Coventry, were the only years in which I enjoyed full family life. I had with me my wife, unimpaired in energy though not always in perfect health, and my three sons—Alastair, Ean and Peter. We were a happy family. The boys were very different in character, but Rugby took an immense interest in them and I think had a feeling that they belonged to the town.

My wife was one of those people whose actions are beyond analysis, yet few can have had a greater or more far-reaching influence. She never assumed any obvious public position. She neither made speeches nor openly advocated causes, but behind the scenes she was the vital influence that inspired and directed any organisation in which she was involved. As one of my churchwardens said to me when we were leaving Rugby, " We may get another man who is as good a Rector as yourself but we will never get another Mrs. Baillie." With my marriage, my work acquired a new and added value ; for it became, and always remained, *our* work even though on the surface it appeared mine. I can only describe the difference by comparing it to a view seen first on a dull grey day and later lit and transformed by glorious sunshine. This complete unity with my wife accounts for my infrequent references to her when describing my work.

The second of the important factors that now entered my life lay in the person of George Dawson. Dawson was anxious to come into the house and after a year or two he occupied the position of butler, though he was still very young. It did not take my wife and I long to appreciate that his character and remarkable organising ability were capable of taking the burden of domestic management entirely off our shoulders. We never had the least cause to worry, knowing quite well that everything would run easily. During the first World War when he was taken away we perhaps realised most fully Dawson's unique qualities ; we found we

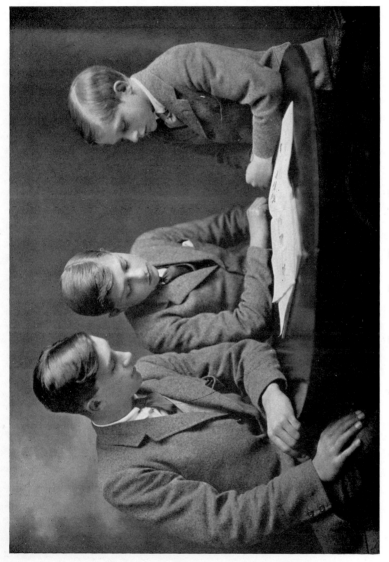

ALASTAIR, EAN AND PETER BAILLIE, AT RUGBY

were simply incapable of managing a house, and what a humiliating discovery it was. From the day that he returned to us everything dropped back as if by magic into position and life again flowed smoothly. To have such a dependable, unshakable person as Dawson was of enormous value to us, especially as hospitality played such a large part in our busy lives.

One other who for forty-seven years has played a great part in the background of my home is Amelia Newman, originally my wife's maid. After my wife's death we realised her full value and she became housekeeper-housemaid. With Dawson she has managed my home ever since. Now, whenever I meet any of my friends their first inquiry is always of Dawson and Newman.

That part of the Rugby picture filled out by my personal life is best represented in our summer holidays, typical as they were of the whole spirit informing my home circle.

At that time people in country houses were ready to receive friends or relations whenever they liked to offer a visit. Between us, my wife and I had innumerable houses in Scotland where we were sure of a welcome and it would have been perfectly easy to ride from house to house. Since, however, my wife found it tiring to go somewhere fresh every night, when she had to dress and often sit among strangers, we took our ease at an inn on alternate nights, though we invariably stayed in some house for two nights in the middle of the week and over the week-ends. For five days each week we used to travel between thirty and thirty-five miles a day ; on our first tour carrying our things with us in our saddlebags but afterwards with Dawson accompanying us in a pony-cart, which was much more convenient. Our second tour was our longest : during it we covered seven hundred and fifty miles and stayed at twenty-seven different houses. People were much amused by our visits, which were certainly unique.

After children came and my wife was not as strong as she had been, we went more often for our holidays to my wife's home in Shropshire. When my son Alastair was three years old, however, we decided to try something more adventurous and we bought a caravan. It was just an ordinary gipsy affair, which we painted gaily. The first year my wife and I travelled on our ponies while Alastair, with Dawson and my secretary Sudworth, was in the caravan. We had fitted two large awnings, which were rolled up on each side of the vehicle when we were moving. Whenever we called a halt these awnings were unrolled to form two good-sized tents, one serving as a kitchen and the other as a bedroom for the men. The whole experiment turned out to be a glorious success.

After our initial venture we spread ourselves a bit. We added two tents to our outfit; in one of which slept the governess and the children while in the other were accommodated Dawson and two other male servants. There were also a pony-cart for my wife, a much smaller cart with a Shetland pony for the children and governess—though the children were on their feet more often than not—and a luggage cart. We always had relays of men guests, two at a time and staying for a fortnight. Dawson, who had studied with great advantage under our cook, Mrs. Whittall, produced wonderful food from our little stove. At night we would secure permission to camp in some field, or if we visited a friend's house, we camped in the park. When visiting, however, we always refused to have a meal at the house but gave dinner parties in camp, when Dawson never failed to astonish those we entertained by his dinners.

The camp in the early morning presented an amusing sight. There would be my wife sitting on the steps of the caravan, in her aquascutum, doing her hair and we men in pyjamas shaving in a little glass attached to the props of one of the awnings. The children meantime were probably playing cricket, while Dawson was cooking.

When the boys went to school, our caravanning had to stop. August is too late for real pleasure in camping as the insects are too many and the evenings too short. But while it lasted, wandering at will over England and generally travelling on alternate days, it was a splendid life, especially for the children. The refreshment of a holiday spent entirely in the open air, with time counting for nothing, is unbelievable. Rain never worried us, since if you live in the open things dry so easily, and at night we were always pleasantly tired and slept well. In all our expeditions we managed to see a great deal and the boys, especially Ean, developed a real love for natural history. Someone (I never knew who) wrote a long article in *The Times* about our tours, not referring to me by name but simply as " a distinguished ecclesiastic ".

CHAPTER II

COVENTRY

IN 1912, at the earnest request of Bishop Huyshe Yeatman-Biggs of Worcester, I moved from Rugby to Coventry and entered on an extremely interesting experience.

In the Middle Ages Coventry was one of the foremost cities in England. It had an immense cathedral, many splendid monasteries and two fine parish churches, whose spires are still famous ; its trade guilds were opulent and active, and a Parliament was twice held there. Up to the Reformation the Church was the basis of all the city's greatness. But with the Reformation the cathedral and the monasteries were destroyed, trade disintegrated and the guilds were ruined, until at last nothing was left within the city walls but picturesque relics of a flourishing past. Nevertheless, in spite of the loss of the cathedral, a nominal importance still attached to the then centre of the united diocese of Coventry and Lichfield. During the Civil War the city closed its gates against Charles I and in consequence the tide of its fortunes sank still lower : with the Restoration, Charles II punished it by making a breach in its wall and changing the title of its bishopric to Lichfield and Coventry.

No longer the county town and with no kind of dignity remaining to it, Coventry was yet on the eve of a great revival. In France the persecution of the Huguenots by Louis XIV drove refugees into England, among them silk weavers who settled at Coventry and developed their industry, making the city prosperous again for nearly two hundred years. As the weaving was done in houses instead of factories, the usual disadvantages and difficulties of an industrial revival were largely avoided. The city regained its dignity through its rich silk magnates, who lived in state in beautiful old houses and dispensed a sumptuous hospitality.

In the middle of the nineteenth century Gladstone signed a treaty with France which, by letting in French silk, killed the weaving industry of Coventry almost in a day. So abject became the poverty to which the city was reduced that all manner of charities were started in London to help its starving population. Lord Leigh, the much-loved Lord Lieutenant of the county, also threw himself into the task of helping the townspeople out of their straits.

The next stage in Coventry's ill-starred municipal story was reached when a commercial traveller, working for a small factory which made sewing machines, went to Paris and there saw the first modern-type bicycle. Realising its immense trade possibilities, the man bought it and urged his English directors to switch over to the manufacture of such machines. His advice was followed and a boom began. The consequent increase in the population was housed without any care for the preservation of the city's beauty. Old buildings were demolished and, with overnight building, many parts became extremely squalid. Happily, a contemporary artist made sketches of all the best buildings that were lost, emphasising the terrible destruction that was carried out. Except for the three historic churches, the two beautiful alms-houses, the Guildhall of St. Mary and a few of the old-time houses, nothing was left. The old city gates had been destroyed some years before. Money, however, came pouring into Coventry. Ultimately American competition began to kill the bicycle business but an even greater era of prosperity opened when the town attracted a large number of the chief motor factories.

Socially, Coventry's vicissitudes had produced curious conditions. The various factories were controlled by limited liability companies, a few of whose leading men lived inside the city ; local government was in the hands of a small group of people belonging to the silk period, no longer weavers, of course, but members in every sense of the former class. At their head was a remarkable man, Colonel Wyley. His authority was tremendous, but it rested entirely on tradition. In no way was he associated with the new industrial population, who had not even begun to be interested in city life.

Coventry, therefore, had become little more than a large aggregate of people. Although the Church might have provided a centre of unity, the town had never been one parish and no single church was able to claim headship. Additionally, the Church as a whole had been affected by the city's changing fortunes. The parishes worked quite independently of one another, while there had been a series of clerical scandals which had wrecked the prestige of the clergy. In one parish, for example, there was still living a former vicar who, having been turned out for drunkenness, supported himself by working as a jobbing gardener. So low had the good name of the clergy sunk that soon after my arrival a leading layman said to me : " It comes to this—if you want to be respected here you will have to win that respect in spite of your cloth." There was a local rule that no clergyman could become a member of the education authority. The Church stood for absolutely nothing in the eyes of the people. If numbers continued to attend the old churches it was simply from tradition.

Most serious of all was the fact that Coventry was quite isolated from the life of the county. It had no common interests or points of contact whatever with the surrounding country. Moreover, by an incredibly stupid act earlier in the century, Warwickshire had been divided from Lichfield and joined to Worcester, so that even the name of the original bishopric was gone. At last Coventry was just a town that happened to stand in the county, with at most a vague tradition of its former greatness attaching to it.

The Bishops of Worcester had grown acutely conscious of the existing state of things. The first step was the making of Birmingham into a diocese, but that left the rest of Warwickshire completely isolated. In my own case, so inaccessible was Worcester that I had been three years Rector of one

of the most important parishes in Warwickshire before I
had seen my cathedral, when I visited it as a tourist. The
only solution seemed to lie in the creation of a new diocese,
of which Coventry should be the centre, the enormous and
glorious parish church of St. Michael being ideally suited
for a cathedral.

The task of creating the new diocese was undertaken by
Bishop Yeatman-Biggs, who erected St. Michael's into a pro-
cathedral. A vacancy in the vicarage gave him a chance of
appointing a sub-dean, but in John Masterman his was not a
fortunate choice. In many ways a first-rate man, Masterman
in this case lacked the gifts needed for leadership. As a result
the enthusiasm which the creation of the pro-cathedral temporarily aroused died down. After Masterman left to become
Bishop of Plymouth, the Bishop came to me and said in view
of the prestige I had already gained in Rugby and throughout
Warwickshire, the only chance of retrieving the situation was
that I should take St. Michael's. Knowing the full extent of
the difficulties involved, it was a heartbreaking job to undertake. At the same time I realised that that way my duty
clearly lay. My acceptance was the only act of real personal
sacrifice to which I have been called.

In the beginning the Bishop did not make my task any
easier. At my institution, in front of a tremendous crowd,
he talked with enthusiasm about his own plans and ideas
but entirely omitted to mention me. He neither com-
mended me to the people nor wished me well in the considerable undertaking that lay before me. Of course it was
purely an accidental oversight on his part, but it created a
bad impression. People inevitably wondered what I had
done to annoy him that he should ignore me in so marked
and deliberate a fashion. There was one thing, however,
that heartened me very much : the leaders of every civil
and religious organisation in Rugby, including even the three
political parties, without telling me sent to the Mayor of
Coventry a round-robin commending me to the people of
the city.

The Bishop told me I was not to regard myself as the vicar of a parish but to devote myself entirely to building up the idea of the cathedral. I had first to discover a house with a garden, which would enable me to bring together people from town and country, in the same way as Rugby, only on a bigger scale. The vicarage of Holy Trinity was large and had a garden, but was inconveniently placed a long way from the church, whereas that of St. Michael's was very small but convenient for both churches. Just then the vicar of Holy Trinity, a fine old man who had been there for years, died and his successor, who was of the utmost help to me afterwards, gladly exchanged vicarages with me. The arrangement, however, would not permanently meet my requirements and eventually I found an alternative place near the station, which had belonged to a local motor magnate. The house was much too big, but nearby were some admirable stables, which I bought and converted into a house suitable to my needs. But in addition to considering my new home in relation to my own work I also bore it in mind as a future residence for the Bishop, who, indeed, finally came to live in it.

My initial step in preparing the way for the new diocese was to unite the new parishes in feeling so that they could achieve corporate action and give a corporate witness. The first of my many efforts to attain this end was the organising of a great procession of all the parishes and choirs through the town. The procession threw a revealing light on the conditions which previously had so weakened Church prestige. A worker belonging to St. John's, one of the few actively worked parishes we had, remarked to me : " This is a note-worthy occasion. I've been working for St. John's for twenty-five years and this is the first time I've met someone from another parish in connection with the Church's work." The beginning of a corporate witness of that sort at once altered the entire situation : people began to realise that the Church stood for something.

In the previous generation Nonconformity had been the

strongest religious influence in the town. It had over-shadowed the Church but, while still doing good work, it had lost much of its vitality. When I invited the Noncon-formist ministers to join us in any work that could be done jointly, and to attend a monthly meeting of the clergy and ministers to discuss the general needs of the Church in Coventry, they accepted cheerfully and gave us their loyal support.

We had only succeeded in making a start when in 1914 war came and, as it was to turn out, brought my big oppor-tunity. My original plans were knocked on the head ; on the other hand, the spirit of a common war-time cause, with a uniformity in work and interest, gave a wonderful impetus to the development of corporate unity within the city. Several first-class men came into the smaller parishes and with almost magical rapidity the old discredit into which the clergy had fallen melted away, and the right of the Church to leadership in many of the town's activities was accepted. The religious work in the parishes naturally gained in consequence of the fellowship created.

My wife at this time was responsible for some work that gained her considerable credit and reputation. Girls were flocking into war industries and in the end some thirty thousand of them had come to the town. My wife organised a body of ladies to help her find suitable lodgings for the girls as they arrived. This entailed visiting a great many houses whose tenants did not ordinarily take lodgers and persuading them to do so by way of war work. When the accom-modation thus gained proved insufficient to cope with the ever-increasing numbers of workers, the Government built hostels, consulting my wife as to their construction and equipment. In this connection there was one amusing in-stance of officialdom. No looking-glasses having been pro-vided for the rooms, the official verdict was that if they wanted to see themselves the girls could go to the bath-rooms and lavatories. My wife insisted that if the girls were expected to maintain their self-respect, they should be encouraged to care about their appearance, and for that looking-glasses in their own rooms were essential. Yet it was only after a struggle that she succeeded in carrying her point.

Girls in industry on such a scale were quite a new problem. Most of the girls had never before left their homes, which in many cases were in villages, and they were being suddenly plunged into a huge population absolutely on their own. There were, of course, certain people who at once raised a cry as to their bad behaviour and immorality. But experience taught us the exact contrary. Inevitably some did give grounds for complaint, but the vast majority impressed us by the strength of principle they showed in the preservation of their self-respect. My wife's work was so thorough that, where we had knowledge of her arrival, no girl failed to find a carefully selected, respectable lodging awaiting her. When this work was quite finished and no fresh girls were coming, the Government appointed a lady at an appreciable salary to take over the job.

It was during this time that Queen Mary, accompanied by Princess Mary, visited Coventry to view the munition works in the town. There was nothing, during the course of the day, that we left out of the tour : historical buildings, philanthropic institutions, industries of every kind, the hostels for girl workers—all were seen in turn. And it was then I had my first sight of what I was one day to know so well : the Queen's extraordinary ability to concentrate on and absorb every last detail of whatever is immediately before her. I recall witnessing on that occasion one instance of the way in which this attribute had cultivated her powers of observation and memory. At the great Siddeley works, the chairman of the company took us into a large department filled with machinery. The Queen looked attentively about her and then, turning to our guide, said : "We went last week to such-and-such a factory, where they were making munitions just as you are. But their machinery was different. Why ?" The chairman told me afterwards that it was astonishing ; even an engineer would hardly have noticed the difference unless his attention had been specially drawn to it. Nevertheless, Queen Mary noticed it at once and insisted on having explained to her exactly what it meant. Her rare faculty of concentration always enables the Queen to have a real knowledge and thorough understanding of whatever engages her attention.

Wartime also brought with it to Coventry an exciting task for me, in a stream of Belgian refugees. I formed a committee to deal with the matter and we took over a large country house standing vacant in a park on the outskirts of the town. An appeal for furniture met with a ready response. To produce efficient results we decided only to take people of the same class. As our first batch of refugees came from the Antwerp slums, we confined ourselves to that type, although we had great difficulty in persuading the London committee to fall in with our rule. We were able to take in about a hundred at a time, and I persuaded the Belgian authorities to let us have six Belgian nuns and a priest, to manage the house. The nuns proved invaluable : they were extraordinarily understanding women and were much loved by the people. Coming of a teaching order they were also able to establish a school for the children, which was carried on until the end of the war. In the house each family had a bedroom, while the ground floor reception room was common to them all. The housekeeping was managed by the nuns with the help of the women.

My chief difficulty with the refugees was to check the ardour of my excellent committee, who were always wanting to get things done the way we like them done in England. I remember one special struggle I had in connection with the serving of tea. Apparently it was the Belgian custom to place a large slice of bread covered with apple puree on top of each cup before the tea was served. My good ladies thought this looked unpleasant, but I insisted that the tea was not for us but for the Belgians, and if they liked to have it that way that was all that mattered. Generally the effect of the life of the community—with its social evenings in the lower room, its recreation in the garden and park, and its pleasant orderly atmosphere of home life—was most remarkable. Some of the families were not, at first, very desirable, being slovenly and dishonest. I remember one such family particularly, and how, under the influence of the house and school, they won a new self-respect and dignity of life.

As soon as possible I had the men of the community absorbed into industry, and as soon as they could speak a little English, I transferred the families to lodgings. I then recruited fresh families in their place from London, so that in the end we had had twelve hundred people through our hands. In the case of families who had left the home to live outside, the children continued to come to the school and the older people to visit the house. The atmosphere of freedom and the homeliness we were able to infuse into the colony made our guests very happy, and while most people were constantly complaining of the refugees' ingratitude, we never had the slightest sign of it.

One Saturday evening, on going to the station to meet a new consignment of Belgians, I found a body of bankers and lawyers and professional men accompanied by wives in fur coats, all looking opulent and superior. Of course, it was impossible to introduce them into the sort of household we had established and, after explaining the situation, I said they must stay at the home over the week-end and make the best of it. The next day, being Sunday, I appealed to the vast congregation of St. Michael's for help in our predicament, and by Monday I had everyone installed in suitable lodgings. Only one of the newcomers gave trouble, and was furious at his temporary accommodation in the home. Suspecting him of being German, I gave information to the authorities and it turned out that he was in fact a spy.

When the war ended I received a gracious message from Cardinal Mercier stating that our refugees had been happier than any others evacuated to England, and later my wife and I were decorated by the Belgian Government. Our success was undoubtedly due to our never allowing the home to be treated like an institution. I visited several other houses accommodating refugees, and they all hemmed the inmates in with innumerable rules and restrictions. At one place, I found that the bedrooms were all shut up after breakfast and the occupants herded together in common-rooms without any privacy or family life, the natural consequence being that they continually quarrelled and became very unhappy.

Two or three years after peace had been declared I visited Belgium and spent a delightful day with our priest and the old *Curé* to whom he was *Vicaire*. The *Curé* was a dear old fellow who had passed his life in that one parish, loving his people and loving also the fruit trees in his garden. I asked him what had happened to the fruit when the Germans came. With a great simplicity he answered that as his fruit was just ripening he had gone to the officer commanding the German forces and explained matters. The officer gave orders accordingly, and the fruit remained untouched throughout the occupation : a pleasant example of humanity midst the brutality of war.

I went also to the convent where our dear nuns lived. A stout nun in a starched cap and flowing robes opened the door for me. On my asking to see *Mère* Marguerite, she looked doubtful ; but when I said that I was the *Chanoine* Baillie, with a loud exclamation she threw up her hands and fled. In a few minutes she returned, followed by a flock of nuns, led by *Mère* Marguerite herself. They were wildly excited, and proceeded to take me all over their school. In the meantime they must have sent into the town for every cake that could be found, for they gave me a tea that would have victualled an army, chattering away all the time I ate. One old nun, who was notoriously dour, chattered as loud and long as anyone, and I gathered that her time in England had been the one excitement of her life.

During all this time of war our main question in the Church was still as to how soon the diocese could be formed. The

Bishop had collected large sums of money from the rich people whom he personally approached, but a substantial sum was still needed and had somehow to be raised. The idea of the new diocese, however, had not created any enthusiasm; indeed, Worcestershire was opposed to it. The Bishop accordingly summoned a meeting of the Rural Deans at which the situation was reviewed. Having had considerable experience in organising popular appeals, I stated my belief that an intensive campaign covering only a short period would be the best plan. After some discussion my proposal was accepted, but it was stipulated I must undertake the running of the campaign.

Being given an absolutely free hand, I formed a small, carefully selected committee. We drew up a short leaflet which put the case so simply that nobody could feel bored by having to read it or have doubts as to its meaning. Then, through the Rural Deans, we arranged for a meeting to take place during October and November in every parish in Warwickshire and Worcestershire. Each parish undertook to send an invitation, accompanied by a leaflet, to all its parishioners a few days beforehand. We thus ensured widespread talk simultaneously throughout the two counties. Wherever possible I addressed the gatherings myself, but of course the majority of them had to be taken by other people. There was not a day, however, when I did not speak to at least one meeting. In the end the campaign proved a triumphant success. Not only was the necessary money obtained, making the foundation of the proposed diocese an immediate possibility, but the counties were entirely converted to the purpose behind it all, which served as a preparation for the actual working of the diocese. Warwickshire, especially, became really diocesan-minded.

Whereas, owing to its greater accessibility from all parts of the proposed diocese, many people regarded the county town of Warwick as most suitable for a working centre, the ancient traditions of Coventry, when added to its possession of a church admirably fitted to serve as a cathedral and also its size and commercial importance, outweighed those claims. In 1917 the culminating point of all our work was reached and the diocese was formed. In the meantime Coventry had been largely pulled together and the Church, by learning to work in unity, had recovered much of her prestige. Also, the leadership of Coventry in the county had been firmly established.

During the twenty years I spent in Warwickshire I was forced by circumstances into leadership, in a way which could never have occurred in the normal conditions of a diocese. Even during my later years at Rugby, the Bishop had taken it for granted that I should be the leader in movements of general interest. This had always put me in a difficult position. In Warwickshire there were two Archdeacons who might easily have resented my seeming to be over them, although in actual fact they behaved in a delightful way and no embarrassment ever arose. At Coventry I was admittedly the leader and prime mover in the preparations for the new diocese, and being associated in people's minds with the whole question, it was widely assumed I should be appointed the first Bishop. I knew quite well that that could not possibly come about, while I also felt strongly it would have been the greatest possible mistake. For I believed that, in view of Warwickshire's recent ecclesiastical history, the new Bishop ought to bring in entirely new ideas. At the same time there was the fact that if I remained in the diocese the incoming Bishop might feel awkward in relation to someone who had been forced into the prominence I had been. Equally, of course, if I suddenly resigned it might, and probably would, have been thought I was doing so in consequence of disappointed hopes.

A solution came which cleared all these difficulties away. I was offered the Deanery of Windsor. This was not altogether a new idea to me as I happened to know King Edward VII had considered appointing me when the vacancy should occur, but as I was practically unknown to King George V, I had thought no more about it. I accepted the post with great enthusiasm, full of dreams of what I hoped to do there.

2

As I have previously written, my acceptance of Coventry was a great personal sacrifice, meaning a considerable reduction in my income. When on my arrival in the town it was immediately necessary for me to build a house, I was puzzled as to what I should do, when my Aunt Lady Caroline Wynford died, leaving me one of her heirs.

Aunt Car was my father's eldest sister, of whom in the latter part of her life I saw a great deal. She was recognised as a great beauty when she was a girl, and I knew her as a typical *grande dame* of the old school : witty, amusing and still, despite an unbecoming grey wig, good looking. In her young days she had fallen deeply in love and never afterwards pretended to care for anyone in the same way. It was equally the case with the young man ; years later one of his children told me that my aunt always remained the love of his life. However, very characteristically she made up her mind that it was not to be and married Lord Wynford, one of the kindest and most eccentric of men, who adored the ground she stepped on. On her writing-table were photographs of her husband and her first love in identical frames ; nevertheless, she was an admirable as well as a devoted wife to the end of her long married life. I was fortunate enough on one occasion to witness a touching echo of her past. One day when she was nearly eighty, I had been out driving with her in London and on our return to Grosvenor Square the butler said : " His Grace called this afternoon and left this parcel for your Ladyship." Opening the parcel she found a magnificent ring and a card on which was written : " In memory of a very old friendship." I never saw her so moved.

My aunt loved the world and was devoted to society. Since her husband's health did not allow him to go out at night, however, she always remained at home with him, over a period of nearly forty years. During the day she indulged her social taste to the full and every evening sat with my Uncle Wynford and related with immense wit all that she had seen and heard while she was out. On his side he would sit in entire contentment, occasionally chuckling and, if I was there, saying in a whispered aside, "Wonderful woman, your aunt!" It was a striking example of a woman making a happy home without any foundation of romance.

My Aunt Car had a son and, in those early married days, it seemed that romance and hope had entered her life. But one day, while she was very ill, her monthly nurse got drunk and in her presence dropped and killed the child. From that moment she determined never to give way to her feelings, and at her death I found in her Bible a prayer she had written out for strength never to show emotion. To the end of her days she continued to face life unflinchingly, but her intense and unremitting self-repression produced an effect of hardness and want of sentiment. Yet after her death, amid her vast correspondence I discovered evidence of the breadth of her private sympathy and the astonishing generosity with which she met all claims of human need. Neither I nor anybody else had had the slightest suspicion of such a thing while she lived.

When she was quite old there were still the remains of those habits of thought which had belonged to her younger years when she dwelt in the great world. For example, it had been customary for people in her position to have a French maid. As she grew older this bored her and towards the end of her time she had an excellent Scots girl who, though her Christian name was probably Maggie, was from convention rechristened Louise. Again, when she was over eighty, she once complained to me what a bore it was that the doctors insisted on her going to the South of France for the winter; and then added: "But there is one advantage, it takes you through Paris twice a year and of course you can't get your clothes anywhere else."

Some time after her husband's death her health gave way and she was able to go out very little. I was the only person to whom she talked freely, and the candour of her speech was entirely characteristic. " No one enjoys life more than I do," she remarked to me several months before she died, " but I don't enjoy this life and so I think I shall die. Besides, it would be more convenient to you if I died now, as then you would have my things." (I was then contemplating building my house at Coventry.) Entering into her own tone of thought I answered : " Oh, come, Aunt Car, I don't think it's necessary for you to die for that reason ! " Nevertheless, her attitude persisting, she instructed her servants that they were to telegraph for me when they felt the end was near.

It was a Sunday when I received their telegram, but I was unable to get away till late and did not see her the same night. The following morning she saw the butler and, after settling her housekeeping books, she gave the man some extra money with the remark : " As I shan't be alive next Monday you had better have some money in hand." Throughout the remainder of the week she would not see anybody but myself, though she sat up in a chair during the day. She refused to see even her sisters as she said they would want to cry over her. Against that ingrained fear of emotion that had affected her life so much, I managed at last to persuade her to see them, stressing the pain that otherwise she would inflict. Her agreement, however, was conditional on my warning them against any undue exhibition of feeling. All the week she was dealing with her affairs with me and when she went to bed on the Friday she told Louise, her maid : " I think I have arranged everything with Mr. Albert so I shall die tonight." I went up to her a little later to say good night and, with the words " you'll be kind to Louise ", she turned over quietly and passed away.

PART IV
WINDSOR

CHAPTER 12

NEW BEGINNINGS

FOR twenty-eight years I walked in and out of the Henry VIII Gate at Windsor Castle. Dreaming since of that time, the Gate has become a symbol of the unique character of the life to which it admitted me. During the daytime it was open, though guarded by sentries and policemen ; at night it was closed and no one was admitted without careful scrutiny. The first night that I was shut into the Castle marked an astonishing severance from all my previous interests and activities. We were not a parish, nor did we play an organic part in any diocese. Technically, we were even outside the province of Canterbury. I cannot envisage a more complete divorce from the lessons of my past experience, from the problems of growing populations and church extension—parochial and diocesan—that had occupied my thoughts since my ordination. It is difficult to adapt oneself to such a change, but it was especially difficult at the time of my appointment because the Castle life was still disorganised, following the war.

I had known something of the life within the Castle precincts when I was a child, for I was taken there each year to see my godmother. The personalities of the older residents inevitably coloured my early family life. There were Ponsonbys and Biddulphs, Cowells and Seymours, whose heads were officials of the Court. As a schoolboy I spent a day with Victor Churchill at the Biddulphs' house, to watch the pageantry of Prince Leopold's marriage to Princess Helene of Waldeck Pyrmont. During my school-days also I had been familiar with the figure of Dean Wellesley, whose character, singularly like that of his great-uncle, the Iron Duke, dominated the whole place. It was said that he was the only person of whom Queen Victoria was in awe. Following him, Randall Davidson won a place as guide, philosopher and friend of the whole Royal Family, permeating the life of the Castle with his influence. In the Cloister lived Canon Hugh Pearson, the Vicar of Sonning, who Wilberforce said was the model parish priest of the diocese of Oxford, but who to us was the beloved H. P., my Uncle Arthur Stanley's most intimate friend. All these families fused into a friendly whole. They dined together and the young ones played tennis together in the Chapter gardens. I thought of their community as of a family. A feeling of permanence was induced in the Windsor of those days when, after the Prince Consort's death, Queen Victoria ceased to live in London and consequently gave more time to Windsor, where families of the Court officials remained in residence almost continuously. But when King Edward came to the throne, the life of the families was diverted mainly to London and this side of the old Windsor gradually died.

During an earlier time the Chapter also lived according to a settled order. By the Statutes, the Dean was only the presiding member of the corporate body (his vote in Chapter counting for no more than that of any Canon), but, from the foundation of the Chapel, the Canons had always held outside parochial or other charges, only living in the Castle for their set period of duty each year. The Dean was the only member of the Chapter permanently in residence and he ruled the community, with the Canons acting simply as an advisory body. This was a sound system in many ways—a perfect one when there were men like Wellesley and Davidson in charge. But when in 1891 Philip Frank Eliot followed Davidson as Dean, without Davidson's or Wellesley's dominating personality to hold the Chapter together on these lines, the system collapsed and the Castle ceased to be a truly corporate community. Eliot did not succeed to completely normal conditions within the Chapter. He had as a Canon a man of disturbing personality who constantly fought against the leadership of the Dean. When I was appointed to follow

Eliot, Davidson said to me, "Your great difficulty will be Canon Dalton." On my very first day in the Castle, Lord Stamfordham, the King's secretary, repeated this warning, and added, "It's not too much to say that Dalton has made your predecessor an unhappy man for a quarter of a century." Later, the King sent for me, begging me to try and get on with his old tutor, to whom he was very much attached, but whom he recognised as being difficult to work with. It was obvious to me then that Canon Dalton would play an important part in my life at Windsor. The prospect of his being difficult did not frighten me ; I had often dealt with difficult men, and found that through patience, friendliness and self-control, any barriers could be broken down. In John Neale Dalton I found a man beyond the difficulties of whose character and personality I was not once able to penetrate. I have never lived and worked, day by day and year by year, so intimately with any man as I did with Dalton during fourteen years. I should have understood him, but I certainly did not. Ever since his death, and especially since I began writing this book, I have been trying to digest my experience of him. His personality filled the thoughts of everyone. But he was a force, without being an influence : he reminded me of Arnold's lines on Byron :

> *He taught us little ; but our soul*
> *Had felt him like the thunder's roll.*

Though Dalton's intellect was tremendous and his learning great, no one ever thought of going to him for enlightenment. He used his knowledge to correct or reprove, seldom to encourage. He was without disciples or followers. In some ways he suggested Dr. Johnson. Both had stupendous physical vigour. When we had begun the restoration of St. George's Chapel in 1920, Dalton was over eighty, but he used to run up the great ladders to the roof of the Chapel, several times a day, to see how the work was progressing. Everything he did, including the use of his powerful voice, was informed by this startling vitality until he was over ninety. He had the almost exaggerated force of mind and character of Johnson, but also some of his grave faults. Johnson was irritable, arrogant, self-assertive, dominating, almost brutally rude, and yet a circle of able and sensible men not merely appreciated his fabulous intellectual reach, but felt his personality to have a peculiar quality of lovableness. Dalton too was intensely irritating : he could understand little of what anyone else felt, yet he drew one's affection. There was a story which Davidson told with great enjoyment. When Dalton was a young Canon in Davidson's time there was one Chapter Meeting at which he had been particularly fractious. In those days there was with them the much revered Canon Courtenay, who had all that polish and courtesy and self-restraint which marked the best men in the Oxford Movement. For a time he was patient with Dalton and then, for the first and probably only time in his life, he lost his temper, his beautiful and refined self-discipline vanishing. " I tell you what it is, Dalton," he exploded. " I wish we were back in school-days—I'd kick your bottom hard." I suppose we have all known naughty, irresponsible schoolboys, irritating but helplessly lovable. I think that all who worked with Dalton had had that feeling about him.

Why was Dalton so provoking ? Four years ago, when I began this book, I told a friend at Windsor that my great problem was in explaining Dalton. He said : " You can't explain him in the terms of our generation. He was an Elizabethan." I then set myself to study the character of the Elizabethans, and after a time I realised that my friend was right. Whenever I think of any of Dalton's characteristics —good or bad—I involuntarily turn to some Elizabethan figure for a parallel. When I remember Dalton's rollicking wit and fun, I am reminded of an expurgated Rabelais. His was an abandoned gaiety that could hardly be found in a Victorian. If I think of the infectious gusto of his company at the dinners of the Drapers' Company, of which he was Chaplain, I recognise a quality that is Falstaffian. When I recall his violent outbursts of anger, I think of the age in which the Queen boxed the French Ambassador's ears in public to express her disapproval ; it was this sort of violently expressed censure that Dalton admired. To him, patience and self-restraint were weaknesses to be despised. Then, remembering the curiously circuitous diplomacy which he employed as an alternative to violence in attaining his ends, I realise that this was an Elizabethan tendency, which grew out of the popular teaching of Machiavelli that came to England with the Renaissance. In his remarkable study *On Hamlet*, Señor de Madariaga notes that it was characteristically Elizabethan for the Dane to boast of an involved artifice which he had used in obtaining an end : certainly Dalton delighted in any concession or victory he gained by such means.

The want in Dalton's character of that consistent discipline to which we were accustomed once again paralleled the habits of life of the Elizabethans. They were magnificent in their display of great qualities, but they constantly acted in ways which to us seemed unprincipled. They never approached that strict ordering of personal behaviour which, beginning with the Puritans, ended after three centuries of training in the Victorians, in whose lives, constantly regulated by inhibitions, there developed an extraordinary admiration for respectability which frequently involved the shaping of their consciences to conform with the requirements of public opinion instead of religious duty. In Victorian literature can be seen grotesque illustrations of the type of clergy who gave way to this worship of respectability. This type were at the height of their influence just about the time when Dalton grew up. I think he must have been brought into close contact with them and, with his usual hasty exaggeration, decided that all clergy were unreal, conventional and weak. Had he gone on working in the Church, he would probably have grown out of this exaggeration, and learned that there were a vast number of men not dominated by conventions and inhibitions. But Dalton was taken from his country curacy to live among sailors, at sea, where he was entirely out of association with the clergy. He never worked with them again until he went to Windsor. Consequently there had been no direct experience to disprove his early, hasty evaluation of clergymen. His youthful rebellion against the conventional and the inhibited had hardened into an obsession so that he was unable to approach any relationship with other churchmen with an open mind. In all instances he began by despising them. This habit of instinctive and immediate contempt was Dalton's chief weakness.

His dominating personality, fortified by the absolute independence he had enjoyed during his long period as King George V's tutor, had hindered Dalton from understanding the meaning or the necessity of corporate responsibility. When he returned to clerical life, at Windsor, it was an almost unbearable irritation to him even to *think* that there were other people who had an equal right with him to a voice in the Chapter. He approached every meeting determined to fight over the smallest details, only to prevent his colleagues, whom he despised, from having their way. This point of view in a strong man inevitably made his colleagues miserable. The damage to our Chapter life was no less than the damage to our personal life. His effervescent temperament made it impossible for Dalton to confine his expressed contempt to our meetings ; he broadcast his opinions to people in the Castle. The Canons were usually scholars, chosen for their high character and qualities of mind; but when the lay residents in the Castle were constantly told how contemptible they all were, an unfortunate and dangerous barrier was raised between the laity and the Chapter. I once asked the Chapter Clerk, who had been Dalton's secretary, whether he could remember any dean or canon with whom the old man had worked during his time at Windsor, and of whom he had spoken with respect. He said there was only one—the saintly Canon Courtenay, who had won this approval because he had once lost his temper.

The Dean had to suffer most of Dalton's contempt because the Dean's was the primary influence which stood in the way of his authority. The fact that for at least two or three years after my appointment I was not able to make myself really known to the people in the Castle meant that he had by then prejudiced everybody against me. During this time, Alexander Nairne became Canon, and I noticed that he stood very much aloof from me. After a few years, when we had become very intimate friends, he told me that Dalton had given him such an unpleasant conception of my character that he had avoided any personal intimacy with me. The completeness of this impression throughout the Castle was revealed when an old friend came to see me and said : " I can't understand why everybody here abuses you so." I was quite isolated but for the loyalty and affection of the Lay Clerks and Vergers. Such a state was not conducive to happiness. The amazing thing is that even after I realised the injury his talk was doing me, I never ceased to appreciate Dalton's lovableness. I suppose I saw that his actions were the product of an undisciplined mind and not of a bad heart ; that his weaknesses were constitutional.

The worry and anxiety of the early difficulties in the Chapter were increased by the depressing circumstances of my home life. Following a period of ever-increasing pain and weariness, my wife was gradually succumbing to an illness which ended in her death. Though she faced life with great courage and did what she could, she was unable to throw herself into the life of the Castle and give me the moral support which I had received from her at Rugby. Her influence would have immensely strengthened my position. As it was, I stood alone.

After five years of illness the doctors told my wife that the end was near. All the signs of suffering left her and she was placid and cheerful to the last. Shortly before she died she had us singly to see her for a private talk. Neither my children, my sisters-in-law nor the servants have ever repeated what she told them, but I am sure it was exactly what they each of them needed. To me, smiling, she said : " I want you to bury me next to your mother at Dochfour." In that she gave me just the help I needed. Aware of her immense affection for her mother and family, I had taken for granted that she would wish to be buried at her old home. She had never known my mother, while Dochfour had few personal associations for her. Therefore her request could mean only one thing : that her life since our marriage had found its full expression in me, making her place beside my mother the only possible one. It was then I realised the meaning of the words that Jesus spoke to His Mother and His Friend from the Cross. They had the assurance of His love and I the assurance of hers.

When Constance died I had astonishing evidence of how far her influence had reached. I had many hundreds of letters of sympathy, all of which contained something more than the conventional sentiments. There were letters from practically every servant whom we had had in our house during the quarter of a century of our married life. There were tributes from shop assistants, often in big London stores, who were totally unacquainted with me and had only seen my wife briefly and casually across a counter. One and all, they wrote in order to tell me of the unforgettable effect of that goodness and warmth of spirit that radiated from her.

For a number of years after Constance's death, if I dreamed it was always of her : they were happy dreams. She would be there with her dear humorous smile, watching me. Before long the pain of our separation lessened, the conviction that she still lived growing deeper and stronger within me.

A further break-up of my family life followed my wife's death when the eldest and the youngest of my three sons died. Peter, the youngest, contracted infantile paralysis within the first three days of his first term at Cambridge and died, just as he had begun to enjoy the most vigorous and joyous stage of his existence. Alastair, the eldest, though his life to that time had not been happy, looked forward to the prospect of a bright future when some then-unknown microbe caused his sudden death. Of our family, only Ean and I remained, and with him I began rebuilding my life. Our close and affectionate friendship has endured to make happy my old age.

CHAPTER 13

ST. GEORGE'S CHAPEL

THE difficulties which confronted me on my installation in Windsor lasted to some degree for fourteen years. The real evil of that turbulent time was that I gave way to the contemptible weakness of self-pity, making myself unhappy. My complete isolation from the people living around me and the loss of my wife meant that there was no one with whom I could sympathetically discuss my situation. The one virtue of the period was that it did not breed in me any personal antagonisms : it made me suspect, however, that I was not fit for my job, that I was a failure. Happily I was soon saved from sinking into a morose inactivity by new and exciting interests which grew steadily from the very beginning.

When I arrived at the Castle I found the Deanery in need of drastic restoration which would take many months to complete, repairs not being easily carried out during wartime. My wife remaining behind at Coventry to keep house for the Bishop of the newly created diocese, Huyshe Yeatman-Biggs, I went first to an hotel and then into the vacant house of one of the minor Canons who was absent at the war. Within a few months, when my wife was staying with me at the hotel, I remarked to her one evening : " Thank goodness I shan't have to raise money here." With a laugh she answered : " Don't you believe it. Wherever you go you'll have to do that. The Chapel will probably fall down, or something of the sort." The very next morning, by a remarkable coincidence, I received a report from the Chapter Architect, Harold Brakspear, of a very alarming nature.

The vaulting of St. George's Chapel was in danger of collapsing and restorations were estimated to cost about

£100,000. The raising of this money was clearly my responsibility, and no one, somewhat naturally, had any desire to share it. Once again I was faced with a familiar kind of problem, but in this instance possessed of quite exceptional perplexities. The primary claim was on the Knights of the Garter, for whom the Chapel technically exists. But just at the end of the war, their class was under great financial strain. None of them were in a position to provide large sums : even so, they were very generous in their response and started me with £25,000. That was sufficient for work to be begun, but barely enough even for that ; the cost of the necessary scaffolding alone amounted to £40,000. *The Times* had recently run, with great success, an appeal for the renovation of Westminster Abbey, and it was out of the question for the Press to make another appeal so soon afterwards. Again, since St. George's was generally regarded as a private royal chapel, it was quite wrongly considered as being the concern of the Office of Works. There was no special public to which I could appeal, as there would have been in the case of a cathedral, where a whole diocese could have been roused into a sense of responsibility. Consequently, what was everybody's business became nobody's business.

I interviewed the editors of all the leading papers, telling them my story and asking if there were any useful suggestions they could make. They were none of them able to find a solution to the problem until I was taken to Sir Campbell Stuart at *The Times*, who suggested I should see G. C. Ackerman, his advertising manager, who was in the same building. Ackerman, after listening thoughtfully, said : "There is only one man who can do it, if he will undertake it, and if he won't I can't see how you're going to get the money." He immediately telephoned Sydney Walton, of whom I had never heard, and asked him if he was free for lunch. After lunch Walton and I were left alone and once again I poured out my tale. When he had heard me to the end he was on fire. Sydney Walton is a remarkable man. He remains always in the background behind the scenes, but the number of things he has done and the causes he has carried through are unbelievable. What he most enjoys is to undertake a cause voluntarily, making it a sheer labour of love. Till the money was fully subscribed (a total of £180,000), over a period of nearly ten years, he and I were seeing one another constantly.

Walton's view, with which I entirely concurred, was that in the circumstances a public appeal would have no chance of success. Our object would have to be achieved by bringing the case privately before individual persons sufficiently wealthy to make large subscriptions. Walton further pointed out that it was of no use going promiscuously to such people, many of whom were already so involved in the support of charities as to make it impossible, and indeed unreasonable, to expect them to take up anything new on a large scale. Our hope lay in discovering men who had made money without having yet found any cause to interest them. Of such men, Walton said there were many. As we went on we had to be careful as to the character and business methods of those whose support we sought to enlist. There had been, for instance, the notorious case of the gift to St. Paul's of a gold chalice by a man whose wealth was found to rest on very undesirable foundations. However we negotiated our problems safely. Our success was a tribute to Sydney Walton, without whose tireless work I am sure the money could not have been raised.

Among those whom Walton interested in the work on St. George's was Mr. Frederick Minter, the great London builder. I mention him specially not only because of the way in which he helped us, but because of the close ties of friendship with him, his son and his grandsons that grew out of it for me, and which are flourishing still with the younger generation. He did not offer a big sum of money or ask for any publicity for what he did, but he said that he would be behind me if ever I was in a tight place. At that time we had to find £2,000 every month, and we were most anxious not to involve ourselves in debt. Whenever necessary Minter wrote out a cheque for any monthly deficit with which we were faced. If his aggregate contribution was less than some other gifts we received, the help his assured support gave us was immeasurable.

After several months Frederick Minter said : "I'm so interested in this work now that I should like to do something towards it in my own yard." At first this presented a difficulty, as we had in our employ an excellent builder with greater experience than anyone in England in the restoring of Gothic buildings. Then suddenly I thought of the very thing for our friend to do. The heraldic beasts on the pinnacles of the Chapel had decayed in Charles II's time and Wren had recommended stone pineapples to replace them. The original architect had intended the beasts to help in ensuring stability ; in addition, something was obviously needed at the summit of the building to achieve perfection of outline. While the replacement of the beasts would have added immensely to the beauty of the Chapel, I had been adamant that nothing should be spent on embellishments and, having from inquiry reached the conclusion that structurally they were not of the first importance, I had excluded them from the estimates. I had hoped, however, that a donor would make this restoration possible through a personal gift, and when I suggested it to Minter he jumped at the opportunity. He scrapped a great deal of unsatisfactory experimental work at some cost to himself before, in Joseph Armitage, he found a man who carried the job through perfectly. Lutyens admired Armitage's work for us so much that he employed him for the carving on Government House, Delhi.

Before the Chapel was finished dear old Frederick Minter died. His son, now Sir Frederick, worked with his father during the whole time with an equal enthusiasm, afterwards rebuilding the choir school for us. I felt that the spirit as well as the nature of the help the Minters had given should be recognised, and, at my suggestion, His Majesty graciously made the son a K.C.V.O.

This work of raising money was rather tedious and anxious, but at the same time it had its amusing side, introducing me to a great many people. Above all, it made me a friend of the publicity profession as a whole. They adopted me and called me their Chaplain, and whenever and wherever possible they helped me. None the less, neither Walton nor any other member of the profession either asked or received one penny of payment for the work they did. We were all out for an adventure, and we carried it through.

The actual work of restoration was also an adventure. Originally, Brakspear's attention had been drawn by widening cracks in the vault, which kept dropping plaster. It was impossible accurately to tell the extent of the trouble until the scaffolding was up, and at that stage he believed that he could rectify the weakness by grouting from above. When the scaffolding enabled him to examine the vaulting closely, he was horrified to find that the cracks were very much larger than he had thought. One of them, extending for the full length of the choir, was in places wide enough to contain his hand. Wren, discovering the fissures, had dealt with them by running in lead. In George III's reign they had increased and the architects, by filling them in with plaster, had made everything look tidy. Because of the inadequacy of these measures the process had continued down the years until there were many cracks as wide as that to which I have previously referred. As if this were not enough, Brakspear discovered a much more serious fault. In a layman's language, which is all I can attempt : this type of vault is constructed so that springers, or brackets, are built out from the wall on each side and the centre built on to them. For stability, it is obviously necessary that the springers should be well bonded into the walls. Brakspear discovered that they were not bonded in at all. At once he called in Giles Scott, whom at his request we had appointed as consulting architect, together with an engineer. After a close examination of the Chapel roof, at which I was present, I remember Giles Scott remarking : " Well, one thing is quite clear—there is no scientific reason why this vault should have stayed up for an hour from the time it was built. In cases like this, all one can say, as one often has to say of old buildings, it happens to have stuck."

The middle of the vault had subsided eleven inches, probably immediately after it had been built, and there, providentially, for centuries it had remained.

As I have said, there were cracks on every side and the danger was really imminent, since the cracks were becoming bigger. The widening process was further accelerated when we dealt with the wooden roof above, which had death-watch beetle, so that for some months we were frantically building a platform over the choir on which to erect a network of wooden struts following the line of every individual rib and thus supporting the whole vault. It was the most fascinating work and I loved to climb up to the platform and watch its progress. We next took down the vaulting, one bay at a time, and, numbering the stones, reconstructed it after building fresh springers, properly bonded into the wall. It was an amazing performance, beautifully carried out. There was also a great deal of further work that had to be done. Henry VII's architects who put in the vaulting had shown extraordinary carelessness and left many mistakes that required immediate correction. It is certain that for generations the worshippers in St. George's had been complacently sitting with an enormous danger overhanging them. With the completion of our task it was gratifying that all the doubtings which had attended us at the outset were silenced. So far as I know not one single criticism was ever levelled at Brakspear's work.

For ten years the restoration of St. George's Chapel, with the necessary preparation for it, occupied much of the attention of the Chapter. In November, 1930, the task was done, and though it had been interesting enough it could not but break the continuity of the Chapter's life, and entail, when the undertaking was behind us, the making of an almost entirely fresh start.

Our first question was that of finance. When its estates were taken over by the Ecclesiastical Commissioners, St. George's was given an adequate income, but the war had revolutionised values and it was necessary to revise the whole financial situation. Before his death in 1931, Canon Dalton had for many years managed the finances, and done it very well. Towards the end, however, I became more and more conscious that we were drifting into dangerous straits and accordingly studied the problems involved and prepared a full report on our position. I then handed the report to Dalton who, although he did not resent it, was by then too old to take the matter in hand. Two things helped us : the first was the suspension of one of the canonries, which the King had agreed to leave temporarily vacant, and the other a grant from the State Apartments' Fund. As great numbers of visitors involved us in considerable expense, and as we could not charge admission to the Chapel, the King decided we should have a grant from the State Apartments' receipts. But these two gains, important as they were, did not balance the loss to our finances from the change of values. As soon as the war ended I took one temporary measure in regard to the income of the Lay Clerks, which in the new conditions was quite inadequate and desperately in need of an increase which the Chapter could not afford. My wife and I let the Deanery and went to live in a minor Canon's house. The money we received from this enabled us to provide our Lay Clerks with the necessary increase. Another assistance to us at this time was the Society of Friends of St. George's which we had formed, who took the financial burden of any special work of repair or improvement in the Chapel off our shoulders. A small fund which was of value in doing other special work came from an incident which gave me great pleasure. When I awoke on the morning of the Chapel re-opening after the restoration, a large envelope was handed to me in bed. It contained a beautifully bound book in which were the names of more than four hundred of my friends, and a musical snuff-box, given me by my son, which contained their cheque for £2,500. In the book was written : "This is in no sense a public tribute, but an affectionate thank-offering from your friends." It was intended that the cheque should be used for some memorial in the Chapel to commemorate my wife and I. Even the railwaymen at Slough and Windsor, hearing of the gesture, asked to be allowed to contribute. A suitable use for the capital has never yet been found, but the interest has done some good work, restoring the Rous Chapel as a place for small services in memory of my wife, and the Garter Plates, which were beginning to suffer a good deal from time.

The main financial work was done by Canon Deane when he was made Steward, and Lewis Stainton, the Chapter Clerk. I do not believe that any Chapter has ever had a better or more efficient Chapter Clerk. He was a born accountant, and with Canon Deane, who was also possessed of business ability and immense industry, our finances were established on a sound footing. Some years afterwards I learnt with great pleasure from Deane that he and Stainton had taken as the basis of their constructive work the report which I had earlier given to Dalton.

Meanwhile, the number of visitors to St. George's was increasing every day. The restoration had promoted new interest in the Chapel, and after King George V died there was a desire among people all over the country to come to Windsor and see his grave. Among the large parties who came by charabanc, especially from the Midlands, I remember at least two which numbered over ten thousand. The experience I had had of my Uncle Arthur Stanley's use of the Abbey in educating the home and overseas public to the meaning of English life in Church and State made me very anxious to give a feeling of welcome to the visitors. I spent a great deal of my time in taking parties round the Chapel. The Canons, too, entered energetically into the spirit of the task, so that it was rare to find any time in the day when at least one of us was not busy with this work. Of course, there were a great many visitors to the Castle on Sundays, when it had been the practice to close the Chapel because the Vergers could not possibly be there in the afternoon in addition to their ordinary work. To overcome this we formed a keen body of volunteers who studied the Chapel and gave up their Sunday afternoons to showing the parties round. Many Eton boys assisted us in this way.

With finances settled and the Chapel restored, 1931 brought with it my first real opportunity of consolidating the improved conditions of Chapter work and life. I was convinced that the system to which St. George's had worked since its foundation, by which all Canons held outside posts and were only in residence at Windsor for their turns of duty, in the circumstances of modern life was quite unsatisfactory. For one thing, under this old system the conditions from which I had suffered for fourteen years could easily be repeated. I felt, therefore, that in future the Canons should be all permanently resident. But the actual work of the Chapter, the administration of the Chapel, is not enough to fill the time of a Canon; it is so much occupied in the settlement of details that to concentrate on it as a life work destroys all sense of proportion. The principle that a Dean or Canon of Windsor should regard his position as one from which to do some outside work, which principle Davidson had impressed on me, I believed to be a right one, and especially work as scholars. Bishop Creighton, I believe, used to say that at a University you were too much in the position of living in a house which the workmen were still engaged in building. I believed that in the Castle, Canons could pursue their special line of study free from disturbing influences, and do very valuable work. I privately presented my plan, in the form of a memorial, to the King, as a suggested guide to the principles that should be followed in appointing Canons. I did not think it right that I should be able to nominate actual men; but in my argument, by way of illustration, I suggested that Canon Nairne, as a Bible student, and Dr. Freer, as a student of Liturgiology, would be the desirable type of man. As vacancies arose the King offered them both an appointment. Canon Nairne accepted, to our enormous advantage. Freer, for quite good reasons, refused.

Windsor has very valuable documents, illustrating the life of the Church through a long period, and I most urgently required an historian. Dalton had done valuable work in cataloguing our manuscripts, but nothing more had been done. I therefore welcomed the appointment of Canon Ollard, who came to us with a considerable reputation as an historian. As soon as he was installed I asked him to organise the historical research in the Chapel, the Chapter cheerfully agreeing. Unfortunately, Canon Ollard's health was failing, and he was never able to devote to the work the concentrated energy that it needed. He formed a considerable body of people to assist him, however, and a good deal was accomplished. This work now continues under a good historian—Mr. M. F. Bond.

As Canon Deane was doing an immense work through his writings, his letters, sermons and his leading articles in *The Times*, we very nearly achieved a Chapter which conformed to the memorial I presented to the King. Though as long as human nature exists there will be differences and disagreements, there is, I believe, the right attitude towards the life and work of the Chapter in the mind of all its present members. One special work is now being done of which I have always dreamed—the work of associating the preparation of young men for Orders with the Chapel.

When the immense study of the history of church music which Dr. Fellowes has done throughout his years at Windsor, and the work of a series of distinguished organists who showed how that music should be rendered, is added to all the other study that has grown out of Windsor, it will be seen that St. George's is to a great degree filling the place it should in the life and the endeavour of the Church and Nation.

2

An interest which absorbed much of my attention was the choir and the choir school. Sir Walter Parratt was still the organist, and I believe that he was supremely efficient in making the music fill its true part as the accompaniment of a service. As I am not musical, I cannot profess to estimate him as a musician, but those in a position to judge regarded him as one of the greatest English organists. According to the composer Stanford, who came to live in Windsor during the war, he had one gift in particular : that of preserving, as no one else in his experience, the perfect pitch of the choir.

Stanford would often bring music which he had written specially for the choir, and Parratt used to produce it ; indeed, many of Stanford's works were first performed in that way.

One weakness of dear old Parratt lay in his firm conviction not only that every Lay Clerk was determined not to do his best but was in fact fighting against his effort to produce good music. It was said this point of view originated with old Wesley, the organist and composer. Although Parratt believed what he told everybody outside, that collectively his Lay Clerks were the best in the world, as he aged his weakness took the form of his getting his knife into one man until he had almost driven that man mad. Nothing the unhappy victim could do was right in such cases. Generally, the men admired him enormously and were extraordinarily loyal to him, but his obsession very naturally caused some discomfort in the cloisters. As I always believed in and encouraged freedom of access, the harassed Lay Clerks used to come to me, when it was quite easy to comfort them with a little cheerful sympathy. Yet whenever I talked to Parratt about some case where I thought he had been unjust, he invariably answered : " Ah, you don't know Lay Clerks ! " I remember one really comic instance of his positively inhuman attitude towards them. During the war, eight of the Clerks had been in the Services and we had managed with four who were over military age. As the eight who had been serving were demobilised about the same time, we decided not to have them back in the choir until they could all rejoin together. After five years' absence in the army they were not at their best, and with the close of their first service Parratt rushed into the vestry, his hair, as invariably in moments of excitement, standing on end. " All I can say, gentlemen," he shouted, " is that we've done very much better without you ! " A remarkable speech of welcome that might have hurt the luckless men but for my bursting out laughing, in which after a moment they joined me, the episode passing harmlessly off in a gale of merriment.

One of the Lay Clerks, named Kempton, who was too old

to serve in the first World War, was not too old to hold the fort again in the choir when it was similarly depleted during the second conflict twenty years later. A great record indeed. It was to Kempton, who had had half a century's experience as a Lay Clerk at St. Paul's and at Windsor, that I once spoke about Parratt's curious attitude towards them, and he said : " Yes, but I'm not at all sure there was not a great deal of justification for it fifty years ago." This was a proof of the improved conduct of services over that period. A great friendship arose between the Lay Clerks and myself, and throughout my time at Windsor they showed me a marvellous loyalty for which I can never cease to be grateful.

We had a headmaster at the choir school who was as near to genius as a man can be. His predecessor told me that when he first came as an assistant to Windsor, the headmaster of the school he had just left said : " I really don't know what to say about Fowler, but one thing I can confidently assert, that whatever subject you give him to teach, he'll teach it better than any other man in England." Fowler had also a much beloved assistant master who, after he retired, lived in the cloisters, where he was visited by all the old boys and written to regularly by most of them. Through a long course of years these two men brought the school to a remarkably high standard.

Sir Walter's relation to the boys of the choir was quite different to the Lay Clerks. No one could have been nicer to them. He entertained them and, though he was a severe disciplinarian, they really loved him and responded perfectly to his instruction.

Choir schools have an extraordinary educational value if they are reasonably well run. Nothing develops the mind so much as having something to do every day which the boy enjoys and which he believes to be worth doing as well as possible. The daily service provides this incentive, and the enthusiasm of our boys for the perfection of the service was amazing. No discipline was needed, as the boys themselves would have made it quite impossible for one of their number to have been slack or half-hearted. I became convinced by long experience that a boy from a choir school develops an alertness of mind which enables him to assimilate knowledge more quickly than other boys. One headmaster of a public school told me that he specialised in trying to get boys from the best choir schools because their keenness to work was so effective an example. A great value in choir training is that the boys are every day using magnificent English and hearing it read. Moreover, they have to pay attention to the words and their meaning since they have to express this through their singing. In itself, this cannot fail to enlarge a boy's mind. Then, there is the influence of the great thoughts which are impressed on them, together with that sense of reverence the services instil. A genuine familiarity with the Psalms alone can hardly fail to elevate the mind. Finally, at Windsor there was a constant association with one of the noblest buildings in England. I know the unconscious influence that had on the boys, and how it stimulated their desire to come back again and again for years after they left ; a thing common enough in public schools, but rare in connection with a private school.

In the case of my own family, I took my youngest boy away from his private school and put him into our choir school. The desire of everybody in the Castle to have their boys in the school created a general interest in it. Princess Alice, Lord Stamfordham, Lionel Cust, and the other Castle residents who had sons, were proud to send them to the school. It almost became a family party. The boys went to tea at all the different houses and everyone at the Castle came down to see their little plays. These last were a great feature, being cleverly written by Bridge, the assistant master. The boys sang and acted them while Parratt attended to the music, as did subsequent organists after his death ; Miss Fowler, and the wives of the subsequent headmasters, looked after the dressing and the make-up. Any amount of old boys made a point of coming to see the plays every year.

At Christmas we had a great party in the Deanery, and

never were there such easy boys to entertain. They knew what games they wanted to play and what they wanted to do. There was no rivalry among them and no quarrels. If I thought they had played one game long enough and suggested a change, there was never a murmur. In fine, from the moment they came until they left they generated an atmosphere of intense joyousness.

It is a great pleasure to record that the Rector of Rugby, who after doing grand work was recently made Bishop of Singapore, was one of our old choir boys whom I knew at Windsor.

3

Shortly after we had begun the restoration of St. George's Chapel, we were asked by the Canadian Education Society to tour Canada with our choir. Our first task in the restoration was the Choir, which necessitated the erection of a temporary partition between it and the Nave so that we could fit up the latter as a church and use it for our services. When the work on the Choir was finished and we moved back out of the Nave, a three-month suspension of services was unavoidable. During this period of enforced inactivity in the Chapel, we decided to accept the Canadian invitation. When the arrangements for this were almost completed, the Chapter took panic, deciding that our boys were too young to face a mid-winter trip without endangering their health. Together with the parents and the doctors, I considered this fear quite absurd. In the face of such a warning, however, when the blame for any mishap would have been heavy, we could not fight. It looked as though the scheme would have to be given up when Sydney Nicholson, the organist at Westminster, intervened. Westminster having a double shift of boys, it was easy for one shift to come with us. Accordingly our men and the Westminster boys made the trip together.

Owing to the vacancy in the organistship caused by Sir Walter Parratt's death, Dr. Fellowes was acting as choirmaster and came with us. With Sydney Nicholson, Major Fred Ney, the secretary of the Canadian Education Society, and myself, we were a happy quartet. We also took a master from the Westminster Choir School to carry on the boys' education.

We landed at Halifax and were welcomed with a banquet at which we were given buffalo-meat—the toughest proposition I had ever met. We then boarded our train, which had been specially arranged for us by Mr. Edward Beatty, President of the Canadian Pacific, whom I already knew and greatly liked.

The tour lasted seventy days, of which the majority were spent in the train. Our work and singing were confined to twenty-three days. We went right across the continent to Vancouver, on the way seeing the Rockies and the great Western Plains. Each time we stopped it meant heavy work, there being at least one concert and one great musical service to be given, and quite often double that amount. Our audiences were so vast that we always had, simultaneously, a lantern lecture on St. George's and the Abbey by myself, a lecture on church music by Dr. Fellowes, an organ recital by Sydney Nicholson, lessons in choir training to local choral societies, and a banquet at which I had to speak. The choir sang seventy times in the course of their total working days, while I spoke, lectured or preached an equal number of times. We could not have done so much but for the long journeys in between, which allowed us time to rest and to prepare for our next appearance.

The enthusiasm of the crowds was unbelievable. Winnipeg was illuminated for three nights. At Toronto, where we began with a service in their vast church, ten thousand people were turned away. It was decided to give another service on the next afternoon, between our two concerts. The people started to queue in the snow at eight o'clock in the morning. The same kind of thing happened everywhere. In the places on the plains not only did we have packed audiences but the service or concert was relayed over a radius of a hundred miles, with the local halls and churches packed full, to hear it. Fellowes and I also had great audiences at our lectures, whilst I gained great credit as a speaker among the Lay Clerks, who said I never once repeated myself in the speeches I made at each successive banquet throughout the tour. It was really quite easy, as each place was different and had a marked individuality. At our stopping places we were all billeted out, and the hospitality of our hosts was magnificent. The boys were overwhelmed with kindness and stuffed with all the good things that could be found.

It was indeed a joyous tour as well as a most interesting experience. Moreover, it bore fruit in that the number of boys' choirs in Canada began immediately to increase, until by now they have multiplied by ten. Of course, the enthusiasm we aroused was due partly to our coming from Windsor and Westminster. But it also came from the Canadians not having previously heard English church music of such high quality. Even the Parliament of Ottawa suspended their sitting so that we might sing before them in Parliament House. As my old Cambridge friend, Viscount afterwards Marquess of Willingdon, was then Governor-General, my visit to Ottawa was a double pleasure.

During the trip I was able to gratify a particular interest of my own. It being known I liked meeting the young, at every place a body of young men were invited to spend an evening with me at some private house : they were of every sort— undergraduates, soldiers, business-men and so on. Our talks impressed me, as indeed all Canada impressed me, with the real power of thought that is to be found there. There are countries where one finds greater superficial brilliance among the young on first meeting them, but I have never found any country whose youth has so much individual thought. One was always finding signs of originality. I remember one school, for students of sixteen and over, which had lost about eighty old boys in the 1914–18 War and had collected a large sum of money for a memorial. Instead of erecting a statue or a utilitarian building, they started a collection of the best pictures they could get by Canadian artists who were painting during the war years. The collection was not finished when I saw it, but I found it remarkably interesting and am sure it will form a striking chapter in the history of Canadian art.

I have already paid tribute to the loyalty and friendliness I always found at Windsor among the Lay Clerks ; but it was by our Canadian adventure that the already happy relationship existing between us was forged into something deeper, so that ever afterwards there was an element of real personal affection in our mutual regard.

4

One cannot think of St. George's Chapel without thinking of functions. There were Garter functions, Royal functions, and predominantly, of course, there were funerals, as it is the burial place of the whole Royal Family. Besides Royal and State functions, we had interesting affairs of other kinds : each year there is the gathering from all over England of the picked representatives of the Boy Scouts, which I always felt to be a solemn and thrilling occasion. For twenty-eight years I had to organise all important events of this kind. In most of them I worked with the Lord Chamberlain, who was responsible for the main direction of the services within the Chapel. With regard to funerals, even King George V was satisfied by the way I organised them. He showed that satisfaction by transferring to me a considerable part of what had been the Lord Chamberlain's responsibility. This meant a great deal, for he was inclined to be critical about my work.

On the occasion of the Service of Thanksgiving at the conclusion of the Chapel restoration, I had to undertake the Lord Chamberlain's work as well as my own. King George refused to robe, and consequently no robes were worn ; he also said it was not to be a Garter, but simply a Chapter ceremony. It was nevertheless the King's wish that important people in the nation were asked—people like the Primate, the Prime Minister, the Lord Chancellor, and so on, together with the Ambassadors of those Kings who had the Order of the Garter. That meant that everybody in the Choir had to be seated according to their precedence. It would not have been difficult if I had been certain who was coming ; people kept dropping out and others kept coming in, and the newcomers could not simply be given the seat arranged for the one who had dropped out, because of the question of precedence. To fit each newcomer in consequently meant the re-organising of almost the whole seating of the Choir. The reshuffling of places continued to within a day of the service, nearly driving me demented. And then, amid all my difficulties and constant confusion, King George suddenly worried that I should be bungling things. He sent for Lord Cromer, the Lord Chamberlain, whom he told to find out what I was doing. I afterwards heard to my great gratification that Lord Cromer replied on the spot that if I was in charge the King might be confident that everything would be properly handled. Nevertheless, Cromer came to see me, but found no criticism to make of my arrangements. I am glad that particular work did not fall to me often. The task left me with the profoundest sympathy for the Lord Chamberlain.

Of all our functions, the most beautiful was the Garter ceremony. It had not been held for some years owing to the first World War, and was not held again until after the second World War.

George V's funeral was the most moving function in which ever I took part. I shall never forget standing at the great West Door of the Chapel to receive the coffin, while the procession, with the Archbishops and Bishops and functionaries, was waiting inside. I stood alone, with the tremendous flight of steps leading down to the Horse Shoe Cloisters empty before me, until with solemn music and the tramp of feet the main cortege approached and turned in under the Cloister Arch. Slowly the coffin was borne up the steps, with the heralds on either side, and towards the Chapel door. No death in our memories had so profoundly touched the heart of the whole nation. King George V had become the father of his people; his relationship with them forged during the anxious years of war. I believe that the heart of every man, woman and child among his subjects was sorrowing with us as the coffin ascended to its final resting-place.

CHAPTER 14

YOUTH

THE gloom of my first years at Windsor was very early pierced by one ever-increasing light of happiness. Towards the end of the first World War as, lonely and isolated, I wandered about the Castle precincts, I noticed the young officer on guard and was suddenly conscious of the dullness which his twenty-four hour vigil must entail. Wondering if he would care to dine with me as a change from his routine, I walked down the hill towards the guard-room. Once there, I thought he might think me only an old bore and turned and walked back the way I had come. I did this five times, until at last I gathered courage to pass through the door and up the narrow stone staircase, which led to the guard-room—a small dark room with deep-set windows through which a little light seeped. In one corner was an iron bed and opposite the doorway a table at which the officer sat. He was a tall, thin lad with a good clean face. When he saw me he jumped up and gave me welcome. We were shy of one another, but that evening he came to dinner. After that first jolly evening, it became a habit for the officer on guard to dine with me at the Deanery every night, opening a relationship between us that gave me an intimate knowledge of the thoughts and feelings and difficulties of the young. In 1917 the traditional reserve of English boys dissolved in the seriousness of the life in which they found themselves. Sitting with me after dinner they were gay and jolly, full of their interests and amusements. Before leaving on their rounds, however, they began after a time to ask me whether they might come back when they had finished their duty : this always meant that they wanted to talk to me about themselves. Death was prominent in all their minds, the idea of it daily being reinforced by news of casualties among their friends overseas. They were none of them afraid of dying—some had already been to the front and returned wounded—but the knowledge of its imminence gave to them all a keen perception of the more significant things in life, and they wanted someone to whom they could talk.

I sat, saying very little, while they went on quietly—in the main confessing their faults and sins and weaknesses. They neither pretended to be good nor boasted of being bad : theirs was an intense humility, conscious of failures and mental muddle, revealing a natural simplicity of mind which witnesses the capacity for holiness belonging to us as made in the image of God. I never gave advice, for which I have a horror in regard to the deeper spiritual questions. Besides, I have found that if you can help a boy to think out his difficulties for himself, he will ultimately make a choice which demands a sacrifice greater than anything you would have dared suggest. Almost invariably the atmosphere between us during those late hours in my study became so solemn that it seemed natural to both of us to go into the Chapel before we parted, and by the light of a lantern to kneel together at the altar rails in silent prayer. I have never at any time felt nearer to Christ ; the immense capacity of love which those boys' talk awoke in me made me feel His presence listening too. Our association was so vital a thing that I refused to take my holiday that year rather than miss one night of their confidences.

For my own part, although our friendship could not alter the intrinsic difficulties which I had to face as Dean, this great experience appreciably mitigated the feeling of frustration in my work. For the boys, I could not tell whether I had helped them spiritually, but our intimacy, in revealing the practical conditions of their life as soldiers, allowed me materially to assist them. They made me an honorary member of their Mess. They brought to me all the gossip of life in the barracks. Often, two or three would shyly come to me and ask whether I would go with them to a theatre in London.

Their Colonel and Adjutant once said that if they wanted to know anything about any young officer, they came to me. I had a proof of this when the Colonel and I went to see a draft off to France. I had often heard the boys say that he was continually complaining about their work and seldom encouraging them, so when he said to me : " You know everything the boys think—I wonder if you can help me to improve my work ? " He was in bad health and consequently over-anxious. Gently as I could, I told him what the boys said. The next morning the officer who came on guard asked me : " What have you been doing to the Colonel ? He's been falling over himself encouraging us. We all said you must have been talking to him." How proud and pleased I was when later the Colonel and Adjutant told me, as they told the King, that I had greatly improved the morale of their young officers.

All this was the beginning of an association with every Battalion of Guards, which lasted for twenty-eight happy years. The habit of the officer on guard dining at the Deanery endured throughout this period, as did my honorary membership of each Officer's Mess, my being elected by each new Battalion.

Peace brought with it a fundamentally different atmosphere to our relationship. The young soldiers were no longer under constant strain to make them feel the need of a confidant. Nevertheless, our association helped to keep me young. I hope, if any of them read what I have written here, that they will understand all their friendship meant to me.

At the outbreak of the second war with Germany, circumstances ordering life in the barracks were such that my experience of 1914–18 could not be repeated. Besides, the whole mental atmosphere of the struggle was different. In 1914 it had been a long time since we had thought of war, and consequently our emotions were kindled and all of us were strung up and excited. In 1939 we had had ample opportunity to digest our experience of twenty-five years before. The result was that people inhibited their emotions and hid their thoughts—as a Frenchman said, the English went into the war like people entering an operating theatre. Even so, there did spring up for me with the Guards at Windsor an additional relationship—with the men—which also gave me an immense amount of pleasure and happiness.

A company of between two and three hundred Guardsmen were quartered in the Mews, and I thought I should do something about them. Our service at the Chapel being quite unsuitable for them, I asked the King if he would allow me to make part of St. George's Hall into a temporary church, where I could have a service for them on Sunday. He not only agreed to my request but said that he might attend the service himself. When he was at Windsor he always did so, together with the Queen and the Princesses. I had a choir from among the men with some ladies of a voluntary choir at St. George's to come and help. Mr. Ogilvy, one of the Eton music masters, used very kindly to play the organ and also practise the choir before the service.

I felt that if I was going to make the services really useful, the men must know me as a man. Accordingly I went every morning to the guard-room for an hour or so and then attended their dinners.

I also had eight Guardsmen to tea once a week, the Company Office selecting them so that everyone should have their turn. These teas gave me as much pleasure as any social gatherings I ever had. During the meal I set about breaking down any shyness. After tea, when the ice was broken, we all moved into my sitting-room and there they were able to relax and talk with absolute freedom. As they arrived at four and I never turned them out till seven, I really did get to hear something of their minds. They enjoyed it immensely, often telling me that what they especially liked was being invited into somebody's home. Their Commanding Officer, Major Phillips, was as good a manager of men as I have ever come across, and he did all he knew to help me. His name cropped up at one of our teas and his praises were sung with great enthusiasm. Finally one of the men said : " The fact is, he's a soldier on parade, and a father to us off." You could not have bettered the description.

There was a quite indirect factor which played no small part in bringing us all together. For many years I had always played medicine ball with the house boy before breakfast. Since the war, however, I had no house boy. At first one of the men on the Tower who watched for aeroplanes used to take his place. When the watchers' job was taken over by the Pioneers, their Commanding Officer was willing to help me, only we were unable to arrange the times. I therefore approached Major Phillips, who allowed me to have two men from the guard-room every morning. At first they were inclined to hang back, but after a few days the sergeant told me that the whole guard used to volunteer, thinking it rather fun. They grew proud of me, too, because from long practice I could beat them at it, though I was nearly eighty. One morning we were all greatly amused, I remember, when the new officer in command of the Pioneers met the officer on guard at my gate and watched us playing. After a time he remarked, "I understand there was talk of our men doing that. I don't believe they could stand up to it !"

Gradually was strengthened the bond between us, with the result that the St. George's Hall service came to mean a great deal. The men genuinely entered into it, and it was very instructive to watch their faces as I preached. They invariably listened ; fairly often they got interested ; sometimes they appeared really moved. In any case the service was always a happy experience for me. If the King had some bishop or other ecclesiastic staying for the week-end, he used to suggest my asking them to preach ; but in the ordinary way I did so myself.

An annual excitement for the Guardsmen's choir was when, with the officers and myself, they went round singing carols at Christmas. We began with the King and Queen, who came down to listen and talk with the men and then gave us refreshments. After that we went on to some of the houses in the precincts. It was all the greatest possible fun and we enjoyed it greatly.

I valued my association with those Guards boys beyond expression. I had had a lot to do with boys of the same sort throughout my parochial years, but the quarter of a century between the wars had altered them considerably. For one thing I never found the later product among them the least ashamed of being religious-minded. I remember at one of our tea parties, as they were all going, being asked by some-body whether there was a Communion at the Chapel the following Sunday which he could attend. It was asked per-fectly naturally, but that would not have been the case before the first World War. Equally, no one ever pretended in the least to being religious, which was, I think, a very wholesome sign : after all, those boys were becoming men, and if they could face the question of religion unself-consciously, many of them would be certain to find their way to it in time.

The Guards sergeants were splendid, especially our old Sergeant-Major Dewbury, a most lovable man who was very popular with all ranks. It will always be one of my proudest memories that the sergeants gave me a banquet when I was leaving Windsor ; a rare honour which I immensely appreci-ated. A very good banquet it was, too—both as regards food and company.

2

The Guards at Windsor were not my only latter-day associa-tion with the young. Since my childhood in Germany, when I had fallen under the spell of Holbein's famous Darmstadt *Madonna and Child*—which I used to gaze at when visiting with my mother one of the Hesse Princesses, to whom the painting belonged—I had steadily developed an intense love of art. When frequently I went to London in connection with raising money for the restoration of St. George's, I took the opportunity to visit all the smaller picture galleries and exhibi-tions. Whenever I saw things I liked I endeavoured to meet the artist responsible for them, and these generally turned out to be young men. It was natural that they should appreciate my interest in their work—the more especially since it was not unintelligent interest—and we mostly became friends. As our relationships developed they began to give little parties for me, until I had quite an extensive circle of young friends. I became familiar with young writers, actors and members of all that world which centres round the arts. They made it quite clear that they liked my company. I was constantly being asked to parties at studios or lodgings, and always at the invitation of the young.

When I was young I liked the old, but when I passed middle age I found myself liking the young more and more, and for the same reason. If you are young the old talk to you from a different background, and there is a certain excitement in looking into the past through their talk ; if you are charging headlong into middle age the young are exciting because they are looking at life from a point of view different to yourself. And so at the parties to which I went I listened to the floods of youthful talk with a vivid interest. I think that the old when they were talking to me in my youth, and the young when I was listening to them in my old age, enjoyed my company because I was a good audience—a sympathetic, appreciative audience, free of humbug. With my young friends I never pretended to be interested but really was adventuring into an uncharted experience, just as years previously I plunged into the exciting newness of my district at Tyne Dock. A number of respectable people looked down their noses at these parties and told me that they thought I was lowering the dignity of my office : the fear of this never worried me unduly. A man who wants to be a man must never allow himself to be governed by the prejudices of respectability. I was concerned, however, to ensure that my presence in so-called Bohemian circles did not degenerate from kindly familiarity into contempt. When young men give to an older man their affection and respect, he can hardly fail to be of help to them ; it is only if and when he loses that respect that he becomes contemptible. I remember a don at

Cambridge who liked keeping undergraduates' society. He brought himself down to our level, and how we despised him.

During the gayest evenings I spent with my young artists, I gained confidence in our relationship from the knowledge that no one told a story or said anything which was likely to have shocked me. As long as that mark of their regard for my feelings remained, I knew that there could be no harm and that there might be a great deal of good in my encouragement of our familiar intercourse. As with my young Guards officers and men, by degrees our acquaintanceship turned itself into something deep and enduring. I shared in times of sorrow and trial, and, where marriages occurred, often had babies brought to me to christen.

If I succeeded in being of use to these boys, it was because they all knew what my real feelings were about them. My attitude towards them was once well expressed when I was sitting with two lads in their rooms. I had been discussing some jolly quality I had discovered in another boy, when one of my companions suddenly said : "The mistake you make is that you think us much better than we are." His friend replied immediately : "Don't be a fool ! It's not what we *are* that the Dean thinks well of, but what he believes we *may be*." It was the truth. I had learned to approach people in this way from my mother, and I always felt how much she would have been at home in the little world of my new discovery, as well as how gay she would have made its company and parties.

3

My association with young people brought me inevitably and specially into touch with those in the theatre. I love the theatre and I love plays, but I think I love the theatre people even better than the plays.

I was quite small when I had my first theatrical experience. It was the somewhat grim drama, *Rip Van Winkle*, in which Jefferson played, and I was extremely frightened. From time to time during the holidays I began to get more accustomed

THE AUTHOR'S MOTHER, LADY FRANCES BAILLIE

to acting. As I passed through London on my way back to school, a bachelor friend of the family generally took me to the theatre. One night, when I was about fifteen, he took me to an after-theatre supper at the Fielding Club in Covent Garden. The Beef Steak being closed, the long table was crowded with most of the leading actors of the day. Dear old Corney Grain, whom I was afterwards to know very well, amused at seeing a boy there, invited me to sit next to him. Kemble took my other side, and together they devoted themselves to entertaining me. Opposite I had Irving and Toole. It was the most gorgeous fun. At the end, my friend having devoted himself a little too liberally to champagne, instead of his taking me home, I took him. Hallam Tennyson, also, was always kind to me, not only taking me to plays but behind the scenes after the last curtain to see some of the great actors and actresses.

When I was up from Cambridge at the end of a Season, I renewed my contact with the theatre and saw a good deal of actors. I became great friends with that adorable old artist, Mrs. John Wood. When quite a young curate I also met Beerbohm Tree and, though we did not meet again for some time, he never failed to send me tickets for every new play he produced. After I was ordained, except for an occasional play, that side of my life came to an end. The gap in my relations with the theatre lasted over twenty years, ending when I went to Windsor.

The young who are engaged in the arts have often certain drawbacks, or at least they lack advantages that the majority of others enjoy. Most of us have been largely sustained and strengthened by our roots in a home, and by having mixed with great varieties of people. But boys following an artistic career are in very many cases divorced from such influences. Not only do they generally live in lodgings, but sometimes they are even alienated from their homes by an antagonistic attitude to the work they have chosen. They are without roots, therefore, and inclined both to associate almost exclusively with boys of their own sort and to be preoccupied with their own interests, which is bad, or at least difficult, since that kind of atmosphere develops a false standard of values. All too easily they may become slack and accept the hollow facile values of a small circle in which vanity is fed by a mutual exchange of compliments that attempts to compensate them for the loss of their self-respect. Of course, among these young artists a narrow artificiality only exists to a limited extent. When a boy is really devoted to art, and is not just talking about it, he will not shrink from any amount of sacrifice or the hardest work.

In no branch of art is the cultivation of character more necessary than in that of the actor. On the stage, indeed, a man has simply got to work or he will go under. The fashion in which actors learn to allow nothing to stand in the way of their work produces noble qualities of heart and mind. I have known a boy carry on at every performance all through an attack of jaundice; anybody who has had jaundice can appreciate the immense concentration of will required by such an effort. Yet normally this high quality of devotion informs the whole acting profession. Another factor conducive to the formation of character in the theatre is that it requires a group effort. An actor has to study constantly how to give and take, though there are some who are selfish and want all the limelight to themselves. On the other hand, it is astonishing how many stars are found to take infinite trouble in giving the youngest actors in their company every possible chance. My old friend Leslie Henson once found a man of real promise in the provinces and, after bringing him into his company, encouraged him to such an extent that he built the man up into being almost a rival to himself.

For the many actors I have known well, I have a great respect and affection: additionally, I owe them a great deal. Recently I was asked to take a service for a neighbour, who was short-handed. I had a slight attack of lumbago and, since a retired man of eighty-seven might not unreasonably on that account be excused from active work, I was greatly tempted to say No. But then I said to myself: " An attack of lumbago, unless it was very bad indeed, wouldn't make an actor shirk his job—so why should it with me?" I took the service.

There are one or two theatrical personalities, no longer living, who contributed much to the happiness of my life. One of them was Marie Tempest, who was just eleven days my senior. I recollect the time when she made her first great reputation in light opera, bringing to it a charm and a quality of voice which has rarely been equalled. I also recall how she abruptly brought that first phase of her career to an end, and ventured into serious comedy. I have often heard her fellow artists comment on the courage with which she risked her established popularity by the change. I firmly believe, however, that if those by whom she was surrounded had allowed it, she could have made a third name even as she became an old woman, by devoting herself to serious drama. As it was, her agelessness in whatever she did was nothing short of marvellous. The polish of her acting remained to the end, and if it became a little mechanical, it was wonderfully little so. I am convinced that she could have attained to her old spontaneity through a stimulating third adventure.

At her funeral a sermon was preached which seemed to me altogether to miss the point. The preacher said that her great contribution was that she made people laugh. Laughter is a wholesome thing, and she certainly did make them laugh, but it was quite a side issue in her life. He real contribution to the world was the tremendous strength of character which made her always give of her best, no matter what question of health, what private anxiety or sorrow, might stand in the way. Before making an entrance she played Patience for an hour in her dressing-room, after she had made up. She gave her whole attention to the game in order to free her mind from anything that might disturb her concentration on her part. This game of Patience sometimes amounted to heroism, as when her husband was in his last illness. Her regard for her audience conditioned her every thought. When we were both over seventy I remember lunching with her one day, when suddenly she said to me : " You mustn't be offended, but I'm going to be personal. You've let your teeth become so bad that they're spoiling your appearance. Remember that you and I have both a public, and that we owe it to our public to make ourselves as pleasant to look at as possible. You must go and have your teeth done." For my part I had ceased to think my appearance mattered, but I accepted her point and went mutely off to my dentist, who made seven extractions.

The tremendous discipline she continually imposed on herself, so that she might give the very best of which she was capable at every performance, made her seem a little hard, since she exacted from other people the same discipline she gave herself. Those who acted with her found her standards severe. Yet she never desired to obscure an actor or actress ; she only sought perfection in every performance. Many who played with her have told me that, while they found the experience extremely trying, it taught them a lot. If she was hard after a fashion, nothing ever killed her essential kindness of heart. Once when playing at a theatre in New York, the best dressing rooms, of which naturally she had one, were on the ground floor, while the minor members of the cast had to climb innumerable stairs to reach their own. Someone casually mentioned that the stairs were extremely bad for one of the young actors, who was consumptive. She said nothing, but the following evening the dressing rooms had been changed —the young actor finding himself in her room, and she occupying his little quarters at the top of the house. Typically, she snapped at anyone who mentioned it, or who tried to thank her for what she had done.

Her tremendous sense of duty was partly due to her upbringing. She had had a Puritan grandmother, and she herself remained at heart a Puritan to the end of her days. Whatever else might be said of her, there was no denying that she was a great woman with a great character, and an exquisitely accomplished actress.

A second picture that stands out in my mind is of another actress, also in her own way a great woman but in her later years a sadly pathetic figure. Connie Ediss had also had her day in the musical comedy, where she was perhaps the most popular of all the reigning stars. She had a delicious, roguish humour which amounted to genius. I shall never forget her singing her most famous song, the chorus of which went—

> *I'd have horses with nice long tails,*
> *If my papa was the Prince of Wales.*

The night I heard her sing it, the Prince of Wales was in a box, enormously enjoying it all. I did not know her then and the next time I saw her was years afterwards, when she was with a provincial company. She was taking Marie Tempest's part in *Passing Brompton Road*, and of course her conception of it was totally different from that of Marie. Nevertheless, I thought it a brilliant performance, as I made a point of telling her when we met some time later. "Oh," she said, "I'm very glad you liked it. You see, I couldn't act it like Marie Tempest. She acted it like a woman who might have passed Brompton Road ; I acted it like a woman who could never have passed it."

The real power of Connie Ediss was shown in that remark of hers : instead of giving her audience a bad imitation, she conceived a new and powerful interpretation within what she knew to be the limits of her own capacity. In that lay her first great and noble quality—she was the humblest minded woman I ever knew. Not having been spoiled by her success, she never grumbled at the long and weary years of struggle she endured in the provinces. It is my belief that those responsible for the discovery of stage talent made a great mistake in not judging her capable of straight acting. When she was past her original musical comedy work, they were apparently unable to see in her anything beyond an entirely uneducated woman who had possessed a trick of charm that made her popular as a comedienne.

I came to know her well just after Leslie Henson brought her back to serious work in London, giving her good parts in his productions. Cyril Maude had also done his best for her, and she had one remarkable success as a cook in one of his plays that fully justified Leslie Henson's interest. Once, when staying with my brother Augustus in Scotland, my niece Fanny and I drove into Edinburgh, where we saw that a new play of Leslie's was being tried out with Connie Ediss among the cast. The piece was, I think, called *The Night of the Garter*. I decided we must wait and see it, if possible taking Connie to supper afterwards. When she came, bubbling with pleasure, she was in her gayest and most amusing mood. In the middle of supper she asked my niece what she would like to do with her life, and when Fanny replied that she sometimes thought she would like to go on the stage, Connie declared with great emphasis : " No, no, don't do that ! If I'd known what the stage was, I'd never have become an actress. I'll tell you what I should have been—I should have been somebody's cook, and a very good cook too ! " She pressed us both to come and see her at her home and sample her cooking, but unfortunately we never managed it. She gave her home in a Surrey village the delightfully humorous name of " Connie Cot " ; all the more humorous, I thought, when I learned it was a flat over the local bank.

One of the fine qualities of Connie Ediss's character was that she never spoke of anyone having been unkind to her. On the other hand, she never tired of talking of the kindnesses she had received, especially from Cyril Maude and Leslie Henson. She used to say : " Dear Leslie ! he didn't need me a bit. But he's just so kind that he made places for me in his plays." Towards the end of her life her health gradually gave way. Once, when she was really ill, I went to see her in hospital. It was obvious that the nurses were simply devoted to her. She lay there quite placidly, talking always of the things people had done for her. Over the next few years she wrote me pathetic, uneducated letters, all of them breathing the same beauty of character. She never referred to her great days as an actress, though her eyes would twinkle if I reminded her of them. I think she was one of the most lovable creatures I have ever come across, and I cannot but feel a woman to be great when she possesses humility as genuine as hers, along with such an intense capacity for loyalty and gratitude.

Among his fellow actors and friends there are many for whom the name Robert Haslam will stand for a great deal. In my case, he became almost a son. I do not know that I have ever met anyone so sincere, so absolutely conscientious and with so great moral courage. He had had a good education at Rugby, but he was not really suited to the stage. I was once deploring to a brother actor of his, who had been a great success and who was very fond of him, the fact that I did not believe Robert would ever make a good actor. " No, " was the reply, " I don't think he will. His character is too completely sincere. To be a successful actor you must have a touch of the poseur, and he hasn't the touch." And that was perfectly true. Indeed, as a man he almost awed one by the dignity of his heart and mind. Once, when he was going away for some time to America, I said to him that I wished he would sometimes say a prayer for me, as I found life very difficult. He promised to do so, but added : " My difficulty is that I can't pray like other people. I can only pray if I really mean something. I can't repeat platitudes to God." That sincerity was the whole basis and quality of his moral make-up.

When Robert returned from America he was very ill with septic glands and went into a nursing home where he was successfully operated on. After the operation he was astonishingly treated, and in a few days they said he was quite fit to leave. As I thought they were neglecting him so much that anything was better than leaving him there, I fetched him in a car and, taking every possible precaution, took him to Windsor. Putting him straight to bed I called his stepmother, who was very fond of him and was a trained nurse, to come and look after him. He was very ill and she was terribly shocked by what I told her of the nursing-home. In a day or two he contracted pneumonia and died. His death caused an intense outburst of sorrow and sympathy from his fellow actors and actresses. It was no mere passing emotion, but a real sorrow. Whenever they spoke of him the stress was laid on the influence his character had had on every company in which he acted. Nor was it only the young actors who said that, but the great stars as well, whilst I felt that I had lost another son.

What I may call my farewell to the stage took place just before I left Windsor. One day Ivor Novello telephoned from his house at Maidenhead to say that the Lunts were staying with him and asked if he might bring them to lunch at the Deanery. I did not know them, but I had an immense admiration for their acting and was delighted. When they arrived I told them that as I was very old I found going up to plays in London had become too tiring for me, and that consequently I had not seen the play they had been acting in, which had just come to an end. A little later Alfred Lunt said : " But if you can't come up to us, why shouldn't we come down to you ? " I thought it was a joke and laughed, but he insisted : " No, I really mean it " ; and she chimed in : " I think Alfred's quite right. It is a play that would act just as well in a room as on the stage."

Accordingly, a day having been fixed, we divided my drawing-room, which was very large and had windows down one long side, into two halves lengthways, providing a stage almost as long as that in a theatre. We had no platform, no scenery, no curtain, no make-up, and for lighting, only the daylight from the windows opposite the actors ; while the small audience for which I had room occupied two rows of chairs in front of the windows. The performance was by the whole of the Lunts' company. The only time I have been gripped by acting in an equal degree was by Sarah Bernhardt in the *Dame aux Camélias*, in the scene where her lover visits her when she is dying of consumption. All our small audience felt the same. We did not feel that we were watching a play but that we were present in a real and very moving scene from life. Even the Lunts said that they felt the special circumstances so much, that they did not think they had ever given a better performance.

I like to feel that I ended my active association with the stage on such a peak of experience. It was an example of that splendid capacity for generosity which actors can show. Down to the smallest detail, the Lunts insisted on making the occasion a gift, refusing to let one penny of cost fall on me. They would not even let me give the actors hospitality, but took a room at an hotel where they all went for a meal afterwards. Their performance was not only the most marvellous exhibition of what acting can be, but a perfect display of the most generous kindness. I fancy there can be nobody else who has witnessed acting in quite such conditions. At the time, we carefully refused to give the matter to the Press, but I now feel I should like to let people know of this characteristic gesture of two great actors. And there was one final, supremely graceful touch that moved me beyond words. I said I was very sorry that there would be room only for a very small audience. My friends replied : " We don't mind if there's nobody except you. We are coming to show you the play."

CHAPTER 15

THE DEANERY

WHEN my wife died our children had reached an age when they were a great deal away from home. Though they came to me whenever they could and our ties always remained the closest, in becoming men they had developed interests and associations beyond the orbit of our intimate family life. I was fortunate at this time in having friends who meant much to me, foremost among them being my brother Augustus's daughter, Fanny, and a young writer, Hector Bolitho.

At the end of the 1914–18 War, Bolitho, a third-generation New Zealander, decided to come to England. Some time after his arrival, when the Chapter required a writer for some work at Windsor, he was recommended to us. He stayed with Canon Dalton several times during the following year and he came to know and to love Windsor. He went to South Africa to edit a magazine, then he returned and took a cottage in Essex. But he had fallen under the spell of the Castle, and in one of his letters to Dalton he said how much he would like to work in the historical atmosphere of Windsor. Dalton always liked to help the young and he showed me the letter. I thought immediately of a mass of letters written by my aunt, Lady Augusta Stanley, to my mother, who had preserved them and left them to me on her death. I knew that these letters, with their wealth of historical interest, personal colour and charm, were worth publishing. I asked Hector Bolitho to spend a week-end with me at the Deanery. After dinner, on the evening of his arrival, I gave him a volume of Lady Augusta's letters to read in bed. Next morning we discussed the possibility of editing them. He was enthusiastic and so we decided to do this work together.

214

Thus began a relationship which gave me another son and which gave him, in the interesting people he constantly met at the Deanery and in the whole atmosphere of our home, a new and exciting background to his life. When we had published the first volume of Lady Augusta's letters they were so successful that we edited a second one, which, in turn, led on to further work together. In the end Hector Bolitho had lived at the Deanery for five and a half years, and happy and productive years they were for both of us.

Fanny spent many months each year with me, being always present at our busiest time in the summer. Popular with boys and girls, and with the enchanting quality of never being bored with anything we were doing, she was of the utmost use to me, as was Hector, in creating in the Deanery the kind of centre I had known during my youth at Westminster. I had as an example the wonderful work my Uncle Dean Stanley had done in making understood, both at home and abroad, the place that Westminster Abbey held in English life—mainly through his having made the Deanery at Westminster a social centre. Accordingly, I encouraged people of every kind to come to me, offering them hospitality of one sort or another, showing them the Chapel and the Castle and letting them be present at a service. This grew into a considerable undertaking, especially in summer. One year we counted the people who had received some form of hospitality at the Deanery during May, June and July, and they amounted to over a thousand. At least half of this number were foreigners, which I felt was particularly important since Windsor has a curious prestige overseas as the centre of English life. It was my hope that every foreigner who took home pleasant memories of Windsor would feel more kindly towards England and so become an apostle of the goodwill which is so much needed after a war. During my travels overseas I had also acquired the habit of discovering some young man, just at the end of his university career, who I thought would profit from spending some time in England. These I would invite to stay for a year at Windsor, where they were able to gain an insight into English life. I believe this was useful work in helping to create some kind of international understanding. Quite apart from this we found our visitors an interesting and vital element in our home.

It is impossible to list the guests we received, but they covered a wide field. I recall at least six sovereigns, besides many princes. There came statesmen ; ambassadors and generals ; singers, pianists and other musicians ; actors, artists ; writers and journalists ; professors and clergy ; and boxers and other athletes. The fact that I did not so much select my guests as simply accept them, no matter who they were or what they did, gave to our society a constant feeling of excitement. More often than not, our parties were extremely mixed. I remember one luncheon at which we had a Hungarian bishop, a young German prince and his aide-de-camp, a Swiss doctor, an American film actor, and the editor of a fashion paper. On one most successful week-end, we had a foreign ambassador and an English comedian with their wives. Such parties could not fail to be interesting.

Of musicians, the greatest from all over Europe came to us and we used frequently to have their wonderful music at the Deanery. Though I seldom asked people to sing, as I did not think it fair, many would volunteer. I remember taking the chief soprano of the Berlin Opera, who was a Swede, over the Chapel, when suddenly she said, " What a wonderful building this must be for singing. " I replied, " It is—and why shouldn't you try it ? " Except for our party the Chapel was empty. Stepping on to the little platform of the Lectern she sang us some Swedish hymns, which were extraordinarily beautiful. In connection with our own choirs singing in the Chapel, I remember Toscanini's amazement at its perfection without any use being made of a conductor. It is regrettable that this special feature, which has characterised English church music since the fourteenth century, is in some cases dying out, certain organists having developed the habit of conducting part of the service.

Though I was shy of asking people to sing, I had no scruples in asking instrumentalists to play, especially after a distinguished pianist once said to me, " Your difficulty won't be in getting us to play—it'll begin when you try to stop us." Fortunately I had a piano which all pianists loved playing on. I remember Malcolm Sargent, who was a special friend, once suggested that he and Edith Baker, the famous exponent of jazz music, who was also staying with us, should test the relation of jazz to classical music by alternately playing jazz and Beethoven. A most interesting experiment. Then again, there was George Chavchavadze, who, after playing to us, would entertain us with a talent which I think was even more remarkable than his piano playing and of which the public knew nothing—that of singing folk songs of all nations. Though he did not have a very good voice, he sang them more perfectly than anyone I ever heard. We were also visited by a quartet, one member of which has since become famous as Barbirolli the conductor. After dinner we used to go with them into the Nave of the Chapel and there in the dim light they would play to us.

Of all the great foreign musicians, the two who became my closest friends were Madame Jeritza and Madame Suggia.

Jeritza was the most opulent personality I ever knew. Absolutely natural, she took colour from the surroundings in which she found herself. She once came to lunch with three great ladies and was the most perfect *grande dame* of them all. On the other hand, when she rowed a party including myself in a small boat on the Attersee, where she had a villa, she was simply a grinning schoolgirl alive with the wildest spirits. It was this quality which made her a great actress, and I venture to think that she was an even greater actress than she was a singer. She was tall, with a superb figure, a face which, if not classically beautiful, gave the effect of beauty and a head crowned with a heavy mane of corn-coloured hair. I remember when I was staying at her villa I used to get up early and have my coffee in the garden. One morning about a dozen people trooped in with musical instruments and sat down. I had not the least idea who or what they were, but presently Jeritza appeared and greeted them warmly. After the arrival of my fellow guests, of whom there were two or three, the visitors gave us a concert. I learned afterwards that they were the Street Singers of Vienna. They formed a society which annually selected a King and Queen, and the new King and Queen had come with a selection of members to serenade Jeritza. She threw herself into the affair with the most infectious abandonment : laughing, cheering, clapping, an audience in herself and such as few artists can have had. It must have been a wonderful occasion for the humble street musicians. Afterwards I told her : " You may be a great singer, but there's one thing I'm quite certain of—you're much greater as an audience ! " And with a schoolgirl grin, she answered me : " I think I am. I do enjoy it so."

That was the secret of her charm. I remember a high-brow Hungarian speaking critically of her, saying that she was not as perfectly trained as some others, and so on. I allowed that that might be quite true, but pointed out that none the less most people enjoyed hearing her much more than they did the other singers. One year, when she was singing at Covent Garden, she was coming to me for a week-end when the Court were in residence. The Sunday before her arrival I dined at the Castle and mentioned her visit to the Queen, who said : " Oh, do tell her that we're so sorry we've not been able to go to Covent Garden to hear her. We do like her singing so much." At the end of the evening she repeated her message. I mentioned our conversation to the Master of the Household, and said : " Why don't you ask her to come and sing after dinner next Sunday, without having any party ? " They did invite her, and the effect upon her was to produce the wildest excitement. Walking up to the Castle she was bubbling all the way. With exquisite judgment she had dressed simply in a plain white frock, without any jewels. Baron Poppa Podrazy, her husband, and Beletzza, who was then conducting the Italian Opera at Covent Garden and came to accompany her, went with us. The King and Queen received us in the green drawing-room and were, of course, charming to them. We then moved into the red drawing-room, where there was a piano. She was nervous, but as soon as she started this disappeared. She began by singing two arias, followed by some English ballads quite beautifully rendered, which is no mean feat for a foreign opera singer. After that she went on singing, the King and Queen encouraging her through a long series of songs. It was a triumphant success, and as we walked down the hill afterwards she seized my arm in her impulsive, delightful fashion. "People have often asked me what was the happiest day of my life," she declared. "I have always said I do not know. Now I shall say *this* is." From that day, whenever she came to England, she telegraphed to me as she landed from the boat and sent me tickets, whenever I could go, for every opera in which she appeared.

Budapest was ringing with a story characteristic of her when I visited it. There was an old Count Batthyány, who was the leader of the sporting world and had been a great friend of King Edward VII. Although eighty-four years old, he dined every night at his club and, after two hours' sleep on a sofa, went on to a night club where he stayed until four in the morning. He made himself a little ridiculous by priding himself on his success with the ladies. He said to Jeritza : " The other day I rang up someone on the telephone. They gave me the wrong number, but when I heard the voice at the other end, I knew that it was a pretty woman, so I asked her to tea with me. We met and had tea, and after dining together and going to a play we went to a night club—I had a great success ! " He saw something in Jeritza's eyes, however, that he did not quite like and quickly added : " Don't you believe me ? " " Oh yes, I believe that you met her and that she was charming, and that you had the evening together and were a great success," she assured him sweetly. " What then don't you believe ? " " Oh," she said, " I don't believe that telephones were invented then."

Madame Suggia I used to meet constantly at the house of Mr. Hudson, the owner of *Country Life*, where she stayed when in London. He was a great friend of mine as well and allowed me a room in his house when I had to spend the night in town. Suggia always pretended to be jealous of my admiration for Jeritza, and once when a snapshot was taken of us together she sent me a copy, with written on the back : " Not Jeritza, only Suggia." She often used to play to me for hours on end in Hudson's drawing-room, and as a 'cellist I suppose in her own time she was supreme. In London she was the great musician who expected deference, the Suggia of Augustus John's well-known portrait. But some years after, when I went to Portugal and visited her at Oporto where she lived with her doctor husband, I found a different woman : she was a simple housewife interested in all the ordinary concerns of life, and quite delightful in a new way.

Apart from the world of music and the arts, contemporary history was transformed into a human document for us through the number of people whom we encountered at the Deanery with a place in the affairs of the time. There were the Amir of Afghanistan, who was afterwards deposed ; the Shah of Persia (who provided an unimpressive figure as a fat little man, quite young, in a frock coat with brown boots and a billycock hat), also afterwards deposed ; King Fuad of Egypt, who had the most perfect manners I had ever seen ; the Crown Prince of Japan, later the Emperor, with whom we had a jolly lunch at the Castle as guests of the Prince of Wales, who, in the wildest spirits, encouraged an atmosphere of joyous fun in the party ; the Crown Prince of Italy, the King of Spain, and many more. Three Ambassadors who came to the Deanery became my very great friends : Count Ahlefeldt of Denmark and his wife ; Olivera of Brazil and his wife, who were great favourites in London society ; Quo of China, a man of great intellectual powers to whom I took particularly. At a banquet in London,

Quo made a speech which to my mind was a perfect example of oratory, astonishing for a man speaking in a foreign language.

Two friendships which stand a little apart from the rest of this period in my life, but which hold a special place in my affections, concern two professional boxers.

The first of these was Paddy Peters, who was in the Irish Guards when I met him, and used to come to the Deanery in the morning and give me physical exercises. His was a beautiful nature such as one does not often meet, being perfectly simple, natural and unself-conscious, and in his friendship absolutely whole-hearted. He was full of fun and we had endless jokes together. When I was seventy, he insisted on my learning to box, always hoping that I should be burgled as he wanted me to have the opportunity of knocking the burglar down. When first I knew him he was the champion welter-weight of the Army, Navy and Air Force. After he left the Army, he became an instructor in boxing to the Air Force at Uxbridge, but all through that time he came to me whenever he could for my exercises. When visiting him in his home, I accidentally discovered a mark of his regard which touched me very much. He had a framed photograph of me in his room, and his baby daughter had been taught to salute it every night before she went to bed. Paddy eventually took a party of the R.A.F. to South Africa for a boxing tour, and they were all killed in an aeroplane accident. His religion, like his friendship, was entirely unself-conscious, woven as it was into the intimate fabric of his life. He was a Roman Catholic, but did not feel that to be any bar to our sympathy. If to love God and your neighbour as yourself·is the mark of a true Christian, Paddy Peters was a great Christian indeed.

When I first met Joseph Rottenburger, he had retired from the ring and had become a masseur. He was successful in finding a great many clients in Paris but quite unable to secure his fees from most of them. In the end, having collected what he could, he bought a little *estaminet* in his native town of Mulhous, where I once visited him with my chauffeur and friend, Len White.

At the outbreak of the last war, Joseph joined the Army. During the course of his service he was nine times wounded, three times a prisoner and three times escaped. Blown up in a lorry in which everyone else was killed, and stripped by the blast of all his clothes, he hung half-conscious in a tree, the temperature below freezing ; his life was only saved by a happy chance : one of his arms was over a branch so that his weight pressing down on to it stopped the circulation and prevented his bleeding to death. After the collapse of France he made his way down into Algiers, rejoined the Army and served to the end of the war. In the seventeen years of our friendship, hardly a month has passed without Joseph writing to me. Even throughout the war I received letters which kept me posted as to all his experiences.

When peace came and Joseph returned to Mulhous it was to find the business of his *estaminet* wrecked. For a time he managed a bar in a Paris hotel, before emigrating to Canada and from there to the United States. Before he left for the other side of the world he flew over to England to say good-bye to me.

Despite the inevitable racial differences between Joseph and Paddy, they enjoyed a common simplicity and directness of nature that fine, clean boxing always develops in men. Jackson, the great boxer of the Regency, must have had very much the same sort of character. In his own day there was no one more respected, and reading about him one feels he was one of the greatest gentlemen in all the vulgar society of that period. I have known Len Harvey only slightly, but I believe he is another man of the same type. Naturally, coarse-minded men are coarsened by fighting, but finer natures are refined still further by the sport.

Every year St. George's Chapel was closed for six weeks for cleaning. During this six weeks I was free to leave Windsor. While my wife lived, as her health made it impossible for us to travel far, we simply went to her old homes at Brancepeth and Burwarton. In 1922 and 1923, as she thought I was feeling the strain of my work and in need of a complete change, she urged me to go abroad myself. I did not like leaving her, but I came to the conclusion that it would worry her less if I agreed, and that I might amuse and cheer her by letters describing my travels.

In 1922 I decided to visit Germany and Austria to study the changes war had produced. Once there, I found these changes to be remarkable and, in many ways, hopeful. Had a stable government been formed at that time, the whole history of the next seventeen years might have been altered. But the sudden possession of an elective government by a people unused to the habits to democracy led only to muddle, so that twenty-two parties were represented in the Reichstag. Years of these political conditions brought Germany to the verge of complete moral collapse, killing hope in the minds of the young and preparing them to accept the one ostensibly clear-cut and constructive policy of Hitler's Nazism. I was not conscious of this in 1922. Indeed, in a letter home I wrote, " Nothing, I think, will drive [Germany] again into militarism unless it is driven by despair."

When I revisited Southern Germany and went on to Hungary in 1931, I saw that the despair I had so feared already had hold of the people. It would have been an altogether sad journey for me but for my visit to Crown Prince Rupprecht of Bavaria, at his castle at Hohenschwangau. The small castle, perched high on a rock, had been entirely restored in romantic Gothic of about 1830. Everything is Gothic, even the piano. The ornaments are all Gothic ; the coverings of the chairs are stamped with heraldic Gothic ; the walls are frescoed with knights and palmers and all the figures belonging to mediæval romance, in the incredibly clean condition that German painters of that date always portrayed them. It was the most complete and deliciously comic thing I ever saw. But the Crown Prince loves it and would not have a thing altered, because it amuses him so. I had a beautiful sitting-room at the top of the tower, with on one side a turret from which I had a stupendous view over the plain to Munich, and on the other side, lying at my very feet, something more beautiful in a still lake surrounded with steep wooded hills. There was an entrancing elderly servant, in a pale blue livery with enormous silver buttons, who looked after me, and, if he could avoid it, never let me move without his help. From the moment he brought my coffee in the morning till the moment when he helped me to undress for bed, he was always on the watch for what he could do and, wherever possible, forestalled my every wish.

Rupprecht is one of the most agreeable men, as well as the most perfect conversationalist I have ever encountered. He has an immense width of interest and experience ; his knowledge of art is well known ; and as a story-teller I seldom met his equal. One of his stories I will never forget. A friend of his, travelling in Canada, penetrated the forests in the far north, where he found a small Trappist monastery. He was given hospitality, and that night at supper the Abbot relaxed the rule of silence. The monks, who were elderly men from different countries, had been in the monastery for at least thirty years. They had never heard of the 1914–18 War ; they had heard no news of the world since they had left their own countries ; they had never seen a newspaper or read a modern book. The way in which the Prince described the sudden awakening of the monks' interest, evoking the flood of their eager questioning about public events and their homelands, was moving to a degree beyond belief.

With an enormous sense of humour, the idea that most amuses the Prince is that he is the legitimate King of England.

When he came to stay with me at Windsor he was delighted
by being received in London by the White Rose Society
and presented with a white rose. One day a friend of mine
while walking in Germany heard following him slowly along
the road a German who was whistling Jacobite airs. Going
up to him, my friend said : "I must apologise, but how
does it come that you are whistling Scots tunes ?" "Well,"
answered Rupprecht, with a twinkle in his eyes, "you see,
I'm really your King !"

From Hohenschwangau I travelled into Hungary, to experience there the last sunset flush of the picturesque old Hungarian society. I was made a member of the great club in
Budapest and met many of the most interesting Hungarian
public men. I got to know Count Apponyi, the veteran
statesman and great orator; Count Batthyány, of whom I
have told a story in connection with Jeritza ; and Prince
Festetics, who kept up all the traditional state of the ancient
Hungarian nobility. The Prince was the last *grand seigneur*
in Europe, and a splendidly refined, public-spirited old man
he was. When I visited his country place I saw all the
magnificence of the old régime. At the door of his house
was a long line of servants in livery with at one end a monumental butler and at the other a chasseur in green with a
plumed cocked-hat. In a moment they had stripped off my
coat. Then, opposite me, the great doors opened to reveal
the little master of it all with great dignity walking slowly
down the grand staircase to meet me, across his shoulders
an Austrian cloak. I felt that I was an ambassador being
received by Louis XIV.

During this time in Hungary I stayed with Count Mikes,
Bishop of Szombathely, who became a great friend and later
stayed with me at Windsor. With a mind curiously typical
of the old régime in Hungary, he was possessed of an effervescent humour and great intelligence. Like myself, he had
in many ways preserved the layman's outlook of his youth,
together with a quite remarkable sympathy with the young.
Of great taste, he had furnished his town palace in Szombathely

and his country house perfectly. He kept a very good cook and an excellent cellar, and loved entertaining.

As the leading spirit in the Royalist Party in Hungary, it was from his country house that the last Emperor Charles made his final bid for the throne, and during the Bolshevik rule under Béla Kún he was imprisoned and condemned to death. While in his cell awaiting execution, he saw a bug come out of the wall. " Poor little thing," he remarked to the insect, " I shall not be here tonight, so you can live." But then his reprieve came and he said to the bug : " Poor little thing, I shall be here tonight, so I am afraid you must die." Somehow his butler organised his escape, and when the Bolsheviks left he returned gaily to his former work.

Count Mikes' favourite recreation was lawn tennis, which a Papal Nuncio once rebuked him for playing. To use his own words : " I answered that in the Middle Ages I should have had fighting, which would have given me exercise. Now I need tennis to give me exercise, so I continue to play. Ridiculous man ! " He was the first Bishop who paid a visit to the Pope in an aeroplane.

When I was staying with him the Bishop sent me to see the great monastery at Pannonhalma. It is a prodigious place, though of no great architectural interest, being mainly built in the early nineteenth century. The rooms are vast, and there is a great library ; there is also a picture gallery which contained the worst collection of pictures I have ever seen. The Abbot received me with great courtesy, professing to regard me as a brother because I was head of a community at St. George's. When he took me in to lunch, I found a hundred monks at long tables in the great rococo refectory, which was older than the other buildings. I sat next to the Abbot at the high table, and, to my consternation, in the middle of lunch the monks rose in a body to their feet and drank my health. I should think it must be the only occasion on which an English clergyman has been toasted by a hundred Benedictine monks. But all the clergy I met in Hungary treated me as a brother clergyman and *not* as an excommunicated heretic.

So many countries which used to recall only a host of interesting and amusing experiences now bring to my mind the sad thought of the havoc which the late war has caused and of the misery to which many of my friends have been reduced. I have never been able to agree with Lord Vansittart's persuasion that a German by virtue of his nationality alone is essentially bad. That curious gospel has been preached about other nations within my memory. In my young day the horror of Napoleonic France still overhung men's minds and you heard Frenchmen spoken of in just the same way as you now hear people speak of Germans. I do not believe the wisdom of the world to be increased by judging men in nationalities and proclaiming in splendid self-righteousness their racial inferiority ; certainly, I am sure it has not tended, nor is likely to tend, to foster the peace of the world. Moreover, history does not justify it, nor does my own experience.

Between my continental tours, I made two trips to the United States, the first and longest in 1923. Friends in New York had invited me to stay with them if ever I crossed. Accordingly, when I decided to make my journey, I simply boarded a ship without any further preparations. On arriving, however, my friends were in the country. When they learned of my arrival they immediately telephoned the Arthur James's, asking them to receive me, which they did. With characteristic American hospitality I was taken into their home and given rooms where I could receive visitors. As I was Dean of Windsor, invitations poured in and the James's, seeing the amount I managed to pack into every day, said that I had come to America to teach the Americans how to hustle. I may have hustled, but the turmoil of those ten days I spent in New York, even though I enjoyed them, I never wished to repeat.

I do not think you see America at its best in the east coast towns. They are too big, too noisy and too rich. I cannot enjoy dinner parties, for instance, such as were given for me in the kindest spirit in New York, when there were between fifty and seventy people present. It was splendid hospitality, but I did not find it agreeable—especially as Americans are addicted to after-dinner speaking. I once created great amusement by pointing out at a banquet that after-dinner speaking was more difficult for an Englishman than an American because Americans were brought up to regard it as a fine art carefully to be cultivated, and Englishmen were taught to regard it as a bad habit scrupulously to be avoided.

At the time of this first visit a good deal of trouble was being taken to promote good feeling between the two countries recently allied in war. I was very much gratified when Lord Burnham, who had been in America while I was there, later stated publicly in London that I had done more than anyone else in that direction. He may have exaggerated, but at least it did imply that I had done something.

After leaving New York I went to most of the Universities, where I asked to be allowed to stay in the Fraternity Houses and meet the students, instead of staying with the authorities : and a jolly experience it was. Then, travelling north as far as the Canadian border, I penetrated for a few days into Canada and was given a most interesting dinner by Mr. Mackenzie King at which I met a good many of his Cabinet Members. To the west I got as far as Chicago, where I was caught by the fiercest whirlwind of transatlantic activity with which I had so far been faced. This whirlwind took the shape of an enthusiastic Southerner who, after hearing me speak at a public meeting, rushed round to see me and irresistibly swept me into pledging myself to a long series of speeches throughout the Southern States. The whirlwind pursued me even during my fulfilment of the somewhat arduous programme he had mapped out for me, telegrams suggesting additional items arriving in a continuous stream. One of them, I remember, proposed that I should leave my train at four in the morning and, during the interval before the next train arrived, visit Ambassador Page's grave. I pointed out that while I should have been prepared for almost any sacrifice to see Ambassador Page in the flesh, the sight of his grave was less compelling.

In the end I had travelled an immense number of miles, stayed in every kind of house in towns and villages, and experienced all manner of amusing and interesting incidents. During the two months and a half the whole experience covered, I never once stayed at an hotel and had only one meal other than a party.

In all fairness I must pay tribute to one beautiful American trait. In England when a man in my position is asked to speak, sometimes involving considerable travelling and expense, it is blandly assumed that he will happily shoulder the responsibility for any outlay incurred. Although in a position to accept this responsibility—and having always done so—I have nevertheless resented it. This does not of course apply in the case of small parishes, but I recall one instance when I was asked to speak at a big luncheon club in one of our most important manufacturing cities. At the luncheon, the chairman mentioned to me that they were going through bad times, declaring that he personally had lost one hundred thousand pounds : such a statement made it sufficiently clear that he must have a good deal left. I was left to return to London with nothing but the sense of my own virtue to cheer me, having spent several pounds on the journey. Americans never do this. After every speech I delivered, a cheque—a very liberal cheque—was pressed into my hand, and while I remonstrated I could not but recognise it as a very fine quality in their character. Indeed, I was paid for practically every expense of my tour.

During my second tour, when I motored with my niece, Fanny Baillie, round Western America, stayed on a ranch in Wyoming and among the film actors in Hollywood, I saw still another side of American life. The people of the little cowboy towns of the West have an astonishing charm, because they are not afflicted with any consciousness of class distinction. Over most of the world, when people talk of their objection to class distinction, they mean that they object to anyone having a social position higher than their own. The Westerners simply would not know what you were talking about if you mentioned any such thing. They mix together with a naturalness which is delightful and with manners most perfect. One story I was told seemed to me to typify the spirit of that picturesque and romantic part of the world. Only forty years previously the widely scattered houses were always open to travellers, who were at liberty to enter and make a meal off whatever they could find. Such hospitality carried only one condition : if any visitor did not wash up before leaving they were liable to be shot. I was assured that this penalty was no idle tale ; it had been known to happen more than once.

Fanny and I spent a week in Hollywood, where, as I knew so many English actors, I was given an exuberant welcome by the Film Society, and lunched at their studio with the Marx Brothers. We then travelled south to the border of Mexico to spend a night at Uma, which is reputed to be the hottest place on the entire American continent. A local saying has it that a Uma man died and went to Hell, where he had to ask for an extra blanket.

The number of foreign visitors I had received and was receiving every day at Windsor ensured that there was some one in almost every country whom I could visit during my yearly holiday. Indeed, Finland and Bulgaria were the only countries in which I did not possess at least one potential host. However, I did not always avail myself of my overseas friends' hospitality. For two consecutive years I travelled with my second son in his little car.

Our first tour took us through Northern Spain, moving south as far as Toledo. Spanish history had always a special interest for me, while Spanish art attracted me very much. On our way down and back, also, we looked over a number of French cathedrals.

Ean and I made our second trip to Denmark, where Baron Rosencrantz was our host. I wonder if anyone has realised

THE AUTHOR WITH HIS SON EAN, LEAVING THE KING'S LEVEE AT ST. JAMES'S PALACE, MAY 1928

why Shakespeare took Rosencrantz and Gildenstern as the names of his two young nobles in Hamlet? I discovered an old guide book in which was given a list of the great families of Denmark in Shakespeare's day, and those two names were the only ones possible for use in poetry. The rest, including such uneuphonious words as Bugg and Thott and Brake, were such as must have sounded comic in a foreign language. It was exciting to find in a small church near the Baron's house, the monument of a Rosencrantz of Shakespeare's time and of his wife, who was a Gildenstern.

Starting our tour from the Baron's beautiful place at Rosenholm, we went to almost all the Islands, and stayed in the superb country houses for which Denmark is noted. It was a most enjoyable holiday, without a single hitch until our poor little car burst into flames on the way to our boat, and we had to be ignominiously towed for some fifty miles in the rear of a fish cart.

After the end of our second tour I came to the conclusion that, enormously as I enjoyed touring with Ean, who was a perfect travelling companion, it was a mistake for him to spend his holidays with me, seeing that we were together for the remainder of the year. Accordingly, when on the year following I proposed to pay a visit to Italy, as I know no Italian and had no companion available, I went to a little restaurant I used to frequent near Leicester Square, and saw an Italian head waiter whom I knew well. I told him I wanted a young Italian who could talk English to come with me and act as a sort of courier, and asked if he knew of a suitable man. "Yes," he said, "I know a man who would suit you exactly—it is myself!"

Indeed my Italian friend was a marvellous companion. In the evenings he played the piano to me in little country inns, or told me amusing war experiences while we wandered through the towns of the Apennines and saw pictures and buildings. He was able to take me to hotels to which most tourists never went, impressing on the proprietors my extreme importance, so that I was made very comfortable. At Sienna we saw the great Fiesta, one of the most remarkable mediæval survivals in Europe.

During the trip I was puzzled as to why he was always trying to edge me towards Turin, until, when we at last arrived there, I found it was his home. His mother had inherited a small villa in the Asti Valley, to which she and the boy's father, who had been a great draper in the town, had retired. He took me to stay with them and we dined in a little courtyard behind the villa, beneath a deep blue velvet sky spangled with stars. On one side was a vineyard sloping up the hill; on another a high trellis fence covered with vines separated us from the farmyard next door. In the farmyard the family were holding their Indian corn harvest, sitting with their friends singing among the corn, shelling it. The principal tenor of the village was their guest that night and sang delightfully.

The chief fruit of my travels was the immense acquaintance-ship I gained in so many different countries, bringing them back with me to Windsor to enrich our home life. Friends from abroad were constantly visiting us; all sorts of links were continually being formed with Europe and the rest of the world; so that I think an even more shattering sorrow came to me from the war than to most people—it was not only my enemies that were suffering but my friends.

3

When each year my holiday came to an end and I returned to Windsor, it was like travelling back to an intimate family circle where the happiest of excitements still awaited me: that of re-living the adventures of my tour in talk with the residents of the cloisters—the Lay Clerks, the organist, the Canons and all their families. We had indeed become an intimate and happy community. I used from the first to leave the Deanery front door always open, encouraging everybody to walk through it and up to my study without ringing the bell. By degrees, the Canons adopted the same habit, so that we were able to drop into each other's houses to talk whenever we felt inclined. I owe a great deal to this freedom of intercourse, since the Canons were all men of considerable ability, having been appointed for that very reason. It was extraordinary the breadth of knowledge covered within their ranks. I found myself surrounded by houses where I could always go for information on any subject. For instance, no one could have required a better authority on mediæval life than our Canon Ollard.

When I wanted general information, I went to Canon Anthony Deane. He always knew the best book to recommend on any subject; he always knew the dates and facts of any incident in which you were interested. Moreover, his information was as accurate as the range of his knowledge was wide. But he was not an original thinker. His great gift was in rendering the best thought and knowledge of the time into small change for the use of ordinary men. The incredible concentration and energy with which he employed that gift was testified to in the long list of books he had written, all of which had an enormous sale, and in his preaching, lecturing, broadcasts and articles in *The Times*. The limit of his achievement is impossible to calculate. He was not an easy man to know, through shyness having encased himself in a defensive armour that made people think him conceited and sometimes even arrogant. This was a mistaken judgment which tended to alienate him from his neighbour and made him suffer. I fancy that I came as close to terms of intimacy with him as was possible; certainly I had great affection for him.

Canon Alexander Nairne was Deane's exact opposite. Whenever, as was often the case, I went in to see him because I was puzzled and wanted light to clear my mind, he always seemed to be doing nothing. It might easily have been thought that he was an idle and indolent man, which would have been a complete misjudgment. An artist in temperament, his relation to religion was a contemplation of the beauty of truth. He hated definitions, and as a preacher and writer he was consequently not easy to follow. Deane used to say Nairne's method was to leave out the alternate lines. In reality he had no method ; he just suggested what he had learned by contemplation. When I took a problem to him, he never answered my question and appeared to wander off on to something quite irrelevant, sometimes going to a bookcase and fetching a book to read some poem which did not seem very much to the point. Before I left him, however, my puzzle had invariably been resolved. His teaching was not instruction but a mental irritant, stimulating thought.

After I had known him for ten years, I once remarked to his great friend, Bishop Headlam : " I've no more idea today of what Nairne believes about anything than I had ten years ago." " No," Headlam agreed, " and there's nothing he'd hate so much as to think that you had." As Nairne never defined his own beliefs, he had no wish for you to define yours ; all definition was to him a limitation. He stood before the vast mystery of truth and let it soak into him, and I found he had the power of enlightening me as few other men, before or since.

I must mention one aspect of my association with Nairne that I found especially delightful. As he was a Fellow of Jesus College I was able sometimes to go and see him when he was in Cambridge. After dinner in Hall, followed by a pleasant spell of talk with the rest of the dons in the Common Room, I would adjourn with him and his great friend Sir Arthur Quiller-Couch, to the former's rooms. Two minds could not have been more sharply contrasted than in this instance of Nairne and Q., but since each admired the other intensely they acted as foils and brought out the best in one another.

I have always seen Nairne and Anthony Deane in the light of the following illustration : Deane was like a Roman road—direct, efficient, attaining his end with certainty but ignoring the country through which he passed ; functioning always magnificently, with an almost arrogant assertion of power. Nairne was like a river meandering through hilly country—adapting its course to every variety of surface in the ground and constantly fed with streams from both sides ; apparently purposeless and yet enriching and fertilising the whole district through which it passed.

Canon Edgar Sheppard was an amiable man whom people thought futile. His name was continually appearing in the papers at weddings, christenings and funerals, while since such reported instances involved always the socially great he was thought to be a snob who enjoyed ministering to such people. This was totally untrue. He was certainly curiously limited ; indeed, I think he had allowed his reasoning powers to become almost atrophied, since he never read, nor wished to read, a book of any sort. He did, however, possess an overmastering sympathy. He liked taking weddings and funerals and christenings because he felt great sympathy with people at such times, without in the least minding who they were. For every one of the services he took for important people and which appeared in the Press, he took a hundred for insignificant people which were never publicised. No need could come to his attention and fail to call out his sympathy. With a readiness to take infinite trouble in assisting people, he got to know all the police of the London district where he lived, in which Buckingham Palace and St. James's stand. If he was told of any difficulty in one of the men's homes, whether sickness or otherwise, no distance could stop him from going to see what he could do, and no effort that might be required exhausted his patience. He was always ready to travel hundreds of miles to do some kindness on behalf of some quite insignificant person who had no direct claim on him whatever. After his death his wife received three thousand letters of tribute and condolence, mostly from people of whom she had never even heard. It might be natural to laugh about some of Canon Sheppard's foibles, but nobody who really knew anything of his life could fail to feel a deep respect for the greatness of his heart and character.

Canon Ollard, whom I have already mentioned, and Canon Crawley have both now passed away—the former being the last survivor of the Canons at Windsor in my day. In both instances, along with their families, they were among my best-loved friends. Crawley's distinction lay in the transparent sincerity and purity of his character, which inevitably won people's love wherever he went.

Of particular note within our body were the Chapel organists. The three who covered my period of office, besides being the leading men of their profession, all had strong and striking personalities. Of Sir Walter Parratt I have already written. I knew him only in his old age, when he was past his best days, but he was still a very interesting man, not only as a musician but through the varied culture of his mind. As a chess player, for instance, he showed exceptional skill. On one occasion when Bonar Law, who was then Prime Minister, came to stay at the Castle, he said that he wished he could get a game of chess. "But," he added, "you won't have anyone I can play with, as I'm used to only the very best players." The member of the Household to whom he was speaking replied : "Oh, but I believe we can produce the very man for you. We'll send for Sir Walter Parratt." Parratt was fetched and ended by defeating Bonar Law triumphantly. Walford Davis, who succeeded Sir Walter, was another highly individual character and of great charm. When he first arrived, as his house in the precincts was not ready, he and his delightful wife lived at the Deanery for three months, which I enjoyed very much. Walford Davis's ideals of a musical service were quite different from mine, and we by no means saw eye to eye as regards the choir. Nevertheless, the inspiration he was able to infuse into a large gathering, the power he was capable of bringing out of music in a community, amounted to no less than genius. The third of my contemporary organists, my dear friend Doctor Harris, still flourishes. We have had any amount of fun together, especially when, with my niece Fanny and I, he went to take the waters at Kissingen. We toured the country there in search of every link with the composer Bach, and Harris joyously played on all Bach's organs. I was not musician enough to share his understanding of Bach, but I could appreciate his enthusiasm and, with my niece, I thoroughly entered into the spirit of our various expeditions of discovery. Through these three men, the organist's house at Windsor was always a pleasant spot for me, even though there might arise occasional frictions which were bound to occur but which did not, I think, in any way lessen the under-lying affection between us all.

An interesting man, who has played a considerable part in my life for many years, is Dr. Fellowes, who travelled with us as choirmaster on our Canadian tour. His great work as a student of music is internationally known. I sometimes think it a pity that his family never allowed him to take up music as his profession ; the great violinists of the day thought very highly of his ability as a young man, while I am sure he would have found fuller scope if it had been his whole interest. In taking the minor canon's part in the services he contributed something to St. George's which I, as well as many others, appreciated enormously. Though one might often have heard minor canons with finer singing voices, I at least have never known one who could surpass him in the exquisite perfection of his diction. It is still a privilege to hear him take a service, even though his voice has lost much of its power.

Although this community, which had as its centre St. George's Chapel, was always my main concern at Windsor, our society was enlarged by the number of interesting people that were normally resident within the Castle. The per-manent Royal element was supplied by Lord Athlone and Princess Alice, who are mercifully still alive. It would be difficult to find two people more widely respected and beloved, not only in England, but in Canada and South Africa, where the high and responsible positions they held materially has added to the interest of their lives. During the long years when we were very near neighbours and seeing each other constantly, they were as perfect to associate with as anyone could have been.

Among the Court officials whom I knew were four outstanding men. Lord Stamfordham had behind him a long and distinguished career, in which, having worked as Private Secretary first to Queen Victoria and then to King George V, he had seen from the very inside most of the important events in our national life. A wise and supremely able man, he had an admirable mastery over the English language which made his letters quite famous as vehicles for expressing the Sovereign's mind. One very special link between us was that while Davidson was Dean in Queen Victoria's time, they were on very intimate terms. Sir Derek Keppel, Master of the Household, possessed the grand manner of a bygone generation to such an exquisite degree that it was a privilege merely to watch him taking his place during a function. Yet he could be a kind and entertaining friend as well. Another who had served under Queen Victoria was Sir Frederick Ponsonby (afterwards Lord Sysonby), made Deputy-Constable and Lieutenant-Governor of Windsor Castle in 1928. His was that peculiarly brilliant quality of mind that marks the whole Ponsonby family and makes them the most delightful companions. But in my eyes, above all, stood Colonel Sir Clive (now Lord) Wigram, Stamfordham's successor as Secretary to the King and later Deputy-Governor of the Castle. To Sir Clive I owe an immense debt, as through the most difficult years of my time at Windsor he was my one real support. He is still alive, and with his wife remains among the friends for whom I have the deepest affection.

There were two Librarians during my time, one of whom succeeded the other. John Fortescue I had known very many years earlier, as he too had been a great friend of Mowbray Morris. Fortescue was unquestionably a great man of letters. A student of military matters, I believe his monumental *History of the British Army*, which was the chief literary achievement of his life, will always remain a standard work.

As a member of society he had some great merits and one great limitation. He was a magnificent talker but not really a good conversationalist. To sit in his room, or take a walk with him, or have him to dinner with a suitable party, was absolutely delightful ; I have known few people who talked better. But he was lost in the give and take of conversation. If he came to dine, I was always careful to select company who would be interested in things that interested him, since if people drifted into conversation that was outside his interest, he was inclined to withdraw into his shell. But his value, both as a friend and a talker, was first class. He was not made to be a Librarian ; the same limitation from which he suffered conversationally affecting him with regard to books. He was such an immensely gifted man, however, that he fulfilled his Librarianship with competence and thoroughness.

When Owen Moorshead was appointed we gained the perfect Librarian, possessed of much wider interests and greater knowledge than most Librarians. Socially, he proved valuable in a community like Windsor, because his tongue is one which always works for peace and goodwill. One cannot help feeling more in charity with others after talking to him. I hope our regard was a mutual one, for in that case I have a real friend.

Quite recently Major-General Sir John Hanbury-Williams died, yet it is a remarkable fact that his father was born in the eighteenth century. Sir John had a full life, in which he had done and seen a great deal. Among other things, he was in Russia as Military Attaché during the last critical days of the Romanoff empire. In appearance, manners, cultivation of mind, he was the very ideal of the gentleman of the old school, and on his retirement from work he developed such strong hobbies that he was never idle and never bored. He and his daughter were particular friends of mine, so that at worrying times I was able to find nothing so restful and comforting as dropping in for a talk with the old man among his books and pictures.

With Mrs. Carteret Carey I had always a great deal to

do throughout the years at Windsor. Her husband was Governor of the Military Knights, and after he died she remained in one of the Military Knights' houses. She did useful work in the town, of which she was Mayoress, acquitting herself of all her voluntary tasks with great energy and efficiency. Her great contribution to our life was in the interest she took in the choir boys, who were very fond of her. She used to go down to the school and read to them in their dormitories, while she helped to make our Christmas party a success by the energetic way in which she threw herself into all the games. She also worked for many years as Secretary to the Friends of St. George's with great efficiency and devotion. She has lately died after some years of great difficulty and hardship, which she bore with a courage that was the essence of her whole character.

Many indeed are my recollections of Windsor figures and faces, all of which bring back to me memories of affection and kindness.

THE AUTHOR IN THE DRAWING-ROOM OF ST. MARY'S, BALDOCK

With Sylvia Grubb, George Dawson and Amelia Newman

CHAPTER 16

THE ROYAL FAMILY

THE Duke of Connaught used to chuckle at the recollection of his love affair at the age of four with my mother, and his avowed intention of marrying her, while he was delighted when I showed him some letters in big printed characters that he sent her, which I found among her papers. When the Duke died, Princess Beatrice wrote to me saying it had been a comfort to her that I had taken the funeral, since I was one of the very few left who occupied a place in the memories of their young days. Then, again, when I was made Dean of Windsor Princess Christian laughingly said to me, " The Dean of Windsor has always been an awe-inspiring person to me since the days of Dean Wellesley, and it is fun to have a Dean whom you have carried about in your arms as a baby ! " The whole relationship that I enjoyed with our Royal Family was just the kindly regard given to the son of an old friend.

When I went to Windsor I entered into circumstances that makes it impossible for me not to talk about the Royal Family. But, since my mother was always so insistent that it was wrong to gossip about them, I am reluctant to do so. What I have written about the older Princesses and the Duke of Connaught all belong to the relationship which I have described as existing with Queen Victoria. They were children of my godmother, and to them I was the son of someone who had been very closely connected with their home life.

On my appointment as Dean of Windsor my old relationship to the Royal Family was changed into an official connection. The generation to which the new Court belonged were strangers to me, and I was a stranger to them. It was comparable with a man being appointed to a country parish and having to come into fairly intimate relations with the squire and his family. I had to make my own place in relation to those who were practically strangers. I had previously spoken to Queen Mary only twice : once when I danced with her while we were quite young at the last ball given at Carrington House before it was pulled down to make way for the War Office ; the other in King Edward's time, when I went to preach at Sandringham. The latter occasion was the only time I had spoken to King George since we once met as little boys. He and his brother had been brought by Canon Dalton to be shown the Abbey by my uncle, Dean Stanley. As I was just the same age, my uncle took me with the party. I only remember that when we got to Queen Elizabeth's monument Prince George climbed up on it and, gazing on her face, said, " What an ugly old woman ! "

My actual work with the Royal Family at Windsor needs no explanation. It meant seeing them fairly often for the arrangement of all sorts of little things in which we were both involved, and I need not describe it any more than I have described the normal work that I did in parishes. Our intercourse gave me an opportunity of knowing them, not only because I had to do with them myself, but because I became acquainted with all the people who served them. Thus did I grow to understand the estimation in which they were held. In England we have recognised that the character our sovereigns show in their homes and their ordinary life is the real criterion on which we base our loyalty. Now, no one could work as I did without being impressed by the tremendous respect which they have won from those who are most closely associated with them in their daily life. This was so in the case of Queen Victoria, though her training, having given her little understanding of human nature, led her into great mistakes in the training of her children and in her relations with her servants. But still, their respect for her amounted to reverence. People often write about her mismanagement of King Edward's education and how unfair she was with him. It is quite true ; but no son ever grew up with a more intense respect and loyalty to his mother. Both Kings George V and VI rubbed shoulders with other people on equal terms in the Navy before they came to the throne, besides being members of largish families, which gave them a greater knowledge of the world.

The other day a man, who has had for twenty years a small office which brings him constantly into relations with the present King, was talking frankly to me, as an old friend. "I hate the kind of publicity the King gets," my companion said. "It doesn't show the great man he is. And he is a great man—no one who has to do with him every day can fail to recognise it. I'll give you an example of what I mean. On the South African tour everybody was very tired, and naturally the King had more to tire him and occupy his mind than anyone. One morning, when he had had a particularly exacting time the day before, he went for an early ride with his daughters. There was nobody about, though I happened to be out early myself and saw this incident. He was riding past the tents of his escort when he saw a young private run out with a camera. Most people would have said, 'Bother him, can't I be left alone a minute.' Instead of which he stopped and posed for the boy, and then called up his daughters to give him a chance of photographing them. Then he rode on. How many men who were tired and overwhelmed with daily engagements would have remembered to take the opportunity of giving pleasure to a young soldier? That," my friend concluded, "is a great man." And I think he was right. He added : "The same is true of the Queen too. They never forget to notice how they can give pleasure."

I think this is one of the symptoms of the astonishing sympathy with their people which has made our sovereigns understand and adapt themselves to each new generation. Of course everybody knows their consistent devotion to duty ; but this has never become mechanical. They are always thinking of, and interested in, the people they are brought into contact with.

Mr. Gore, in his *Life of King George V*, makes a strange mistake when he includes me in a list of the King's personal friends. It is true, in many cases, that a fairly intimate acquaintance may justify the use of the word *friend*, but King George had the great gift of making and keeping real friends. His friendships were not very many in number and mostly had been formed during his youthful days in the Navy, when he never expected to occupy the throne. As such they remained quite simple and sincere attachments, which endured until he died. In this, one had an especially clear indication of the unusual simplicity and directness of character of which, during his reigning years, the King was to furnish such abundant proof. I never had the opportunity of entering into the ranks of that tried and chosen body.

Incidentally, it is not unamusing now to recall that my installation at Windsor was technically altogether unconstitutional. When, in the first place, I was informed of the King's gracious intention, I was told that the actual offer of the appointment would come from the Prime Minister. Mr. Lloyd George, however, forgot to write the necessary letter and everything went forward without anyone raising any objection.

The remarkable strain of personal humility which had characterised Queen Victoria showed itself, I believe, in both George V and his son, the present King, and contributed equally to their greatness. Indeed, in the case of King George V there were present many of the qualities that had so distinguished the great Queen. She had always shown conspicuous courage, whether physical or moral, and Lord Stamfordham, while acting as King George's secretary, told me how at the time of a great national crisis, when the King had to make a decision of the utmost moment, he never seemed to give a thought to the consequences for good or evil which his course of action might bring on himself.

"Never," Lord Stamfordham emphatically declared, "have I seen a man with such moral courage."

King George cared little for the pomps and ceremonies of kingship. He detested the publicity that his position involved; to do his simple duty was his sole consideration. During the first World War all that it meant and might mean —to his subjects especially—was ever in the forefront of his mind, absorbing his attention to an astonishing extent. He never spared himself in any direction. I well remember his once remarking wearily to me, "I think people hardly realise that I am the only man in England who never has a complete day's holiday." Yet he was kind and considerate in spite of it all, while I doubt if a thought of pride ever entered his mind. If I had to choose an inscription for his monument I should quote, simply:

> His life was gentle, and the elements
> So mix'd in him that Nature might stand up
> And say to all the world " This was a man ! "

In regard to Queen Mary, of course, it is not possible for me to speak. Not only does the whole nation rejoice that she is still alive, but no words of mind could add to the reverence in which she is held. For myself she is much more than a queen. While shut off from active life as I am today, I am made happy by the occasional opportunities she takes of showing she has not quite forgotten me. I hope she will forgive my quoting what she once said to me in a moment of great sorrow, drawing herself up with an incomparable dignity: "There is only one way to meet these things and that is to go straight on." I think that has been the motto of her life.

With the present King and Queen, again, because they are alive, I am prevented from saying much beyond the fact that they have fully maintained the family tradition of kindliness in all their dealings with me, and I believe they deserve the respect which their parents won and which they are winning for themselves.

Now, when I have quite retired from the world, the Royal Family are associated in my mind with countless happy memories. And these inspire me to say, as I watch and listen to everything that concerns them, may God bless them and theirs—and to say it from the very depths of my heart.

CHAPTER 17

BRAINS AND FAITH

I HAVE indicated throughout this book the gradual development of my relation to faith, and the way in which my way of teaching it always dissatisfied me. My faith had been built up for me by my mother, simply by her daily reading of the Lessons with me, without any theological explanation. The result was to give me a knowledge of God and of Jesus Christ as real as the knowledge I had of my mother. But what I knew by faith, though real and the anchor of my whole life, was quite unself-conscious. I took my knowledge of God for granted, as I took the knowledge I had of my mother. Consequently, as a young man, nothing of a sceptical nature had affected me at all, scepticism always seeming to me unintelligible. Just at the time of my ordination, however, I came in touch with the intellectualism of the nineteenth century, which really amounted to this : the conviction that no truth could be imparted, or indeed known, except through the intellect. All my generation, more or less, suffered from this belief. I should have seen the fallacy of it from my own experience, but I did not. I found great difficulty in teaching the intellectual formulas which the books and teaching of the time impressed on us. All through my life what I *knew* was at war with what I *thought* I should teach. I do not mean to say that I never preached out of my own experience, but I think it was rare.

An excellent lady in Plumstead once said to me : "Your sermons are always fluent and sometimes eloquent, but you don't preach the Gospel." Of course the word Gospel was used at that time to express a theological formula which had been very much discredited, chiefly by the Oxford Movement, but I am sure that she did not mean that. I believed her criticism was sound, though I did not understand what the word Gospel really meant. On the other hand, I believe that I did sometimes preach the gospel—that is, preach the faith my mother had given me—especially in the three-hour service on Good Friday, where in the Last Words I felt the revelation of Jesus more clearly than anywhere else. I always found that those addresses had more effect on people than any other sermons I preached, but could not tell why this was so.

Unfortunately it was very late in my work when this confusion in my mind was cleared for me. One day Henry Marten, afterwards Provost of Eton but then Lower Master, asked me to preach in the Lower Chapel at Eton, which the young boys attended. I could not satisfy myself as to a line on which I should preach until the last minute ; as it was not long after Easter I decided to talk about the first word on the Cross. When I came to my sermon I said : " Now, boys, let's talk about bad temper. We all know that it's bad, but we often think that we have some excuse for giving way to it." I then went through the most common reasons for irritation—hunger, fatigue, sickness, pain, injustice, slander, enmity—and when I had done, I said, " Now, boys, I want you to think of Jesus when He had to bear these things." I showed how He was suffering practically every normal cause for irritation and anger and resentment before saying : " How did He behave in those circumstances ? Well, with His enemies crowding round Him, after a night of slander and injustice, when He was hungry and thirsty and utterly tired out, the people round Him heard Him say, as He looked at the crowds that were jeering and hooting at Him, *Father, forgive them for they know not what they do.* You see," I said, " none of the things that happened had shaken His calmness or made Him forget that the condition of their minds was a more terrible thing than His own suffering." I ended : " Next time you feel you are about to lose your temper, think of Jesus on the Cross." I came out of the Chapel feeling humiliated. I thought I had preached a feeble and obvious sermon.

The next day I had a letter of thanks from Marten. It seemed warmer than such letters usually are, but I thought nothing of that, as he was a great friend. So it passed out of my mind.

The following Sunday, my youngest boy, who was in the Upper School at Eton so that he had not been in Lower Chapel, said to me when he came for lunch, " What were you doing in Lower Chapel last Sunday ? "

" I don't know what you mean. I was preaching there," I said.

" Yes," he said, " but the school is buzzing with your sermon."

" What do they say about it," I asked.

" Oh, they say that you preached religion."

I was completely confused. Why should the boys pick out this sermon from among the sermons they heard every Sunday and say it was about religion ? The next day I went to see the Lower Master's sister, who had been in Chapel and who was an extremely intelligent woman. As soon as I got there, she burst out : " I can't tell you what your sermon has meant both to the boys and masters. We have sermons every Sunday and the preachers give us their theories and opinions and generally bore us. You took a difficulty of life that we are all conscious of straight into relationship with Jesus, and we all felt that you had given us light on our lives." Then she went on to say : " When we were young we went to the Temple Church, as my father was a leading lawyer. All the lawyers used to go Sunday by Sunday to hear Dr. Vaughan's sermons. Do you think they'd have gone to have their brains instructed by his theories and opinions ? They'd have thought, ' We're quite as clever as he is ', and his sermons would have bored them. But he did what you did on Sunday week and that was why they went to hear him."

Naturally this set me thinking and I realised that I was wrong in believing that religious truth must be taught through the intellect. I remembered that what was good news, or

Gospel, as preached by the Apostles, was not an intellectual thing but the story of a Man's life in leading His friends ; in time their learning by His perfectness to believe Him when He said He was a revelation of the Father. When they came to preaching this story, they did not attempt to address people's intellects. Gradually I became conscious of the many things that we know, and some of the most important things which are not learned by our brains. I saw that host of things we learn through the senses. And then I asked, how do we know people ? The brain can tell us a lot *about* people, but it cannot tell us how to know them. The cleverest man does not necessarily know his children as well as some quite ignorant woman. We know people through a separate faculty—the faculty which the Bible calls love. If that is so of people it must be so of God too, since He is a person. There is another reason why the intellect cannot be our chief faculty for acquiring any knowledge beyond that of purely material things. God calls Himself the Father, not of the clever people, or highly educated people, but of all men. Can we think that He would differentiate so cruelly as to make man's knowledge of Him dependent on his intellectual powers and intellectual definitions ? No—the Gospel must be intelligible if it be really a Gospel sent by God. And it *is* intelligible *because* all men can learn how to know a person.

So I believe that we must base our teaching as the Apostles did, on the knowledge of Jesus Christ and Him crucified, which is what St. Paul told us. Our sermons and teachings must be addressed to the faculty by which we can know people, and not to intellectual theories and definitions. This falling back on the intellect has been the weakness of all ages and, in different forms, has caused the failure of every great religious revival. To intellectualise is tempting because it is easy and satisfies our vanity, but it means death to faith.

APPENDIX

ALBERT VICTOR BAILLIE

Born 1864.

Trinity College, Cambridge. B.A. 1886, M.A. 1891, D.D. 1918, C.V.O. 1921, K.C.V.O. 1932.

Assistant Curate of St. Mary's, South Shields, 1888–90.

Assistant Chaplain, Missions to Seamen, South Shields, 1890–1.

Assistant Curate of St. Paul's, Walworth, and Domestic Chaplain to Bishop (Davidson) of Rochester, 1891–4.

Assistant Curate of St. Mark's, Plumstead, 1894–5.

Vicar of St. Margaret's, Plumstead, 1895–8.

Rector of Rugby, 1898–1912. Rural Dean of Rugby.

Hon. Canon of Worcester, 1905–8.

Hon. Canon and Chancellor of St. Michael's Collegiate Church, Coventry, 1908–17. Sub-Dean, 1912–17.

Appointed and installed Dean of Windsor, 19th December, 1917.

Resigned September, 1945.

INDEX

253

INDEX